Mystical Verse and Prose

Poesías y prosas místicas

Mystical Verse and Prose

Poesías y prosas místicas

A Dual-Language Book

St. John of the Cross

Edited and Translated by
STANLEY APPELBAUM

DOVER PUBLICATIONS, INC.
Mineola, New York

Bibliographical Note

This Dover edition, first published in 2007, is a new selection from a standard Spanish edition of the works of Saint John of the Cross (see Introduction for first and early editions), together with a new English translation by Stanley Appelbaum, who also made the selection and wrote the Introduction and footnotes.

Library of Congress Cataloging-in-Publication Data

John of the Cross, Saint, 1542–1591.
    [Poems. English & Spanish]
    Mystical verse and prose = Poesías y prosas místicas / St. John of the Cross ; edited and translated by Stanley Appelbaum.
        p. cm. — (Dual-language book)
    ISBN 0-486-45123-2 (pbk.)
    1. John of the Cross, Saint, 1542–1591—Translations into English. I. Appelbaum, Stanley. II. Title. III. Title: Poesías y prosas místicas.

PQ6400.J8A2 2007
861'.3—dc22

2006050213

Manufactured in the United States of America
Dover Publications, Inc., 31 East 2nd Street, Mineola, N.Y. 11501

CONTENTS

Longer titles of works will be found in the Introduction. Full chapter titles will be found on the pages given. The numbering of poems (1–8) has been introduced in this Dover edition to streamline cross-referencing.

Noche oscura / Dark Night

Cántico espiritual / Spiritual Canticle

Llama de amor viva / Living Flame of Love

INTRODUCTION

Life

Juan de Yepes y Álvarez, the future Saint John of the Cross, was born in 1542 in Fontiveros, near Ávila (Old Castile, central Spain), a small town with a population of about 5,000 at the time. His father, a Toledan textile merchant of remote noble ancestry, had there met and married a poor weaver, and, disinherited for wedding a commoner, had learned her trade. Juan was the youngest of three brothers. (The middle brother died in childhood; the eldest brother, Francisco, became very pious, after a rowdy youth, and in later years often visited Juan in different parts of Spain as an aide.) Left a widow when Juan was five, the boys' mother received little help from her wealthy in-laws. After an unsuccessful attempt to better their lot in nearby Arévalo (1548–1551), the family moved to Medina del Campo, the area's thriving trade-fair center with some 30,000 inhabitants. There Juan entered a parochial school for poor children and orphans, and apprenticed himself to masters of various manual trades, none of which caught his fancy.

Put to work in a local convent church, Juan became a nurse in its associated hospital for contagious diseases, attending a Jesuit school in his spare time and acquiring a solid classical secondary education (1559–1563); upon leaving this school, he joined the Carmelite order as a friar, taking the name-in-religion Juan de Santo Matía (John of Saint Matthew). The Order of Our Lady of Mount Carmel (named for the mountain overlooking present-day Haifa, which had been sacred to Baal before Elijah linked it to the Jewish, and thus later, the Judeo-Christian tradition) was founded in the Holy Land by crusaders around 1150; its original ("primitive") rule was very strict and ascetic, but by the sixteenth century, the Carmelites had become comparatively lax, living by a more worldly ("mitigated") rule.

From 1564 to 1568, Juan was in Salamanca, attending both the prestigious local Carmelite college and the best university in Spain (the great religious writer Luis de León, 1527–1591, was then on the theology faculty). The most crucial encounter of Juan's life took place there: with (the future Saint) Teresa of Ávila (1515–1582), in 1567. She had come to Salamanca to found her second reformed Carmelite convent there (her new, reformed nuns were called Discalced, or barefoot, though before long they wore sandals), and to scout for a friar who could do the same for males. The ascetic, contemplative Juan was recommended to her, and she enlisted him in her cause, talking him out of transferring to the highly reclusive Carthusians. In 1568, he founded the first Discalced Carmelite friary in the hamlet of Duruelo in the extreme west of Ávila province, taking the definitive name of (Fray) Juan de la Cruz, and becoming subprior and master of novices. (In 1570, the friary moved to Mancera de Abajo, three miles away, and Juan journeyed to Pastrana, east of Madrid, to found another house.)

In 1571, Juan became rector of the first Discalced college, located in the famous university town Alcalá de Henares, east of Madrid (where Cervantes was born in 1547). In 1572, Teresa summoned him to the convent of La Encarnación, her headquarters in Ávila, as confessor and spiritual adviser to her nuns. Before her departure in 1574 (Juan stayed until 1577) they worked together very closely; in these years she was at the height of her mystical experiences. In 1576, Juan attended the Carmelite chapter (national meeting) at Almodóvar del Campo (Ciudad Real province, La Mancha region), where the resentful unreformed branch clashed angrily with the reformers.

Late in 1577, Juan's "mitigated" opponents arrested him (the arrival of a new, misinformed papal nuncio in that year endangered the reform for some time). After being whipped and manhandled, he had to ride a mule over the wintry Guadarrama range before being imprisoned in the Toledo Carmelite friary, in a tiny, stuffy, poorly lighted cubbyhole, where his conditions were worse than Spartan. After six months, a new, more humane warder supplied him with paper to write down poems, and occasionally let him out of the room for necessary chores. This new situation ultimately allowed Juan to make an adventurous, risky escape in August 1578, finding refuge for two months with sympathizers in Toledo. Later that year, he attended another chapter in Almodóvar, this time a breakaway congress of Discalced Carmelites only, and was briefly excommunicated for doing so. At that chapter he was appointed as superior of the friary of El Calvario, in the far north of eastern Andalusia (Jaén province, just south of La Mancha); henceforth he was to be extensively associated with Andalusia. On his way to El Calvario, he stopped at the Discalced convent in nearby Beas de Segura; the prioress, Ana de Jesús, was to be important later in his life.

In 1579, Juan became the founder and rector of the first Andalusian Discalced college, in the large manufacturing town of Baeza (in the center of Jaén province; population 50,000), which had the finest university in the region; he continued to visit the Beas convent as confessor and spiritual adviser. In 1580 (the year Juan's mother died), the Carmelite reform was rescued by a papal brief (warmly fostered by King Felipe [Philip] II) establishing separate religious "provinces" for the order's two branches. Each branch was now headed by a "provincial," also called "vicar provincial."

In 1581, at the first separate Discalced chapter under the new dispensation, in Alcalá de Henares, Juan became third *definidor* to the provincial (the *definidores* were close assistants to the provincial, in line for replacing him if he died or became incapacitated). Later that year, he was sent to Ávila to escort Teresa to Granada, where a Discalced convent was to be founded; a previous commitment elsewhere prevented her from going to Granada, and the convent there was founded in 1582 by Ana de Jesús, formerly of Beas, with Juan in attendance. In Granada, on a hill across a gorge from the Alhambra, the Discalced friary of Los Mártires had been founded in 1573; its community now elected Juan as prior (he also confessed the local Discalced nuns). In 1583, at the second legal Discalced chapter, in Almodóvar (at which it was determined that priors were henceforth to be elected only at chapters), his priorate in Granada was renewed (an aqueduct he then built at Los Mártires is still standing).

In 1585, at a Discalced chapter in Lisbon (Portugal was annexed to Spain from 1580 to 1640), he was named second *definidor*. At another chapter, in Pastrana, invoked later that year by the rigorous new provincial Nicolás Doria, Spain was divided into four Discalced areas, and Juan was named vicar provincial of Andalusia, with his residence in Granada. Henceforth he had to travel far and wide throughout the region; at Seville he made some bad enemies within his own branch of the Carmelites because of his strictness. In 1586, he founded Discalced friaries in Córdoba, La Manchuela (Mancha Real, close to the city of Jaén), and even distant Caravaca (beyond the eastern border of Andalusia, in the Murcia region). In that year he suffered two serious illnesses, one when near Córdoba, and the other while on his way to a meeting of *definidores* in Madrid. At that gathering, Doria, with Juan in opposition, had the Carmelite rite changed from the Jerusalem to the Roman observance, and permission was granted to have the late (Saint) Teresa's books printed. Also in 1586, Juan accompanied Ana de Jesús to Madrid to found the Discalced convent there.

At a chapter in Valladolid in 1587, Juan lost his ranks of *definidor* and vicar provincial, but was reconfirmed as prior of Los Mártires in Granada. In 1588 (the Armada year), at a chapter in Madrid which established a new council for governing Discalced affairs, Juan was named third councillor (of six) and first *definidor* (under Doria as vicar general); he was also reunited with his native Castile, as prior of the friary in Segovia, the foundation of which he had guided from his Andalusian base two years earlier. (Segovia was also made the seat of the [transitory] new council [until 1590].) The Segovia foundation had been subsidized by the pious and wealthy widow Ana del Mercado y Peñalosa, whom Juan had met in 1582, and who had become so devoted to him as her spiritual adviser that she followed him to Segovia.

In June 1591, Juan continued to oppose Doria's proposals at a chapter in Madrid. He was stripped of his offices, and was slated to be sent as a missionary to Mexico (though not unwillingly) when he refused to continue as prior in Segovia. Sent to Andalusia to recruit eleven fellow missionaries, he was again humiliated and persecuted, this time by his enemies among the Discalced. At the friary of La Peñuela (on the southern, Andalusian slopes of the Sierra Morena, just west of Las Navas de Tolosa, site of the 1212 battle, a turning point in the Reconquest of Spain from the Moors) Juan's right leg became inflamed, making him feverish. Refusing to go for treatment to Baeza, where he was so well known, he chose the unfamiliar city of Úbeda, not far away. There the local prior also bore him a grudge, and he was improperly handled. The ailment (probably blood poisoning) spread painfully through his body, and he died in Úbeda on December 14, 1591.

Juan de la Cruz was beatified in 1675 and canonized in 1726. In 1738, his feast day was established as November 24; it was later moved to December 14, the anniversary of his death. In 1926, he was declared a doctor of the Church (one of only thirty-odd throughout history whose writings are considered authoritative guides for Christian conduct and belief). In 1952, in recognition of the supreme quality of his best verse, he was named patron saint of Spanish poets. In addition to the major books excerpted in this anthology and discussed below, his surviving works include brief bits of advice for members of religious houses, some religious aphorisms, a few letters, and miscellaneous fragments; other items, known by name or other references, have been lost; also, some spurious works have been attributed to him in the past.

Saint John of the Cross, a short, slight man, was humble, approachable, and inspirational to his followers. Though he was ascetic and learned, and underwent occasional blank periods or trances, he could also be a hands-on laborer for his various friaries, firm but lenient with the friars he supervised, taking them on excursions to enjoy the natural countryside he loved so well, and giving individual attention to their problems. A converter of sinners and an exorcist, he was duly suspicious of engineered miracles, but did perform some miracles of his own, being especially known for accurate predictions.

Works

Poetry

Saint John of the Cross is considered one of the very greatest Spanish lyric poets, if not the greatest, though we possess only a handful of his poems, and about half of those are less highly regarded than the rest. Some of his poems were published in the posthumous first edition of a large number of his works: *Obras espirituales que encaminan a una alma a la perfecta unión con Dios* (Spiritual Works Which Set a Soul on the Path to Perfect Union with God), printed in Alcalá de Henares in 1618 by the widow of Andrés Sánchez Ezpeleta. The "Cántico espiritual," however (which was given that name in a 1630 edition of his works, evidently with reference to "Canticles," the Vulgate Bible name for the King James's "Song of Solomon"), was not published in Spanish until the 1627 Brussels edition of his works (along with the prose commentary on it of the same title), though it had already appeared in a 1622 Parisian edition, in French. All of this refers to the saint's first version of the verse and prose *Cántico* (*Cantico A*); the definitive version (*Cántico B*) was first published in the 1703 Seville complete-works edition, issued by F. de Leefdael. The saint's poetry was influenced by the Bible, by folk lyrics, by the courtly verse in the various Renaissance *cancioneros* ("song books"), and by the Italian-influenced pastoral poems of the great Garcilaso de la Vega (1501?–1536), whose work had already been recast *a lo divino* (in the religious vein) by Sebastián de Córdoba Sacedo (1545?–1604?) in 1575. Saint John's poetic conceits (such as an intensive use of oxymoron) are characteristic of the Siglo de Oro (Golden Age), in the vigorous early part of which he lived and wrote. As in much mystical literature, his imagery often verges on the erotic. Some information follows on the individual poems selected here (the few omitted are generally considered inferior; some, even mediocre and tedious); the numbering of the poems from 1 to 8 (the numbering of their *stanzas* is a universal practice) has been introduced in this Dover edition for brevity in references.

1. "En una noche obscura": This poem (or at least its first three stanzas) is the basis of the linked prose commentaries *Subida del Monte Carmelo* and *Noche oscura*. Its Italian-influenced prosodic scheme is called *liras* in Spanish. Its full title as it appears in the *Subida* is: "Poem in which the soul sings of the happy fortune it had in passing through the dark night of faith, naked and purified, to union with the Beloved." In the poetry section of the 1618 edition, it is titled "Poem of the soul rejoicing in its attainment of the lofty state of perfection, which is union with God, by the path of spiritual renunciation." It is thought to have been written between 1579 and 1581.

2. "Cántico espiritual": This poem is the basis of the prose commentary of the same name. It, too, is written in *lira* stanzas, and it is closely inspired by the biblical Song of Solomon. Its full title as it appears in the definitive version (B) of the commentary is: "Poem between the soul and her Bridegroom." The first version of the poem (A), thought to have been begun (first 31 stanzas) in 1578 in the Toledo prison, and continued between 1582 and 1584, comprised only 39 stanzas. When the commentary was undertaken, beginning in 1584, Saint John moved many stanzas into a new sequence to suit a more logical exegesis of the poem. The present stanza 11 is said to have been written and added (making 40 stanzas) in 1586. It is the full definitive version of the poem (B) that appears in this Dover edition. The poem traces the soul's entire spiritual itinerary from first setting out toward union with God to final achievement of it; its final stanzas reflect the bliss of that state (to the extent possible in this life). The poem has been called "one of the most beautiful works of European lyric poetry of all time."

3. "¡Oh llama de amor viva": The basis of the prose commentary *Llama de amor viva,* it is also written in *liras.* Its full title as it appears in the definitive version (B) of the commentary is: "Poem made by the soul in close union with God, her beloved Bridegroom." In the 1618 edition, it is "Poem of the soul in close communication of loving union with God." It is thought to have been written between 1582 and 1585 (or, more specifically, 1584, or 1584–1585) for the above-mentioned Ana del Mercado y Peñalosa, who was also the dedicatee of the prose *Llama.*

It is unnecessary to say anything more about the content of poems 1–3 at this point, not only because the commentaries they inspired are discussed below, but also because this volume includes so much written about them in Saint John's own words.

4. "Vivo sin vivir en mí": The full title is "*Coplas* [the specific lyrical-ballad stanza form of this poem] of the soul aching to see God." It is thought to have been written between 1582 and 1585. Dissatisfied with anything this life has to offer, the soul yearns for the real, eternal life, and the sight of God in glory only possible after death.

5. "Que bien sé yo la fonte que mana y corre": The full title is "Song of the soul that is pleased to know God through faith." It is thought to have been written in prison in Toledo in 1578. God, the divine fountain in three Persons, is hidden in the Communion bread and can only be known in the darkness (renunciation of worldly things and eclipse of the intellect) brought on by faith.

6. "Entréme donde no supe": The full title is "*Coplas* written on the occasion of an ecstasy of deep contemplation." It is thought to have been written between 1582 and 1585. The "unknowing" caused by the phaseout of the human intellect in close converse with God is superior to all earthly knowledge.

7. "Un pastorcico, solo, está penado": The full title is "Another poem, refashioned into a religious motif, about Christ and the soul." It is thought to have been written between 1582 and 1585, though the evidence for this is not strong. The shepherd lad is Christ, Who is crucified in the last stanza; the shepherdess is the faithless soul, whom He threatens. The poem is a brilliant religious transformation of a known secular love song.

8. "Tras de un amoroso lance": The full title is "Another religious version by the same author." It is thought to have been written between 1582 and 1585; again, it was based on a popular song, no doubt about love. Here the narrator finally achieves his goal (union with God) through such salutary practices as self-abasement and the embracing of spiritual "darkness."

The Major Prose Works

The eminent Spanish poet Luis Cernuda (1902–1963) once wrote: "Few things exist in our language as beautiful as the works of Saint John of the Cross. I am not speaking of his poetry only, but also of his prose." And the saint's chief biographer aptly characterized the major prose works: "He embodies supreme intelligence in the *Subida* and the *Noche,* Near Eastern imagination in the *Cántico,* and a blazing heart in the *Llama.*"

In the reign of Felipe II, the bulk of Spanish prose writing was religious. The Carmelite authors, in particular, strove to harmonize the emotion of the Augustines and Franciscans with the intellectuality of the Dominicans and Jesuits. As a mystic seeking close personal union with God in this life, Saint John of the Cross was influenced by certain books of the Bible, by certain Church fathers and medieval writers (such as Saint Bernard, 1090–1153), by important German and Flemish authors of the Middle Ages and early Renaissance (such as Master Eckhart, ca. 1260–1327, and Jan van Ruysbroeck, 1293–1381), and by the mystical writers in Arabic (extensively translated in Spain; there was a specifically Arabic tradition of religious prose commentaries on preexisting poems). (It has been said that Saint John wrote commentaries on his own boldly stated poems to defend their orthodoxy.) As a Renaissance man, and a man wishing to be of immediate use to the often unlearned or even illiterate friars and nuns under his direction, Saint John, though versed in Latin theology, wrote in Spanish. (Other great Spanish mystics of his own day, all of whom used the vernacular, included the above-mentioned Saint Teresa and Luis de León, an Augustine friar, as well as the ascetic Dominican friar Luis de Granada, 1504–1588.) A distinctive feature of Saint John's prose works is his superb extended comparisons, inspired literary images introduced to illustrate difficult philosophical concepts; major examples in the present anthology will be found in: *Subida,* book II, chapter 5, sections 6 and 9; *Noche,* book I, chapter 1, section 2; *Noche,* book II, chapter 8, section 3; and *Llama,* prologue, section 3 (a metaphor that permeates and structures the whole work). (The numbering of sections within chapters, retained in this edition for convenience of reference, dates back to an important edition of the complete works in the early twentieth century.)

The major works actually form a single escalating sequence, both chronologically and thematically, which may be summarized as follows. [*Subida,* book I:][1] Certain souls chosen by God long for the closest union with Him possible in this life. Toward this end, as an active agent, the soul must mortify the senses (its lower part) by ascetic practices, and must renounce worldly things; all this leaves the soul in a state called "night" (the word is also applied to related psychic phe-

---

1. The *Subida/Noche* complex is a commentary on the first three stanzas of poem 1.

nomena; compare poem 5; the resulting eclipse of normal knowledge is described in poem 6). [*Subida,* book II:] Not only the senses, but the spirit as well, must be actively (voluntarily) exercised in the higher, rational part of the soul; the first stage entails purifying the soul's power of intellect by means of the "theological virtue" faith. [*Subida,* book III:] To complete the active reformation of the spirit, the soul's two other powers must be purified: "memory" by hope, and the will by charity. All this activity is aided by meditation. [*Noche:*] But this purification cannot become total without God's operations on the senses (book I) and the spirit (book II), during which the soul is a passive recipient. At this more advanced stage, the soul is in contemplation. The desired union is achieved. [*Cántico,* the commentary on poem 2:] The entire trajectory just described is reviewed in different terms, with different literary images (such as spiritual marriage) and with a different theological mechanism, the three paths: purgative, illuminative, and unitive. At the end, the actual state of bliss in this union (in this life) is described. [*Llama,* the commentary on poem 3:] But all this can be even more intensely felt; in this new situation, the soul is impatient to die in order to attain the ultimate union and see God's glory in heaven (compare poem 4). The individual prose works:

Subida del Monte Carmelo. The "ascent" idea had been used before, in the 1535 *Subida del Monte Sión* (Ascent of Mount Zion) by the Franciscan friar Bernardino de Laredo. Saint John of the Cross supplied a schematic diagram of his Mount Carmel, but his text is not topographical (as Dante's *Divine Comedy* is, for example). The *Subida,* which was left incomplete, is thought to have been written between 1579 and 1585. It was first published in the 1618 *Obras espirituales* (see "Poetry" section, above). A long subtitle reads: "Treats of how a soul can prepare to arrive quickly at divine union. Gives advice and doctrine, to beginners as well as proficients, very helpful for their learning to slough off all worldly things, to remain unentangled in spiritual matters, and to live in the utmost nakedness and freedom of spirit, as required for divine union." This book, like its direct continuation (or component part) *Noche oscura,* is the author's most thoroughly scholastic work, very rigorous in logic and full of theological subtleties. Its style is sometimes dry and rugged, and its argumentation occasionally obscure.

Many chapters[2] have been selected here from *Subida* because it is

---

2. The excerpts in this Dover anthology are always complete chapters (or other complete subdivisions), without exception.

basic to the entire prose oeuvre, introducing much of the thought patterning and specific terminology used in every commentary by the author. From book I we have included the prologue, with its statement of purpose; the first definition of "night"; and some explanation of the soul's sensory nakedness and how it is achieved actively, with at least some reference to every line of poem 1, stanza 1. (The first and last chapters of book I are here.) From book II we have included the introduction to the active purification of the intellect by faith, and one good sample chapter from a sequence that constitutes a veritable mini-treatise on ecstatic visions, hearing voices, etc. From book III we have included chapters concerning the active purification of the will by charity, and of the memory by hope, as well as an interesting chapter on religious images (statues and paintings).

Noche oscura. Though separated from *Subida* in the first (1618) edition (creating an editorial tradition that has never been abandoned), the *Noche* is clearly a continuation of it, and an integral part of it, commenting on the same poem but containing the exposition of the soul's *passive* role in achieving divine union. Proof that Saint John considered these two apparently separate works as one appears in: *Subida,* book I, chapter 1, section 2; *Subida,* book I, chapter 13, section 1; *Subida,* book II, chapter 2, section 3; *Subida,* book II, chapter 6, section 8; and, most conclusively, in *Llama,* discussion of stanza 1, section 25 (this *Llama* reference also reveals that the title *Noche oscura* for this part of the treatise goes back to Saint John himself!). The *Noche* is thought to have been written between 1582 and 1585, though earlier dates have also been conjectured. There is no significant subtitle. The style is similar to that of the *Subida,* with occasional signs of becoming more fluid and easy.

Selections here include the very beginning (the introduction to the passive purification of the soul—book I, senses; book II, spirit—through God's own intervention) and the very end, where the book breaks off abruptly.[3]

Cántico espiritual. Like poem 2, on which it is based, two versions of this prose commentary (A and B) are extant. *Cántico A* is thought to have been written in 1584; the revision, *Cántico B,* between 1586 and 1591 (it is from this definitive version that the Dover selection was made). *Cántico A* was first published in Spanish in the 1627 Brussels edition mentioned in the "Poetry" section, above (with

---

3. One reason for not including more of the *Noche* here is that Dover has already reprinted the complete 1935 translation of it by E. Allison Peers under the title *Dark Night of the Soul* (ISBN 0-486-42693-9).

the same preceding 1622 French edition); *Cántico B,* in the 1703 Seville edition cited in the same place. The subtitle reads: "Explanation of the poem that treats of the love practiced between the soul and the Bridegroom Christ, in which some points and effects of prayer are touched on and explained. Written at the request of Mother Ana de Jesús, prioress of the Discalced nuns in the convent of San José in Granada. 1584." (This prioress has been prominently mentioned in the sketch of Saint John's life given above.) The style of *Cántico B* already shows the author at his best. The complete stanza-by-stanza and line-by-line analysis is fervent, lucid, and arresting, though the argumentation occasionally requires close attention. Some scholars consider the *Cántico* to be Saint John's supreme prose work.

The selections here include the prologue (which has been called a "veritable treatise on the esthetics of the delirium which ought to characterize all authentically mystical literature") and the entire discussion of the first stanza and the last two (39 and 40).

Llama de amor viva. Called by at least one critic "the most sublime" of Saint John's books, it is a completely preserved commentary on poem 3. It was first published in the above-mentioned 1618 Alcalá edition, and is extant in two versions (A and B), not widely divergent in wording, though version B is somewhat longer (B is used in this Dover edition). *Llama A* is thought to have been written between 1585 and 1587 (thus, after the writing of *Cántico A;* the *Llama* is referred to in *Cántico B); Llama B,* between 1586 and 1591. The subtitle reads: "Explanation of the poem that treats of the very close, ennobled union and transformation of the soul in God, written in prayer by Father John of the Cross, Discalced Carmelite, at the request of Doña Ana de Peñalosa." (This noble lady has been mentioned in the biography above.) The style is coruscating with ardor, like a particularly stirring sermon, as befits the subject matter: the most intense union with God possible on earth. There is barely a trace of stiffness or obscurity in this prose that has been called "impassioned and fiery."

Selected here are the prologue and the uncut discussion of the first stanza: the longest single excerpt in this anthology, exemplifying the fullest exposition of the author's thought while he is writing in his best vein.

Postscript. Very little is extant in Saint John's own handwriting (none of his poems or major prose works),[4] but there are sufficient

---

4. The longest item in his own hand is a thirteen-page copy he made of a nun's autobiography.

manuscript copies of each work by other hands to assure authenticity and provide a good text. As has been seen, all the first editions appeared a generation or more after his death; in the subsequent centuries, editors of his works have made use of a greater variety of extant manuscript copies. There is no definitive critical edition yet, the earliest attempt having been made about 1750. One of the two basic complete-works editions in the early twentieth century, the underpinning of all that have followed, is the one prepared by Father Gérardo de San Juan de la Cruz, published in Toledo from 1912 to 1914 by the Viuda é hijos de (Widow and Sons of) J. Peláez. There are several English translations of the complete works, the earliest having appeared in 1862.

The Nature of This Edition

The Spanish text of this Dover edition is discreetly modernized in spelling and punctuation, though it does not tamper with the sources lexically or syntactically. The new English translation, which aims at completeness and accuracy (it faces the Spanish original, and, like all Dover dual-language books, has a pedagogical aspect), avoids paraphrasing and that apparent smoothness which is often achieved by omissions, condensation, and rearrangement of sentences and paragraphs. Thus, it strives to reflect the very long sentences of the original, which are sometimes rambling, but often have great cumulative power and rhetorical sweep.

Terms from scholastic philosophy and theology are often retained, so as not to falsify the author's purpose (thus, for example, we keep: substance, essence, discourse, proximate, possible intellect, and memory [in its technical use as one of the soul's three powers]); "supernatural" is retained, though it is always equivalent to "heavenly" or "divine," never referring to weird or uncanny terrestrial phenomena. But when confusion of meaning was highly likely, we have altered some terms; for instance, we have used "propensity" instead of the technical "habit," and "perception" instead of "apprehension" (there is never a connotation of vague fears or forebodings).

The reader may at first be jolted by one odd convention adopted here from the practice of earlier English translators, though he will rapidly grow accustomed to it: the use of "she" and "her" when referring to the soul (the feminine noun *alma* in Spanish; also feminine in the biblical languages Hebrew, Greek, and Latin). Not only does this help to achieve clarity amid a true jungle of pronouns in the text (without repeating the noun "soul" ad nauseam): the soul in the text is almost always personified, standing for "person" or "bride," and is the actual speaker in the three supreme poems (1–3), on which the major prose commentaries are based.

Biblical quotations have been given in the King James version wherever this was possible. When it was not (because the author's exegesis following a quotation was too closely based on the exact wording of the often very different Latin Vulgate rendering, or even the author's own Spanish version), a new literal translation has been made (or the substance of the quotation has been worked into the main text); in such cases, the citation of biblical book, chapter, and verse has been prefaced by a cautionary "[compare]." All names of biblical books, however, and all citations of chapter and verse, in the translation refer to the King James version, whereas the Spanish text always gives the Vulgate references, which sometimes differ, especially in the Psalms.

Mystical Verse
and Prose

Poesías y prosas
místicas

Poesías

1. "En una noche obscura"

1. En una noche obscura,
   con ansias, en amores inflamada,
   ¡oh dichosa ventura!,
   salí sin ser notada,
   estando ya mi casa sosegada:
2. a escuras y segura
   por la secreta escala, disfrazada,
   ¡oh dichosa ventura!,
   a escuras y en celada,
   estando ya mi casa sosegada;
3. En la noche dichosa,
   en secreto, que naide me veía
   ni yo miraba cosa,
   sin otra luz y guía
   sino la que en el corazón ardía.
4. Aquésta me guiaba
   más cierto que la luz del mediodía
   adonde me esperaba
   quien yo bien me sabía,
   en parte donde naide parecía.
5. ¡Oh noche que guiaste!,
   ¡oh noche amable más que la alborada!,
   ¡oh noche que juntaste
   Amado con amada,
   amada en el Amado transformada!
6. En mi pecho florido,
   que entero para él solo se guardaba,

Verse

1. "On a dark night"

1.   On a dark night,[1]
with longings, afire with love
(oh, happy fortune!),
I went out without being detected,
my house being calm now.
2.   In the dark, but feeling safe,
by the secret ladder, in disguise
(oh, happy fortune!),
in the dark and in concealment,
my house being calm now;
3.   in the happy night,
secretly, with no one seeing me
and I looking at nothing,
with no other guiding light
than the one burning in my heart.
4.   This light was guiding me
more surely than the light of noon
to where I was awaited
by Him whom I knew so well
in a place where no one else was present.
5.   O night that guided me!
O night more charming than the dawn!
O night that joined together
the Beloved and His sweetheart,
the sweetheart transformed in the Beloved!
6.   On my flowery bosom,
which had been kept intact for Him alone,

1. This is the poem commented on in the two-part prose treatise *Subida del Monte Carmelo* and *Noche oscura*. The adjectives nodifying the speaker ("I") are feminine, since the narrator is the soul (*el alma*).

3

allí quedó dormido
y yo le regalaba,
y el ventalle de cedros aire daba.

7. El aire del almena,
cuando yo sus cabellos esparcía,
con su mano serena
en mi cuello hería,
y todos mis sentidos suspendía.

8. Quedéme y olvidéme,
el rostro recliné sobre el Amado;
cesó todo y dejéme,
dejando mi cuidado
entre las azucenas olvidado.

2. Cántico espiritual

1. ¿Adónde te escondiste,
Amado, y me dejaste con gemido?
Como el ciervo huiste,
habiéndome herido;
salí tras ti clamando, y eras ido.

2. Pastores, los que fuerdes
allá por las majadas al otero:
si por ventura vierdes
aquel que yo más quiero,
decilde que adolezco, peno y muero.

3. Buscando mis amores
iré por esos montes y riberas;
ni cogeré las flores
ni temeré las fieras,
y pasaré los fuertes y fronteras.

4. ¡Oh bosques y espesuras,
plantadas por la mano del Amado!,
¡oh prado de verduras
de flores esmaltado!;
decid si por vosotros ha pasado.

He fell asleep in that place
and I kept caressing Him,
and the fan of cedars sent a breeze.

7.   The breeze from the battlements,
while I was toying with His hair,
struck my neck
with its serene hand,
suspending all my senses.

8.   I lingered and forgot who I was,
I bent my face over the Beloved;
everything ceased and I abandoned my self,
leaving my cares behind
forgotten amid the lilies.

2. Spiritual Canticle

1.   Where have You hidden Yourself,[2]
Beloved, leaving me moaning?
Like a stag You fled
after wounding me;
I sallied forth after You, calling out, but You were gone.

2.   You shepherds who may go
yonder to the knoll past the sheepfolds:
if by chance you should see
Him whom I love best,
tell Him I am languishing, suffering, and dying.

3.   In quest of my Darling
I shall traverse those mountains and riverbanks;
I shall not gather flowers,
I shall not fear wild animals,
and I shall pass fortresses and frontiers.

4.   O woods and thickets,
planted by the hand of the Beloved!
O verdant meadow
enameled with flowers!
Tell me whether He has passed your way.

---

2. This poem is the basis of the prose commentary of the same name. The chief speaker is the bride (cf. the Song of Solomon).

5.   Mil gracias derramando
      pasó por estos sotos con presura
      y, yéndolos mirando,
      con sola su figura
      vestidos los dejó de hermosura.

6.   ¡Ay!, ¿quién podrá sanarme?
      Acaba de entregarte ya de vero;
      no quieras enviarme
      de hoy más ya mensajero,
      que no saben decirme lo que quiero.

7.   Y todos cuantos vagan
      de ti me van mil gracias refiriendo,
      y todos más me llagan,
      y déjame muriendo
      un no sé qué que quedan balbuciendo.

8.   Mas ¿cómo perseveras,
      ¡oh vida!, no viviendo donde vives,
      y haciendo por que mueras
      las flechas que recibes
      de lo que del Amado en ti concibes?

9.   ¿Por qué, pues has llagado
      aqueste corazón, no le sanaste?;
      y, pues me le has robado,
      ¿por qué así te dejaste
      y no tomas el robo que robaste?

10.   Apaga mis enojos,
      pues que ninguno basta a deshacellos,
      y véante mis ojos,
      pues eres lumbre dellos,
      y sólo para ti quiero tenellos.

11.   Descubre tu presencia,
      y máteme tu vista y hermosura;
      mira que la dolencia
      de amor, que no se cura
      sino con la presencia y la figura.

12.   ¡Oh cristalina fuente,
      si en esos tus semblantes plateados
      formases de repente
      los ojos deseados
      que tengo en mis entrañas dibujados!

5. "Pouring forth a thousand graces,
   He passed hastily through these groves
   and, beholding them as He went,
   by His mere presence
   He left them clad in beauty."

6. Alas, who will be able to cure me?
   Surrender Yourself truly now;
   please no longer send me
   messengers from today on,
   for they are unable to tell me what I want.

7. And all those who roam around
   report a thousand gracious things to me about You,
   and all of them wound me more deeply,
   and I am left dying
   by some words or other that they keep stammering.

8. But how do you persist,
   O life, not living while you live,
   and being caused to die
   by the arrows you receive
   from your inner conception of the Beloved?

9. Why, since You have wounded
   this heart, have You not healed it?
   And, since You have stolen it from me,
   why have You remained this way,
   not taking the spoils of Your theft?

10. Soothe my griefs,
    since no one else is able to dissipate them,
    and let my eyes see You,
    since You are their light,
    and I wish to have them merely for Your sake.

11. Reveal Your presence,
    and let the sight of Your beauty kill me;
    observe that the pain
    of love is not cured
    except by actual presence and form.

12. O crystal fountain,
    if only in your silvery mirror
    you could suddenly give shape to
    those longed-for eyes
    which are engraved within me!

13. ¡Apártalos, Amado,
     que voy de vuelo!
               Vuélvete, paloma,
     que el ciervo vulnerado
     por el otero asoma
     al aire de tu vuelo, y fresco toma.
14. Mi Amado, las montañas,
     los valles solitarios nemorosos,
     las ínsulas extrañas,
     los ríos sonorosos,
     el silbo de los aires amorosos;
15. la noche sosegada
     en par de los levantes del aurora,
     la música callada,
     la soledad sonora,
     la cena que recrea y enamora.
16. Cazadnos las raposas,
     que está ya florecida nuestra viña,
     en tanto que de rosas
     hacemos una piña,
     y no parezca nadie en la montiña.
17. Detente, cierzo muerto;
     ven, austro, que recuerdas los amores,
     aspira por mi huerto
     y corran sus olores,
     y pacerá el Amado entre las flores.
18. ¡Oh ninfas de Judea!,
     en tanto que en las flores y rosales
     el ámbar perfumea,
     morá en los arrabales
     y no queráis tocar nuestros umbrales.
19. Escóndete, Carillo,
     y mira con tu haz a las montañas
     y no quieras decillo;
     mas mira las compañas
     de la que va por insulas extrañas.
20. A las aves ligeras,
     leones, ciervos, gamos saltadores,
     montes, valles, riberas,
     aguas, aires, ardores
     y miedos de las noches veladores:

13.   Turn them aside, Beloved,
for I am flying!
            "Return, my dove,
for the wounded stag
appears on the knoll
in the breeze of your flight, and enjoys the coolness."

14.   My Beloved, the mountains,
the lonely sylvan valleys,
the strange islands,
the sounding rivers,
the whistling of the enamored winds;

15.   the night as calm
as the east winds of dawn,
the silent music,
the sounding solitude,
the supper that refreshes and ignites love.

16.   You men there, hunt the vixens for us,
for our vineyard is now in bloom,
while we make
a cluster of roses,
and let no one appear on the mountain.

17.   Stop, dead north wind;
come, south wind, awakener of love,
blow through my garden
and let its fragrances run,
and my Beloved shall pasture amid the flowers.

18.   O maidens of Judea,
while amid the flowers and rosebushes
the ambergris wafts its perfume,
remain on the outskirts
and do not try to touch our threshold.

19.   Conceal Yourself, Dearest,
and turn Your face to the mountains
and do not try to speak;
but look at the girl friends
of her who travels through strange islands.

20.   "You light-winged birds,
lions, red deer, leaping fallow deer,
mountains, valleys, riverbanks,
waters, winds, heat,
and fears of the sleepless nights:

21.   Por las amenas liras
      y canto de serenas, os conjuro
      que cesen vuestras iras
      y no toquéis al muro,
      por que la esposa duerma más seguro.
22.   Entrado se ha la esposa
      en el ameno huerto deseado,
      y a su sabor reposa,
      el cuello reclinado
      sobre los dulces brazos del Amado.
23.   Debajo del manzano,
      allí conmigo fuiste desposada,
      allí te di la mano,
      y fuiste reparada
      donde tu madre fuera violada.
24.   Nuestro lecho florido,
      de cuevas de leones enlazado,
      en púrpura tendido,
      de paz edificado,
      de mil escudos de oro coronado.
25.   A zaga de tu huella
      las jóvenes discurren al camino,
      al toque de centella,
      al adobado vino:
      emisiones de bálsamo divino.
26.   En la interior bodega
      de mi Amado bebí, y, cuando salía
      por toda aquesta vega,
      ya cosa no sabía
      y el ganado perdí que antes seguía.
27.   Allí me dio su pecho,
      allí me enseñó ciencia muy sabrosa,
      y yo le di de hecho
      a mí sin dejar cosa;
      allí le prometí de ser su esposa.
28.   Mi alma se ha empleado
      y todo mi caudal en su servicio;
      ya no guardo ganado,
      ni ya tengo otro oficio,
      que ya sólo en amar es mi exercicio.

21. By the pleasant lyres
     and the sirens' song, I call on you
     to desist from your wrath
     and not to touch the wall,
     so that the bride may sleep more securely.

22. The bride has entered
     the delightful garden she had yearned for,
     and is reposing to her heart's content,
     her neck reclining
     on the sweet arms of her Beloved.

23. Beneath the apple tree,
     there you were wed to Me,
     there I gave you My hand,
     and you were mended
     where your ancestress was once violated.

24. Our flowery bed,
     enlaced by lions' dens,
     hung in purple,
     constructed of peace,
     crowned with a thousand golden shields.

25. Following your footsteps
     the young women go down the path,
     to the touch of a spark,
     with the spiced wine:
     effluvia of divine balsam."

26. In the innermost wine cellar
     of my Beloved I drank, and when I issued forth
     onto this great fertile plain,
     I no longer knew a thing
     and I had lost the flock I was formerly following.

27. There He gave me His bosom,
     there He taught me detectable knowledge,
     and in reality I gave Him
     myself, omitting nothing;
     there I promised Him to be His bride.

28. My soul employed itself
     and all my wealth in His service;
     I no longer watch a flock,
     I no longer have any other duty,
     for now my task is merely to love.

29.   Pues ya si en el ejido
      de hoy más no fuere vista ni hallada,
      diréis que me he perdido,
      que, andando enamorada,
      me hice perdidiza, y fui ganada.

30.   De flores y esmeraldas,
      en las frescas mañanas escogidas,
      haremos las guirnaldas,
      en tu amor floridas
      y en un cabello mío entretejidas.

31.   En sólo aquel cabello
      que en mi cuello volar consideraste,
      mirástele en mi cuello
      y en él preso quedaste,
      y en uno de mis ojos te llagaste.

32.   Cuando tú me mirabas,
      su gracia en mí tus ojos imprimían:
      por eso me adamabas,
      y en eso merecían
      los míos adorar lo que en ti vían.

33.   No quieras despreciarme;
      que, si color moreno en mí hallaste,
      ya bien puedes mirarme
      después que me miraste,
      que gracia y hermosura en mí dejaste.

34.   La blanca palomica
      al arca con el ramo se ha tornado,
      y ya la tortolica
      al socio deseado
      en las riberas verdes ha hallado.

35.   En soledad vivía,
      y en soledad ha puesto ya su nido,
      y en soledad la guía
      a solas su querido,
      también en soledad de amor herido.

36.   Gocémonos, Amado,
      y vámonos a ver en tu hermosura
      al monte y al collado,
      do mana el agua pura;
      entremos más adentro en la espesura.

29.   Since now, if on the village common
I were not to be seen or found from today on,
you would all say I was lost,
that, going about in love,
I got lost on purpose: but I have been won!

30.   Of flowers and emeralds,
gathered on cool mornings,
we shall make garlands,
blossoming in Your love
and woven into one of my hairs.

31.   Into that one hair
which You gazed at as it flew against my neck:
You looked at it on my neck
and You got caught in it,
and You wounded Yourself on one of my eyes.

32.   Whenever You looked at me,
Your eyes imprinted their grace on me:
therefore You loved me deeply,
and thereby my eyes
deserved to worship what they saw in You.

33.   Please do not have contempt for me;
for, if You have found my complexion to be swarthy,
now You may readily behold me,
for after once beholding me
You left behind grace and beauty in me.

34.   The little white dove
has returned to the ark with the branch,
and now the little turtledove
has found her longed-for mate
on the green riverbanks.

35.   She was living in solitude,
and in solitude she has now built her nest,
and in solitude she is guided
by her Loved One alone,
Who is also smitten by love in solitude.

36.   Let us rejoice, Beloved,
and let us go see in Your beauty
the mountain and the hill,
where the pure water wells up;
let us enter further into the thicket.

37.   Y luego a las subidas
       cavernas de la piedra nos iremos
       que están bien escondidas,
       y allí nos entraremos,
       y el mosto de granadas gustaremos.
38.   Allí me mostrarías
       aquello que mi alma pretendía,
       y luego me darías
       allí tú, vida mía,
       aquello que me diste el otro día:
39.   El aspirar del aire,
       el canto de la dulce filomena,
       el soto y su donaire
       en la noche serena,
       con llama que consume y no da pena.
40.   Que nadie lo miraba . . .
       Aminadab tampoco parecía;
       y el cerco sosegaba,
       y la caballería
       a vista de las aguas descendía.

3. "¡Oh llama de amor viva"

1.   ¡Oh llama de amor viva,
       que tiernamente hieres
       de mi alma en el más profundo centro!;
       pues ya no eres esquiva,
       acaba ya, si quieres;
       rompe la tela de este dulce encuentro.
2.   ¡Oh cauterio suave!
       ¡Oh regalada llaga!
       ¡Oh mano blanda! ¡Oh toque delicado!,
       que a vida eterna sabe
       y toda deuda paga;
       matando, muerte en vida la has trocado.
3.   ¡Oh lámparas de fuego,
       en cuyos resplandores
       las profundas cavernas del sentido,

37.   And then to the lofty
       caverns in the rock we shall ascend,
       which are well hidden,
       and there we shall enter in,
       and we shall taste the juice of the pomegranate.
38.   There You will show me
       that which my heart aspired to,
       and then You shall give me
       there—You, my life—
       that which You gave me the other day:
39.   The breathing of the air,
       the song of the sweet nightingale,
       the grove and its elegance
       in the serene night,
       with flame that consumes but causes no pain.
40.   For no one was looking . . .
       nor was Amminadib present;
       and the siege slackened,
       and the cavalry
       was descending in sight of the waters.

3. "O living flame of love"

1.   O living flame of love,[3]
      you that tenderly wound
      the deepest center of my soul!
      Since you are no longer harsh,
      please complete your task:
      rend the veil of this sweet encounter!
2.   O gentle cautery!
      O delightful wound!
      O soft hand! O delicate touch,
      which tastes like eternal life
      and pays every debt!
      Killing me, you have changed death to life.
3.   O lamps of fire,
      in whose glow
      the deep caverns of sense,

---

3. This poem is the basis of the prose commentary of the same name.

que estaba oscuro y ciego,
con extraños primores
calor y luz dan junto a su querido!

4.   ¡Cuán manso y amoroso
recuerdas en mi seno
donde secretamente solo moras,
y en tu aspirar sabroso
de bien y gloria lleno
cuán delicadamente me enamoras!

4. "Vivo sin vivir en mí"

Vivo sin vivir en mí
y de tal manera espero,
que muero porque no muero.

1.   En mí yo no vivo ya,
y sin Dios vivir no puedo;
pues sin él y sin mí quedo,
este vivir ¿qué será?
Mil muertes se me hará,
pues mi misma vida espero,
muriendo porque no muero.

2.   Esta vida que yo vivo
es privación de vivir;
y así, es contino morir
hasta que viva contigo.
Oye, mi Dios, lo que digo,
que esta vida no la quiero;
que muero porque no muero.

3.   Estando absente de ti,
¿qué vida puedo tener,
sino muerte padescer,
la mayor que nunca vi?
Lástima tengo de mí,
pues de suerte persevero,
que muero porque no muero.

4.   El pez que del agua sale
aun de alivio no caresce,
que en la muerte que padesce,
al fin la muerte le vale.

which was formerly dark and blind,
now with strange excellence
give both warmth and light to their loved one!
4.   How meekly and lovingly
you wake in my breast,
where you secretly dwell alone,
and with your delectable breathing,
filled with goodness and glory,
how delicately you enamor me!

4. "I live without living in myself"

I live without living in myself,
and I hope in such a way
that I die because I do not die.
1.   I no longer live in myself,
and I cannot live without God;
since I am left without Him and without myself,
what will this living amount to?
There will be a thousand deaths for me,
since I hope for my very life,
dying because I do not die.
2.   This life that I live
is a deprivation of life;
and thus, it is a continual dying
until I live with You.
Hear, my God, what I say:
I do not want this life;
for I am dying because I do not die.
3.   Being absent from You,
what life can I have
except to suffer death,
the greatest I ever saw?
I feel pity for myself
because I persist in such a manner
that I die because I do not die.
4.   A fish out of water
still does not lack for relief,
for in the death that it suffers
death finally does it good.

¿Qué muerte habrá que se iguale
a mi vivir lastimero,
pues, si más vivo, más muero?

5.   Cuando me pienso aliviar
de verte en el Sacramento,
háceme más sentimiento
el no te poder gozar;
todo es para más penar,
por no verte como quiero,
y muero porque no muero.

6.   Y si me gozo, Señor,
con esperanza de verte,
en ver que puedo perderte
se me dobla mi dolor;
viviendo en tanto pavor
y esperando como espero,
muérome porque no muero.

7.   Sácame de aquesta muerte,
mi Dios, y dame la vida;
no me tengas impedida
en este lazo tan fuerte;
mira que peno por verte,
y mi mal es tan entero,
que muero porque no muero.

8.   Lloraré mi muerte ya
y lamentaré mi vida
en tanto que detenida
por mis pecados está.
¡Oh mi Dios!, ¿cuándo será
cuando yo diga de vero:
vivo ya porque no muero?

5. "Que bien sé yo la fonte que mana y corre"

Que bien sé yo la fonte que mana y corre,
aunque es de noche.

1.   Aquella eterna fonte está escondida,
que bien sé yo do tiene su manida,
aunque es de noche.

What death can there be that is equal
to my pitiful life,
since the more I live the more I die?

5.   When I think of gaining relief
by seeing You in the Sacrament,
I am caused greater distress
by not being able to enjoy You;
everything leads to more grief
through not seeing You as I wish to,
and I die because I do not die.

6.   And if I rejoice, Lord,
in the hope of seeing You,
on seeing that I may lose You
my sorrow is doubled;
living in such fear
and hoping as I hope,
I am dying because I do not die.

7.   Release me from this death,
my God, and give me life;
do not keep me entangled[4]
in this snare that is so strong;
observe that I ache to see You,
and my woe is so powerful
that I die because I do not die.

8.   I shall now bewail my death
and lament my life
as long as it is detained
because of my sins.
O my God, when will it happen
that I can truly say:
"Now I live because I do not die."

5. "For I know well the fountain that gushes and flows"

For I know well the fountain that gushes and flows,
        though it be night.

1.   That eternal fountain is hidden,
but I know well where it has its dwelling,
        though it be night.

---

4. *Impedida* is feminine: an indication that the speaker is the soul.

2. En esta noche oscura de esta vida,
que bien sé yo por fe la fonte frida
aunque es de noche.

3. Su origen no lo sé, pues no le tiene,
mas sé que todo origen della viene,
aunque es de noche.

4. Sé que no puede ser cosa tan bella
y que cielos y tierra beben della,
aunque es de noche.

5. Bien sé que suelo en ella no se halla
y que ninguno puede vadealla,
aunque es de noche.

6. Su claridad nunca es escurecida,
y sé que toda luz de ella es venida,
aunque es de noche.

7. Sé ser tan caudalosos sus corrientes,
que infiernos, cielos riegan, y las gentes,
aunque es de noche.

8. El corriente que nace desta fuente
bien sé que es tan capaz y omnipotente,
aunque es de noche.

9. El corriente que de estas dos procede,
sé que ninguna de ellas le precede,
aunque es de noche.

10. Bien sé que tres en sola una agua viva
residen, y una de otra se deriva,
aunque es de noche.

11. Aquesta eterna fonte está escondida
en este vivo pan por darnos vida,
aunque es de noche.

12. Aquí se está llamando a las criaturas,
y de esta agua se hartan, aunque a escuras,
aunque es de noche.

13. Aquesta viva fuente que deseo,
en este pan de vida yo la veo,
aunque de noche.

2. On this dark night of this life,
    I know the cool fountain well through faith,
           though it be night.

3.   I do not know its source, since it has none,
    but I know that all beginnings come from it,
           though it be night.

4.   I know there cannot be a lovelier thing
    and that heavens and earth drink from it,
           though it be night.

5.   I know well that no bottom is to be found in it
    and that no one can ford it,
           though it be night.

6.   Its brightness is never darkened,
    and I know that all light has come from it,
           though it be night.

7.   I know its currents are so abundant
    that they water hells, heavens, and nations,
           though it be night.

8.   The current that rises from this fountain,
    I know well, is so able and omnipotent,
           though it be night.

9.   The current that proceeds from these two sources—
    I know that neither of them precedes it,
           though it be night.

10.   I know well that three reside in a single living water
    and one derives from another,
           though it be night.

11.   This eternal fountain is hidden
    in this living bread to give us life,
           though it be night.

12.   Here it continually calls to all created beings,
    and with this water they fill themselves, though in the dark
           because it is nighttime.

13.   This living fountain that I desire,
    in this bread of life I see it,
           though it be night.

6. "Entréme donde no supe"

Entréme donde no supe,
y quedéme no sabiendo,
toda sciencia trascendiendo.
1.   Yo no supe dónde entraba,
pero, cuando allí me vi,
sin saber dónde me estaba,
grandes cosas entendí;
no diré lo que sentí,
que me quedé no sabiendo,
toda sciencia trascendiendo.
2.   De paz y de pïedad
era la sciencia perfecta,
en profunda soledad
entendida (vía recta);
era cosa tan secreta,
que me quedé balbuciendo,
toda sciencia trascendiendo.
3.   Estaba tan embebido,
tan absorto y ajenado,
que se quedó mi sentido
de todo sentir privado,
y el espíritu dotado
de un entender no entendiendo,
toda sciencia trascendiendo.
4.   El que allí llega de vero
de sí mismo desfallesce;
cuanto sabía primero
mucho baxo le paresce,
y su sciencia tanto cresce,
que se queda no sabiendo,
toda sciencia trascendiendo.
5.   Cuanto más alto se sube,
tanto menos se entendía,
que es la tenebrosa nube
que a la noche esclarecía;
por eso quien la sabía
queda siempre no sabiendo,
toda sciencia trascendiendo.

6. "I entered a place where I had no knowledge"

I entered a place where I had no knowledge,
and I remained without knowledge,
transcending all knowledge.

1. I knew not where I was entering,
   but when I found myself there,
   without knowing where I was,
   I understood great things;
   I shall not say what I felt,
   for I remained without knowledge,
   transcending all knowledge.

2. Of peace and piety
   the knowledge was perfect,
   in profound solitude
   understood (by the direct path);
   it was something so secret
   that I remained stammering,
   transcending all knowledge.

3. I was so immersed,
   so absorbed and ecstatic,
   that my sense remained
   bereft of all sensation,
   and my spirit endowed
   with an understanding not understood,
   transcending all knowledge.

4. Whoever truly arrives there
   is lost to himself;
   whatever he formerly knew
   seems very low to him,
   and his knowledge increases so greatly
   that he remains without knowledge,
   transcending all knowledge.

5. The higher he ascends
   the less he understands,
   for it is the shadowy cloud
   that illumines the night;
   therefore whoever knows it
   always remains without knowledge,
   transcending all knowledge.

6. Este saber no sabiendo
    es de tan alto poder,
    que los sabios arguyendo
    jamás le pueden vencer,
    que no llega su saber
    a no entender entendiendo,
    toda sciencia trascendiendo.
7. Y es de tan alta excelencia
    aqueste summo saber,
    que no hay facultad ni sciencia
    que le puedan emprender;
    quien se supiere vencer
    con un no saber sabiendo,
    íra siempre trascendiendo.
8. Y si lo queréis oír,
    consiste esta summa sciencia
    en un subido sentir
    de la divinal Esencia;
    es obra de su clemencia
    hacer quedar no entendiendo,
    toda sciencia trascendiendo.

7. "Un pastorcico, solo, está penado"

1. Un pastorcico, solo, está penado,
    ajeno de placer y de contento,
    y en su pastora puesto el pensamiento,
    y el pecho del amor muy lastimado.
2. No llora por haberle amor llagado,
    que no le pena verse así afligido,
    aunque en el corazón está herido;
    mas llora por pensar que está olvidado.
3. Que sólo de pensar que está olvidado
    de su bella pastora, con gran pena
    se dexa maltratar en tierra ajena,
    el pecho de el amor muy lastimado.
4. Y dice el pastorcico: ¡Ay, desdichado
    de aquel que de mi amor ha hecho ausencia

6.   This unknowing knowledge
    is of such lofty power
    that wise men in their disputes
    can never obtain it,
    because their knowledge does not extend
    to understanding without understanding,
    transcending all knowledge.
7.   And this highest knowledge
    is of such lofty excellence
    that there is no faculty or science
    that can come to grips with it;
    whoever knows how to conquer himself
    with a knowledge not known
    will always go on transcending.
8.   And if you wish to hear it,
    this highest knowledge consists
    in a sublime sense
    of the divine essence;
    it is a work of His clemency
    to cause someone not to understand,
    transcending all knowledge.

7. "A shepherd lad, alone, is grieving"

1.   A shepherd lad, alone, is grieving,
    a stranger to pleasure and contentment,
    His thoughts all centered on His shepherdess[5]
    and His bosom sorely hurt with love.
2.   He does not weep because love has wounded Him,
    for it does not grieve Him to find Himself thus afflicted,
    although He is stricken to the heart;
    but He weeps to think that He is forgotten.
3.   For at the mere thought that He is forgotten
    by His lovely shepherdess, with great grief
    He lets Himself be mistreated on foreign soil,
    His bosom sorely hurt with love.
4.   And the shepherd lad says: "Oh, woe
    to the one who has absented herself from My love

---

5. The human soul.

y no quiere gozar la mi presencia,
y el pecho por su amor muy lastimado!

5.   Y a cabo de un gran rato, se ha encumbrado
sobre un árbol, do abrió sus brazos bellos,
y muerto se ha quedado asido dellos,
el pecho de el amor muy lastimado.

8. "Tras de un amoroso lance"

Tras de un amoroso lance,
y no de esperanza falto,
volé tan alto, tan alto,
que le di a la caza alcance.

1.   Para que yo alcance diese
a aqueste lance divino,
tanto volar me convino
que de vista me perdiese;
y, con todo, en este trance
en el vuelo quedé falto;
mas el amor fue tan alto,
que le di a la caza alcance.

2.   Cuando más alto subía
deslumbróseme la vista,
y la más fuerte conquista
en escuro se hacía;
mas, por ser de amor el lance,
di un ciego y oscuro salto,
y fui tan alto, tan alto,
que le di a la caza alcance.

3.   Cuanto más alto llegaba
de este lance tan subido,
tanto más bajo y rendido
y abatido me hallaba;
dixe: No habrá quien alcance;
y abatíme tanto, tanto,
que fui tan alto, tan alto,
que le di a la caza alcance.

4.   Por una extraña manera
mil vuelos pasé de un vuelo,
porque esperanza de cielo

and does not wish to enjoy My presence,
and My bosom so sorely hurt with love for her!"
5.   And after a long while, He climbed
up a tree, where He opened His handsome arms,
and, hanging by them, He died,
His bosom sorely hurt with love.

8. "In pursuit of an amorous adventure"

In pursuit of an amorous adventure,
and not lacking in hope,
I flew so high, so high,
that I caught up with my quarry.
1.   In order to overtake
this divine adventure,
I had to fly so high
that I was lost from sight;
but nevertheless at this critical moment
I fell short in my flight;
but love was so lofty
that I caught up with my quarry.
2.   The higher I ascended
the more my eyes were dazzled,
and the greatest conquest
was made in darkness;
but because the adventure was one of love,
I made a blind, dark leap
and rose so high, so high,
that I caught up with my quarry.
3.   The higher I reached
in this very lofty adventure
the lower, the more submissive,
and the more downcast I found myself;
I said: "No one can ever catch up!"
and I cast myself down so far, so far,
that I rose so high, so high,
that I caught up with my quarry.
4.   In a strange manner
I surpassed a thousand flights in one flight,
because the hope of heaven

tanto alcanza cuanto espera;
esperé solo este lance
y en esperar no fui falto,
pues fui tan alto, tan alto,
que le di a la caza alcance.

achieves all that it hopes for;
I hoped for this adventure alone
and I was not denied my hope,
because I rose so high, so high,
that I caught up with my quarry.

Subida del Monte Carmelo

Prólogo

1. Para haber de declarar y dar a entender esta noche oscura por la cual pasa el alma para llegar a la divina luz de la unión perfecta del amor de Dios cual se puede en esta vida, era menester otra mayor luz de sciencia y experiencia que la mía porque son tantas y tan profundas las tinieblas y trabajos, así espirituales como temporales, por que ordinariamente suelen pasar las dichosas almas para poder llegar a este alto estado de perfección, que ni basta sciencia humana para lo saber entender ni experiencia para lo saber decir; porque sólo el que por ello pasa lo sabrá sentir, mas no decir.

2. Y, por tanto, para decir algo desta noche oscura, no fiaré ni de experiencia ni de sciencia, porque lo uno y lo otro puede faltar y engañar; mas, no dejándome de ayudar en lo que pudiere destas dos cosas, aprovecharme he para todo lo que con el favor divino hubiere de decir—a lo menos para lo más importante y escuro de entender—de la divina Escritura, por la cual guiándonos no podremos errar, pues que el que en ella habla es el Espíritu Santo. Y si yo en algo errare por no entender bien así lo que en ella como en lo que sin ella dijere, no es mi intención apartarme del sano sentido y doctrina de la santa Madre Iglesia Católica, porque en tal caso totalmente me sujeto y resigno no sólo a su mandado, sino a cualquiera que en mejor razón de ello juzgare.

3. Para escrebir esto me ha movido no la posibilidad que veo en mí para cosa tan ardua, sino la confianza que en el Señor tengo de que ayudará a decir algo, por la mucha necesidad que tienen muchas almas, las cuales, comenzando el camino de la virtud, y queriéndolas nuestro Señor poner en esta noche oscura para que por ella pasen a la divina unión, ellas no pasan adelante, a veces por no querer entrar o dejarse entrar en ella, a veces por no se entender y faltarles guías idóneas y despiertas que las guíen hasta la cumbre. Y así, es lástima

Ascent of Mount Carmel

Prologue

1. To be able to explain and make understandable this dark night through which the soul passes in order to attain the divine light of perfect loving union with God to the extent possible in this life, a greater light of knowledge and experience than I possess would be necessary, because there are so many and such profound dark zones and labors, spiritual as well as worldly, through which happy souls are usually accustomed to pass, in order to attain this high state of perfection, that human knowledge is insufficient to be able to understand this, and experience is insufficient to be able to express it; because only the person who undergoes it will be able to feel it, though not express it.

2. And therefore, to say something about this dark night, I shall rely neither on experience nor knowledge, because both of them may fall short and be deceptive; but, without ceasing to make use of these two factors, as far as I can, I shall take advantage, in everything I have to say (with God's favor)—at least in the most important things and the hardest to understand—of Holy Scripture; with it as our guide we cannot go astray, since the voice speaking therein is that of the Holy Spirit. And if I should make some mistakes from imperfect understanding of what I say with or without the authority of Scripture, it is not my intention to swerve from the wholesome sense and teachings of our holy mother, the Catholic Church, because in such situations I submit and yield altogether, not only to its commands, but also to anyone who may have a better-founded judgment of them.

3. I have been incited to write this not by any potential I find in myself for so arduous a task, but by the trust I have in the Lord that He will help me say something useful because of the great necessity felt by many souls who are setting out on the path of virtue but who, our Lord wishing to place them in this dark night so they can proceed toward union with Him, fail to move forward, at times because they do not wish to enter that union or allow themselves to enter, at times because they do not understand themselves and lack suitable, wide-awake guides to lead them to the summit. And thus it is pitiful

ver muchas almas a quien Dios da talento y favor para pasar adelante, que, si ellas quisiesen animarse, llegarían a este alto estado, y quédanse en un bajo modo de trato con Dios, por no querer, o no saber, o no las encaminar y enseñar a desasirse de aquellos principios. Y ya que, en fin, nuestro Señor las favorezca tanto que sin eso y sin esotro las haga pasar, llegan muy más tarde y con más trabajo, y con menos merecimiento, por no haber acomodádose ellas a Dios, dejándose poner libremente en el puro y cierto camino de la unión. Porque, aunque es verdad que Dios las lleva—que puede llevarlas sin ellas—, no se dejan ellas llevar; y así, camínase menos resistiendo ellas al que las lleva, y no merecen tanto, pues no aplican la voluntad, y en eso mismo padecen más; porque hay almas que, en vez de dejarse a Dios y ayudarse, antes estorban a Dios por su indiscreto obrar o repugnar, hechas semejantes a los niños que, queriendo sus madres llevarlos en brazos, ellos van pateando y llorando, porfiando por se ir ellos por su pie, para que no se pueda andar nada, y si se anduviere, sea al paso del niño.

4. Y así, para este saberse dejar llevar de Dios cuando Su Majestad los quiere pasar adelante, así a los principiantes como a los aprovechados con su ayuda daremos doctrina y avisos, para que sepan entender o a lo menos dejarse llevar de Dios. Porque algunos padres espirituales, por no tener luz y experiencia destos caminos, antes suelen impedir y dañar a semejantes almas que ayudallas al camino, hechos semejantes a los edificantes de Babilonia, que, habiendo de administrar un material conveniente, daban y aplicaban ellos otro muy diferente, por no entender ellos la lengua (Gen 11,1–9), y así no se hacía nada. Por lo cual es recia y trabajosa cosa en tales sazones no entenderse una alma ni hallar quien la entienda; porque acaecerá que lleve Dios a una alma por un altísimo camino de oscura contemplación y sequedad en que a ella le parece que va perdida, y que, estando así llena de oscuridad y trabajos, aprietos y tentaciones, encuentre con quien le diga, como los consoladores de Job (2,11), o que es melancolía o desconsuelo o condición, o que podrá ser alguna malicia oculta suya, y que por eso la ha dejado Dios, y así, luego suelen juzgar que aquella alma debe de haber sido muy mala, pues tales cosas pasan por ella.

5. Y también habrá quien le diga que vuelve atrás, pues no halla gusto ni consuelo como antes en las cosas de Dios, y así, doblan el trabajo a la pobre alma; porque acaecerá que la mayor pena que ella siente sea del conocimiento de sus miserias propias, en que le parece que ve más claro que la luz del día que está llena de males y pecados,

to see many souls to whom God gives the aptitude and favor to move forward, and who, if they only tried to bestir themselves, would attain this lofty state, remaining at a low level of converse with God because they do not want to or know how to, or because no one sets them on the path and teaches them to relinquish their principles. And even when our Lord finally favors them so much that He allows them to proceed even without some prerequisite or other, they arrive very much later and with more toil, and with less merit, because they have not adapted themselves to God, allowing themselves to be set freely on the pure and sure path to union. Since, though it is true that God is carrying them—for He can carry them even when they make no effort—they do not allow themselves to be carried; and thus they make less headway by resisting Him who carries them and have less merit because they do not apply their will, whereby they also suffer more; because there are souls who, instead of surrendering to God and helping themselves, hinder God instead by their indiscreet actions or resistance, acting like children who, when their mothers want to pick them up, kick and cry, insisting on walking on their own, so that no progress at all can be made or, if it is, it is at the child's pace.

4. And so, to afford this ability to let themselves be carried by God when He in His majesty wishes to move them forward, with His aid I shall give teaching and advice to both beginners and proficients, so they can learn to understand or at least let themselves be carried by God. Because some spiritual directors, not having the light and experience of these journeys, hinder and injure similar souls instead of helping them onto the path, acting like the builders of the Tower of Babel, who, needing to supply suitable materials, gave and applied quite different materials because they failed to understand the language (Genesis 11:1–9), and thus nothing was accomplished. Therefore at such times it is a rugged, toilsome thing when a soul cannot understand herself or find anyone that understands her; because it may happen that God carries a soul along a very lofty path of obscure contemplation and aridity, on which she believes she is lost, and that, being so full of darkness and toils, difficulties and temptations, she runs across someone who tells her, like Job's comforters (Job 2:11), that she is suffering from melancholy or despair or a weak constitution, or else that there may be some hidden evilness in her, for which reason God has abandoned her, and thus they usually deem that that soul must have been very evil, since she is subject to such woes.

5. And there may also be those who tell the soul she is retrogressing because she finds no pleasure or comfort in the things of God, as she used to, and thereby they double the poor soul's toil; because it may happen that the greatest pain she feels is that of the awareness of her own wretchedness, in which she believes she sees more clearly than daylight that she is full of evils and sins,

porque le da Dios aquella luz de conocimiento en aquella noche de contemplación (como adelante diremos), y como halla quien conforme con su parecer, diciendo que serán por su culpa, crece la pena y el aprieto del alma sin término, y suele llegar a más que morir. Y no contentándose con esto, pensando los tales confesores que procede de pecados, hacen a las dichas almas revolver sus vidas y hacen hacer muchas confesiones generales y crucificarlas de nuevo, no entendiendo que aquél por ventura no es tiempo de eso ni de esotro, sino de dejarlas así en la purgación que Dios las tiene, consolándolas y animándolas a que quieran aquello hasta que Dios quiera, porque hasta entonces, por más que ellas hagan y ellos digan, no hay remedio.

6. De esto habemos de tratar adelante con el favor divino, y de cómo se ha de haber el alma entonces y el confesor con ella, y qué indicios habrá para conocer si aquélla es la purgación del alma, y, si lo es, si es del sentido o del espíritu (lo cual es la noche oscura que decimos), y cómo se podrá conocer si es melancolía o otra imperfección acerca del sentido o del espíritu. Porque podrá también haber algunas almas que pensarán, ellas o sus confesores, que las lleva Dios por este camino de la noche oscura de purgación espiritual, y no será por ventura sino alguna imperfección de las dichas; y porque hay también muchas almas que piensan no tienen oración y tienen muy mucha, y otras que tienen mucha y es poco más que nada.

7. Hay otras que es lástima que trabajan y se fatigan mucho y vuelven atrás, y onen el fruto del aprovechar en lo que no aprovecha, sino antes estorba, y otras que con descanso y quietud van aprovechando mucho. Hay otras que con los mismos regalos y mercedes que Dios les hace para caminar adelante se embarazan y estorban y no van adelante; y otras muchas cosas que en este camino acaecen a los seguidores dél, de gozos, penas y esperanzas y dolores: unos que proceden de espíritu de perfección, otros de imperfección. De todo, con el favor divino, procuraremos decir algo, para que cada alma que esto leyere en alguna manera eche de ver el camino que lleva y el que le conviene llevar, si pretende llegar a la cumbre deste Monte.

8. Y por cuanto esta doctrina es de la noche oscura por donde el alma ha de ir a Dios, no se maraville el lector si le pareciere algo oscura; lo cual entiendo yo que será al principio que la comenzare a leer, mas, como pase adelante, irá entendiendo mejor lo primero, porque con lo uno se va declarando lo otro, y después, si lo leyere la segunda vez, entiendo le parecerá más claro, y la doctrina más sana. Y si algunas personas con esta doctrina no se hallaren bien, hacerlo ha mi poco saber y bajo estilo, porque la materia de suyo buena es y harto nece-

because God gives her that light of awareness in that night of contemplation (as I shall state later on), and, finding someone in agreement with that belief, someone who says that this is her own fault, the soul's pain and difficulty are increased infinitely, and she usually ends up in a state worse than death. And not content with this, when such confessors think this is caused by sins, they make the aforesaid souls review their lives and force them to make many general confessions, crucifying them again, failing to understand that perhaps this is the wrong time for any of those approaches, but that those souls should be left in the state of purification that God has decreed for them and should be comforted and encouraged to desire that state as long as it pleases God, because until then, whatever the confessors do and say, there is no help for them.

6. With God's aid, I shall discuss this later, and also how the soul is then to behave, and the confessor as well, and what indications there may be to recognize whether the purification of the soul is taking place, and, if it is, whether it is purification of the senses or of the spirit (which latter purification is what I call the dark night), and how one can tell whether it is melancholy or some other imperfection of the senses or the spirit. Because there may also be some souls, or their confessors, who think God is carrying them along this path of the dark night of spiritual purification, whereas perhaps it is only some imperfection in them; and because there are also many souls who think they have insufficient power of prayer though they have a great deal, and others who have a lot though it amounts to practically nothing.

7. There are other souls whom it is a pity to see toiling and laboring greatly and yet retrogressing, seeing the fruit of benefit in things which bring no benefit but hindrance instead, while other souls reap great benefit in ease and calm. There are others who, with the same gifts and graces that God gives them to move forward, impede and hinder themselves and make no progress; and many other things along this path befall those who follow it, joys and griefs, hopes and sorrows: some proceeding from a spirit of perfection, others from imperfection. Of all this, with God's favor, I shall try to say something, so that every person who reads this may in some way get to see the path he is following and the one he ought to follow if he desires to reach the summit of this mountain.

8. And inasmuch as this teaching concerns the dark night through which the soul must go to God, the reader should not be surprised if he finds it somewhat obscure; by which I mean that this will be at the outset when he starts reading, but as he proceeds he will better understand the earlier material, because one thing will explain the other, and later, if he reads it again, I am sure he will find it clearer, and the teaching more beneficial. And if some people are still uneasy with these teachings, it will be due to my scanty knowledge and common style, because in itself the mat-

saria. Pero paréceme que, aunque se escribiera más acabada y perfectamente de lo que aquí va, no se aprovecharan de ello sino los
menos; porque aquí no se escribirán cosas muy morales y sabrosas
para todos los espirituales que gustan de ir por cosas dulces y sabrosas
a Dios, sino doctrina sustancial y sólida, así para los unos como para
los otros, si quisieren pasar a la desnudez de espíritu que aquí se es-
cribe.

9. Ni aun mi principal intento es hablar con todos, sino con algunas
personas de nuestra sagrada Religión de los primitivos del Monte
Carmelo, así frailes como monjas, por habérmelo ellos pedido, a quien
Dios hace merced de meter en la senda deste Monte, los cuales, como
ya están bien desnudos de las cosas temporales deste siglo, enten-
derán mejor la doctrina de la desnudez del espíritu.

Libro primero, CAPÍTULO 1

PONE LA PRIMERA CANCIÓN.—DICE DOS DIFERENCIAS DE NOCHES POR
QUE PASAN LOS ESPIRITUALES SEGÚN LAS DOS PARTES DEL HOMBRE
INFERIOR Y SUPERIOR Y DECLARA LA CANCIÓN SIGUIENTE

> **En una noche obscura,**
> **con ansias, en amores inflamada,**
> **¡oh dichosa ventura!,**
> **salí sin ser notada,**
> **estando ya mi casa sosegada.**

1. En esta primera canción canta el alma la dichosa suerte y ventura
que tuvo en salir de todas las cosas afuera, y de los apetitos e imperfecciones que hay en la parte sensitiva del hombre por el desorden
que tiene de la razón. Para cuya inteligencia es de saber que, para que
una alma llegue al estado de perfección, ordinariamente ha de pasar
primero por dos maneras principales de *noches,* que los espirituales
llaman purgaciones o purificaciones del alma. Y aquí las llamamos
noches, porque el alma, así en la una como en la otra, camina como de
noche, a escuras.

2. La primera *noche* o purgación es de la parte sensitiva del alma,
de la cual se trata en la presente canción, y se tratará en la Primera
Parte deste libro; y la segunda es de la parte espiritual, de la cual habla
la segunda canción que se sigue, y désta también trataremos en la
Segunda y Tercera Parte cuanto a lo activo, porque cuanto a lo pasivo
será en la Cuarta.

3. Y esta primera *noche* pertenece a los principiantes al tiempo que

ter is good and extremely necessary. But it seems to me that, even if it were written more elegantly and perfectly than it now is, only a few readers would profit by it, because there will not be found herein things that are very congenial and delightful to all those spiritual people who like to pursue things that are sweet and have the savor of God, but, instead, substantial and solid teachings, for the one group as for the other, if they wish to attain the nakedness of spirit herein described.

9. Nor is my principal intention to address everybody, but only some people of our holy order of the old, original observance of Mount Carmel, both friars and nuns, because they requested me to do so. May God give them the grace of setting them on the path up this mountain! Since they have already largely divested themselves of the worldly things of this age, they will better understand the doctrine of the nakedness of the spirit.

Book I, CHAPTER 1

CONCERNING THE FIRST STANZA. THE TWO DIFFERENT NIGHTS THROUGH
WHICH SPIRITUAL PEOPLE PASS, IN ACCORDANCE WITH THE LOWER OR
THE HIGHER PART OF MAN. EXPLANATION OF THE FOLLOWING STANZA

> **On a dark night,**
> **with longings, afire with love**
> **(oh, happy fortune!),**
> **I went out without being detected,**
> **my house being calm now.**

1. In this first stanza the soul sings of the lucky lot and fortune she had in emerging from all created things and from the appetites and imperfections present in the sensory part of man because of the disorder of his reason. To understand this, one must know that, if a soul is to attain the state of perfection, she usually must first pass through two main kinds of "nights," which spiritual people call purgations or purifications of the soul. And here I call them "nights" because, in both kinds, the soul travels as if at night, in the dark.

2. The first "night," or purification, is that of the sensory part of the soul, which is the subject of the present stanza and will be the subject of Book I of this treatise; and the second is that of the spiritual part, which is discussed in the second stanza (to follow), and I shall also discuss it in Books II and III with regard to its active aspect, because the passive aspect will be in Book IV.[6]

3. And this first "night" pertains to beginners at the time when God

---

6. Which ultimately became known as the separate *Noche oscura.*

Dios los comienza a poner en el estado de contemplación, de la cual también participa el espíritu, según diremos a su tiempo. Y la segunda *noche* o purificación pertenece a los ya aprovechados al tiempo que Dios los quiere ya comenzar a poner en el estado de la unión con Dios; y ésta es más oscura y tenebrosa y terrible purgación, según se dirá después.

Declaración de la canción

4. Quiere, pues, en suma, decir el alma en esta canción, que salió— sacándola Dios—sólo por amor dél, inflamada en su amor *en una noche oscura,* que es la privación y purgación de todos sus apetitos sensuales acerca de todas las cosas exteriores del mundo y de las que eran deleitables a su carne, y también de los gustos de su voluntad; lo cual todo se hace en esta purgación del sentido, y por eso dice que salía *estando ya* su *casa sosegada,* que es la parte sensitiva, sosegados ya y dormidos los apetitos en ella, y ella en ellos, porque no se sale de las penas y angustias de los retretes de los apetitos hasta que estén amortiguados y dormidos. Y esto dice que le fue *dichosa ventura* salir *sin ser notada,* esto es, sin que ningún apetito de su carne ni de otra cosa se lo pudiese estorbar, y también porque salió de noche, que es privándola Dios de todos ellos, lo cual era noche para ella.

5. Y esto fue *dichosa ventura,* meterla Dios en esta *noche,* de donde se le siguió tanto bien, en la cual ella no atinara a entrar, porque no atina bien uno por sí solo a vaciarse de todos los apetitos para venir a Dios.

6. Esta es, en suma, la declaración de la canción. Y ahora nos habremos de ir por cada verso escribiendo sobre cada uno y declarando lo que pertenece a nuestro propósito. Y el mesmo estilo se lleva en las demás canciones, como en el prólogo dije, que primero se pondrá cada canción y se declarará, y después cada verso.

Libro primero, CAPÍTULO 2

DECLARA QUÉ «NOCHE OSCURA» SEA ESTA POR QUE EL ALMA DICE HABER PASADO A LA UNIÓN. DICE LAS CAUSAS DE ELLA

En una noche oscura

1. Por tres cosas podemos decir que se llama *noche* este tránsito que hace el alma a la unión de Dios: La primera, por parte del término de donde el alma sale, porque ha de ir careciendo el apetito del gusto de todas las cosas del mundo que poseía, en negación de ellas; la cual negación y carencia es como noche para todos los sentidos del

starts placing them in the state of contemplation, in which the spirit participates as well, as I shall say on the proper occasion. And the second "night" or purification pertains to those already proficient, at the time when God now wishes to start placing them in the state of union with God; and this is a more obscure, shadowy, and terrible purification, as I shall say later.

EXPLANATION OF THE STANZA

4. So then, in brief, in this stanza the soul wishes to say that she went out— God releasing her—solely for love of Him, afire in her love "on a dark night," which is the deprivation by purification of all her sensory appetites for all external worldly things and those which had been delectable to her flesh, and also of the pleasures of her will; all of this is done in this purification of the senses, so that she says that she went out, her "house being calm now," her house being the sensory part, the appetites within it now calmed and asleep, and it with them, because no one emerges from the pains and anguish of the inner chambers of the appetites until they are deadened and asleep. And it says here that it was a "happy fortune" for her to go out "without being detected"; that is, with no appetite of her flesh or anything else being able to hinder her, and also because she went out at night, which means that God rid her of all those things, making it night where she was concerned.

5. And this was a "happy fortune," God placing her in this "night," from which she derived so much benefit, and into which she would not have succeeded in entering, because a person on his own hardly succeeds in freeing himself from every appetite in order to come to God.

6. This, in brief, is the explanation of the stanza. And now we must go through it line by line, writing about each one and explaining whatever pertains to our purpose. And the same approach will hold for the remaining stanzas, as I said in the Prologue: first every stanza will be set down and explained, then every line.

Book I, CHAPTER 2

EXPLAINING WHAT "DARK NIGHT" IT IS THROUGH WHICH THE SOUL
SAYS SHE HAS GONE ON TO UNION. ITS CAUSES

On a dark night

1. For three reasons we can say that the name "night" is given to this course followed by the soul on her way to union with God: The first, with regard to the soul's point of departure, because she must continue to do without the appetite of her pleasure in all the worldly things she once owned, and must renounce them; this renunciation and lack are like a

hombre. La segunda, por parte del medio o camino por donde ha de ir el alma a esta unión, lo cual es la fe, que es también oscura para el entendimiento como noche. La tercera, por parte del término adonde va, que es Dios, el cual ni más ni menos es noche oscura para el alma en esta vida. Las cuales tres noches han de pasar por el alma, o por mejor decir, el alma por ellas, para venir a la divina unión con Dios.

2. En el libro del santo Tobías (6,18–22) se figuraron estas tres maneras de noches por las tres noches que el ángel mandó a Tobías *el mozo* que pasasen antes que se juntase en uno con la esposa. En la primera le mandó que *quemase el corazón del pez* en el fuego, que significa el corazón aficionado y apegado a las cosas del mundo, el cual, para comenzar a ir a Dios, se ha de quemar y purificar de todo lo que es criatura con el fuego del amor de Dios; y en esta purgación se ahuyenta el demonio, que tiene poder en el alma por asimiento a las cosas corporales y temporales.

3. En la segunda noche le dijo que *sería admitido en la compañía de los santos patriarcas,* que son los padres de la fe; porque pasando por la primera noche, que es privarse de todos los objetos de los sentidos, luego entra el alma en la segunda noche quedándose sola en fe—no como excluye la caridad, sino las otras noticias del entendimiento (como adelante diremos)—, que es cosa que no cae en sentido.

4. En la tercera noche le dijo el ángel que *conseguiría la bendición,* que es Dios, el cual mediante la segunda noche, que es fe, se va comunicando al alma tan secreta y íntimamente, que es otra noche para el alma en tanto que se va haciendo la dicha comunicación muy más oscura que estotras, como luego diremos. Y pasada esta tercera noche, que es acabarse de hacer la comunicación de Dios en el espíritu, que se hace ordinariamente en gran tiniebla del alma, luego se sigue la unión con la esposa, que es la Sabiduría de Dios, como también el ángel dijo a Tobías que, *pasada la tercera noche, se juntaría con su esposa con temor del Señor;* el cual temor de Dios cuando está perfecto, está también perfecto el amor, que es cuando se hace la transformación por amor del alma con Dios.

5. Estas tres partes de noche todas son una noche; pero tiene tres partes como la noche, porque la primera, que es la del sentido, se compara a prima noche, que es cuando se acaba de carecer del objeto de las cosas; y la segunda, que es la fe, se compara a la medianoche, que totalmente es oscura; y la tercera, al despidiente, que es Dios, la cual es ya inmediata a la luz del día. Y, para que mejor lo entendamos, iremos tratando de cada una de estas causas de por sí.

night to all of man's senses. The second, with regard to the means or path by which the soul must proceed to this union, this path being faith, which is also obscure as night to one's understanding. The third, with regard to the goal she must reach, which is God, Who is likewise a dark night for the soul in this life. These three nights must pass through the soul or, rather, the soul through them, to arrive at divine union with God.

2. In the book about the holy Tobias (Tobit 6:18–22) these three kinds of nights were symbolized by the three nights which, by the angel's orders to young Tobias, he had to pass before he could unite with his bride. On the first, he ordered him to burn the fish's heart in the fire; this signifies the heart fond of and attached to worldly things; in order to start out on the path to God, it must be burned and purged of everything pertaining to created things with the fire of God's love; and in this purgation the devil is frightened away, the devil who has power over the soul because of her clinging to corporeal, earthly things.

3. On the second night he told him that he would be admitted into the company of the holy patriarchs, who are the fathers of the faith; because by passing through the first night, in which she divests herself of all the objects of the senses, the soul next enters the second night, remaining solely in faith—this does not exclude charity, but does exclude all other intellectual notions (as I shall say later)—something outside the realm of the senses.

4. On the third night the angel told him that he would achieve the blessing, which is God, Who by way of the second night, which is faith, continues to communicate Himself to the soul so secretly and intimately that there is another night for the soul on which this communication steadily becomes much more obscure than the earlier ones, as I shall explain later. And after this third night, on which God finishes making His communication to the spirit, which is generally done amid a great darkness of the soul, there then follows the union with the bride, who is the Wisdom of God, just as the angel told Tobias that, after the third night, he would unite with his bride in the fear of the Lord; when this fear of the Lord is perfect, love is perfect, too, and it is then that the transformation of the soul in God through love takes place.

5. Taken together, these three parts of night comprise one night; but it has three parts like our physical night, because the first, the night of the senses, may be compared to our early night, which is when one finally loses the objectivity of things; and the second, which is faith, may be compared to midnight, which is totally dark; and the third, to the end of the night, which is God, being already on the verge of the daylight. And, to understand this better, we shall discuss each of these causes separately.

Libro primero, CAPÍTULO 3

HABLA DE LA PRIMERA CAUSA DESTA «NOCHE»,
QUE ES DE LA PRIVACIÓN DEL APETITO EN TODAS LAS COSAS,
Y DA LA RAZÓN POR QUE SE LLAMA «NOCHE»

1. Llamamos aquí *noche* a la privación del gusto en el apetito de todas las cosas, porque así como la noche no es otra cosa sino privación de la luz y, por el consiguiente, de todos los objetos que se pueden ver mediante la luz, por lo cual se queda la potencia visiva a escuras y sin nada, así también se puede decír la mortificación del apetito *noche* para el alma, porque, privándose el alma del gusto del apetito en todas las cosas, es quedarse como a escuras y sin nada. Porque, así como la potencia visiva mediante la luz se ceba y apacienta de los objetos que se pueden ver, y apagada la luz no se ven, así el alma mediante el apetito se apacienta y ceba de todas las cosas que según sus potencias se pueden gustar, el cual también apagado, o, por mejor decir, mortificado, deja el alma de apacentarse en el gusto de todas las cosas, y así se queda según el apetito a escuras y sin nada.

2. Pongamos ejemplo en todas las potencias. Privando el alma su apetito en el gusto de todo lo que el sentido del oído puede deleitar, según esta potencia se queda el alma a escuras y sin nada; y privándose del gusto de todo lo que al sentido de la vista puede agradar, también según esta potencia se queda el alma a escuras y sin nada; y privándose del gusto de toda la suavidad de olores que por el sentido del olfato el alma puede gustar, ni más ni menos según esta potencia, se queda a escuras y sin nada; y negando también el gusto de todos los manjares que pueden satisfacer al paladar, también se queda el alma a escuras y sin nada; y finalmente mortificándose el alma en todos los deleites y contentamientos que del sentido del tacto puede recebir, de la mesma manera se queda el alma según esta potencia a escuras y sin nada. De manera que el alma que hubiere negado y despedido de sí el gusto de todas las cosas, mortificando su apetito en ellas, podremos decir que está como de noche a escuras, lo cual no es otra cosa sino un vacío en ella de todas las cosas.

3. La causa de esto es porque, como dicen los filósofos, el alma, luego que Dios la infunde en el cuerpo, está como una tabla rasa y lisa en que no está pintado nada y, si no es lo que por los sentidos ya conociendo, de otra parte naturalmente no se le comunica nada. Y así, en tanto que está en el cuerpo, está como el que está en una cárcel oscura, el cual no sabe nada sino lo que alcanza a ver por las ventanas de

Book I, CHAPTER 3

THE FIRST CAUSE OF THIS "NIGHT,"
WHICH IS THE PURPOSEFUL LOSS OF THE APPETITE FOR ALL THINGS;
AND THE REASON FOR ITS BEING CALLED "NIGHT"

1. I here call "night" the purposeful loss of pleasure in the appetite for all things, because, just like night, it is nothing other than the loss of light and, consequently, of all objects that can be seen by means of light; thereby the faculty of sight is left in the dark, without anything; thus, the mortification of the appetite may also be called "night" for the soul, because when the soul purposely loses her pleasure in the appetite for all things she is left as if in the dark, without anything. Because, just as the faculty of sight by means of light feeds and nourishes itself on the objects that can be seen, but cannot be seen when the light goes out, thus the soul by means of the appetite nourishes herself and feeds on all the things that can be enjoyed by her faculties, and when the appetite, too, is extinguished or, rather, mortified, the soul ceases to nourish herself on her pleasure in all things, and thus is left, with regard to the appetite, in the dark, without anything.

2. Let us give an example for every faculty. When the soul loses her appetite for pleasure in everything that the sense of hearing can delight, with regard to that faculty the soul is left in the dark, without anything; and when she loses pleasure in everything that can charm the sense of sight, with regard to this faculty, too, the soul is left in the dark, without anything; and when she loses pleasure in all the sweetness of fragrances that the soul can enjoy through the sense of smell, with regard to this faculty, in just the same way, she is left in the dark, without anything; and also renouncing her pleasure in all the food that can satisfy the palate, the soul is likewise left in the dark, without anything; and, finally, when the soul mortifies herself by giving up all the delights and contentments she can receive from the sense of touch, in the same way, as concerns this faculty, the soul is left in the dark, without anything. So that we may say that the soul who has renounced and dismissed her pleasure in all things, mortifying her appetite for them, is as if in the darkness of night, which is nothing else than a void in her, the lack of all things.

3. The cause of this is that, as the philosophers say, after God infuses the soul into the body, she is like a smooth, clean slate on which nothing is written, and if she did not learn through the above-mentioned senses, she would otherwise be cut off from natural communications. And so, while she is in the body, she is like one placed in a dark prison cell who knows nothing but what he manages to see through the windows of that cell, and

la dicha cárcel, y si por allí no viese nada, no vería por otra parte; y así el alma, si no es lo que por los sentidos se le comunica, que son las ventanas de su cárcel, naturalmente por otra vía nada alcanzaría.

4. De donde, si lo que puede recebir por los sentidos ella lo desecha y niega, bien podemos decir que se queda como a escuras y vacía, pues, según parece por lo dicho, naturalmente no le puede entrar luz por otras lumbreras que las dichas; porque, aunque es verdad que no puede dejar de oír y ver y oler y gustar y sentir, no le hace más al caso ni le embaraza más al alma si lo niega y lo desecha, que si no lo viese ni lo oyese, etc.; como también el que quiere cerrar los ojos, quedará a escuras como el ciego que no tiene potencia para ver. Y así, al propósito habla David diciendo: *Pauper sum ego, et in laboribus a iuventute mea,* que quiere decir: Yo soy pobre y en trabajos desde mi juventud (Ps 87,16). Llámase pobre (aunque está claro que era rico) porque no tenía en la riqueza su voluntad, y así era tanto como ser pobre realmente; mas antes, si fuera realmente pobre y de la voluntad no lo fuera, no era verdaderamente pobre, pues el ánima estaba rica y llena en el apetito. Y por eso llamamos esta desnudez *noche* para el alma, porque no tratamos aquí del carecer de las cosas—porque eso no desnuda al alma si tiene apetito de ellas—, sino de la desnudez del gusto y apetito de ellas, que es lo que deja al alma libre y vacía de ellas, aunque las tenga; porque no ocupan al alma las cosas de este mundo ni la dañan, pues no entra en ellas, sino la voluntad y apetito de ellas que moran en ella.

5. Esta primera manera de noche, como después diremos, pertenece al alma según la parte sensitiva, que es una de las dos que arriba dijimos por las cuales ha de pasar el alma para llegar a la unión. Ahora digamos cuánto conviene al alma salir de su casa en esta *Noche oscura del sentido,* para ir a la unión de Dios.

Libro primero, CAPÍTULO 13

EN QUE SE TRATA DE LA MANERA Y MODO QUE SE HA DE TENER PARA ENTRAR EN ESTA «NOCHE DEL SENTIDO»

1. Resta ahora dar algunos avisos para saber y poder entrar en esta *Noche del sentido.* Para lo cual es de saber que el alma ordinariamente entra en esta noche sensitiva en dos maneras: la una es activa, la otra, pasiva.

Activa es lo que el alma puede hacer y hace de su parte para entrar en ella, de lo cual ahora trataremos en los avisos siguientes.

Pasiva es en que el alma no hace nada, sino Dios la obra en ella, y

if he could see nothing there, he would see nothing elsewhere; and so the soul, except for what is communicated to her by the senses, which are the windows of her prison, would by nature achieve nothing any other way.

4. Hence, if she rejects and renounces what she can receive through the senses, we may correctly say that she is left as if in the dark and empty, since, as the above discussion shows, by nature light cannot enter to her by any other openings than those stated; because, though it is true that she cannot cease to hear, see, smell, taste, and feel, it makes no more difference to her and hampers her no more, if she renounces and rejects all this, than if she did not see, hear, etc.; just as a man voluntarily closing his eyes will be left in the dark as much as a blind man who lacks the power to see. And David speaks the same way on this subject: "*Pauper sum ego, et in laboribus a iuventute mea*," which means: "I have been poor and in toils since my youth" ([compare] Psalm 88:15). He calls himself poor (though he was clearly rich) because his will was not fixed on his wealth, and this was thus tantamount to being actually poor; on the other hand, if he were actually poor but were not so in his will, he would not be truly poor, since his mind was rich and of full appetite. Therefore I call this nakedness "night" for the soul, because I am not here speaking of the outright lack of things—since that does not strip the soul bare if she has an appetite for them—but of the divestment of her taste and appetite for them, and it is this that leaves the soul free and empty of them even if she possesses them; because then the soul is not occupied by the things of this world, neither do they harm her, since she does not concern herself with them: rather, the harm is done by the will and appetite for them dwelling within her.

5. This first kind of night, as I shall say later, pertains to the sensory part of the soul, and is one of the two I mentioned above through which the soul must pass to achieve union. Now let me tell how beneficial it is to the soul to emerge from her house on this "dark night of the senses," to proceed toward her union with God.

Book I, CHAPTER 13

DISCUSSION OF THE MANNER AND METHOD NECESSARY FOR ENTERING THIS "NIGHT OF THE SENSES"

1. Now I must still give some instructions for knowing how, and being able, to enter this "night of the senses." For this one must know that the soul generally enters this sensory night in two ways: one is active; the other, passive.

"Active" refers to what the soul can do, and does do, for her part to enter it; I shall now discuss this in the instructions below.

"Passive" indicates that the soul does nothing, but God works within

ella se ha como paciente; de la cual trataremos en el Cuarto Libro, cuando habemos de tratar de los principiantes. Y porque allí habemos, con el favor divino, de dar muchos avisos a los principiantes, según las muchas imperfecciones que suelen tener en este camino, no me alargaré aquí en dar muchos, y porque también no es tan proprio deste lugar darlos, pues de presente sólo tratamos de las causas por qué se llama *noche* este tránsito, y cuál sea ésta, y cuántas sus partes.

Pero, porque parece quedaba muy corto y no de tanto provecho no dar luego algún remedio o aviso para exercitar esta noche de apetitos, he querido poner aquí el modo breve que se sigue; y lo mesmo haré al fin de cada una de esotras dos partes o causas desta noche de que luego, mediante el Señor, tengo de tratar.

2. Estos avisos que aquí se siguen de vencer los apetitos, aunque son breves y pocos, yo entiendo que son tan provechosos y eficaces como compendiosos, de manera que el que de veras se quisiere exercitar en ellos, no le harán falta otros ningunos, antes en éstos los abrazará todos.

3. Lo primero, traiga un ordinario apetito de imitar a Cristo en todas sus cosas, conformándose con su vida, la cual debe considerar para saberla imitar y haberse en todas las cosas como se hubiera él.

4. Lo segundo, para poder bien hacer esto, cualquiera gusto que se le ofreciere a los sentidos, como no sea puramente para honra y gloria de Dios, renúncielo y quédese vacío dél por amor de Jesucristo, el cual en esta vida no tuvo otro gusto ni le quiso que hacer la voluntad de su Padre, lo cual llamaba él su comida y manjar (Io 4,34). Pongo ejemplo. Si se le ofreciere gusto de oír cosas que no importen para servicio y honra de Dios, ni lo quiera gustar ni las quiera oír; y si le diere gusto mirar cosas que no le ayuden a amar más a Dios, ni quiera el gusto ni mirar las tales cosas; y si en el hablar o otra cualquiera cosa se le ofreciere, haga lo mismo; y en todos los sentidos ni más ni menos, en cuanto lo pudiere excusar buenamente, porque, si no pudiere, basta que no quiera gustar de ello, aunque estas cosas pasen por él. Y desta manera ha de procurar dejar luego mortificados y vacíos de aquel gusto a los sentidos, como a escuras. Y con este cuidado en breve aprovechará mucho.

5. Y para mortificar y apaciguar las cuatro pasiones naturales, que son gozo, esperanza, temor y dolor, de cuya concordia y pacificación salen estos y los demás bienes, es total remedio lo que se sigue, y de gran merecimiento y causa de grandes virtudes:

her and she merely undergoes; I shall discuss this in Book IV[7] when it is time to talk about beginners. Since, with God's aid, I shall be giving many instructions to beginners in that place, because of the many imperfections they usually manifest on this path, I shall not expatiate and give many here, also because this is not the appropriate place for it, since I am now merely discussing the reasons that this transit is called a "night," what is its nature, and how many parts it has.

But, because I feel it would be very abrupt and much less helpful not to give some remedy or advice at once on how to practice this night of the appetites, I have decided to add here the following brief method; and I shall do the same at the end of each of the other two parts or causes of this night which, with the Lord's help, I shall later discuss.

2. Though the instructions that follow here for subduing the appetites are few and brief, I believe they are as useful and effective as they are concise, so that whoever honestly tries to train himself with them will not need any others; on the contrary, in these he will possess all necessary advice.

3. First, let him have the customary desire to imitate Christ in all he does, in conformity with His life, which he should contemplate in order to imitate it and to act in every situation as He would have.

4. Second, to do this properly, let him renounce all pleasure offered to his senses, except when it is purely for God's honor and glory, and let him remain empty of it for the love of Jesus Christ, Who in this life neither took nor desired any other pleasure than to do the will of His Father, calling this His food and nourishment ([compare] John 4:34). I give an example. If he should be offered the pleasure of hearing things that do not redound to the service and honor of God, let him not wish to enjoy or hear him; and if he should be given the pleasure of beholding things that do not help him love God more, let him not desire that pleasure nor behold such things; and if it should be offered to him in speaking or anything else, let him do the same; and equally for all the senses, insofar as he can excuse himself politely, because, if this is impossible, it suffices for him to take no pleasure in these things even though he experiences them. In this way he must try to leave his senses mortified afterward and free of that pleasure, as if in the dark. By taking such cares, he will soon benefit greatly.

5. And to mortify and pacify the poor natural passions, which are joy, hope, fear, and sorrow, from whose concord and pacification these and all other benefits result, the total remedy is as follows (it is of great merit and the cause of great virtues):

---

7. The *Noche oscura.*

6. Procure siempre inclinarse:

no a lo más fácil, sino a lo más dificultoso;

no a lo más sabroso, sino a lo más desabrido;

no a lo más gustoso, sino antes a lo que da menos gusto;

no a lo que es descanso, sino a lo trabajoso;

no a lo que es consuelo, sino antes al desconsuelo;

no a lo más, sino a lo menos;

no a lo más alto y precioso, sino a lo más bajo y despreciable;

no a lo que es querer algo, sino a no querer nada;

no andar buscando lo mejor de las cosas temporales, sino lo peor;

y desear entrar en toda desnudez y vacío y pobreza por Cristo de todo cuanto hay en el mundo.

7. Y estas obras conviene las abrace de corazón y procure allanar la voluntad en ellas; porque, si de corazón las obra, muy en breve vendrá a hallar en ellas gran deleite y consuelo, obrando ordenada y discretamente.

8. Lo que está dicho, bien exercitado, bien basta para entrar en la noche sensitiva. Pero, para mayor abundancia, diremos otra manera de exercicio que enseña a mortificar *la concupiscencia de la carne, y la concupiscencia de los ojos, y la soberbia de la vida* (1.ª, 2,16), que son las cosas que dice san Juan reinan en el mundo, de las cuales proceden todos los demás apetitos.

9. Lo primero, procurar obrar en su desprecio y desear que todos lo hagan y esto es contra la concupiscencia de la carne.

Lo segundo, procurar hablar en su desprecio y desear que todos lo hagan y esto es contra la concupiscencia de los ojos.

Lo tercero, procurar pensar bajamente de sí en su desprecio y desear que todos lo hagan también contra sí, y esto es contra la soberbia de la vida.

10. En conclusión de estos avisos y reglas conviene poner aquí aquellos versos que se escriben en la *Subida del Monte*, que es la figura que está al principio deste libro, los cuales son doctrina para subir a él, que es lo alto de la unión; porque, aunque es verdad que allí habla de lo espiritual y interior, también trata del espíritu de imperfección según lo sensual y exterior, como se puede ver en los dos caminos que están en los lados de la senda de perfección. Y así, según ese sentido los entenderemos aquí, conviene a saber: según lo sensual. Los cuales, después, en la Segunda Parte de esta Noche, se han de entender según lo espiritual.

11. Dice:

6. Let him always try to incline:

not to what is easiest, but to what is most difficult;

not to what is most delicious, but to what tastes the worst;

not to what is most pleasurable, but rather to what gives least pleasure;

not to what is relaxing, but to what is toilsome;

not to what affords consolation, but to what affords disconsolation;

not to the more, but to the less;

not to what is highest and most precious, but to what is lowest and most contemptible;

not to desiring things, but to desiring nothing;

not to seeking after the best of worldly things, but the worst;

and to wish to enter into all nakedness and emptiness and poverty, for Christ's sake, with regard to all that exists in the world.

7. And it befits him to embrace these works wholeheartedly and try to make his will conform to them; because if he performs them wholeheartedly, he will very soon come to find great delight and comfort in them, functioning in an orderly, discreet fashion.

8. When all this has been properly drilled into him, it is quite sufficient to give him entry into the night of the senses. But, to broaden our scope, I shall state another type of exercise which teaches how to mortify "the lust of the flesh, and the lust of the eyes, and the pride of life" (I John 2:16), which are the things Saint John says prevail in the world, and from which all the other appetites proceed.

9. First, try to work toward belittlement of yourself and wish everyone else to do so; this combats the lust of the flesh.

Second, try to speak in belittlement of yourself and wish everyone else to do so; this combats the lust of the eyes.

Third, try to think humbly of yourself, with a view to belittlement of self, and wish everyone else to do so to your detriment; this combats the pride of life.

10. To conclude these instructions and rules it is fitting to add here the verses inscribed on "The Ascent of the Mountain," which is the diagram placed at the beginning of this treatise; they teach how to ascend it, reaching the summit of union; because, though it is true that the subject there is the spiritual, inner life, it also refers to the spirit of imperfection with regard to the sensory, external life, as can be seen in the two paths flanking the road to perfection. And so it is in this sense that I shall understand them here, to wit: with regard to the senses. Later, in Book II of this treatise, they will be understood as pertaining to the spirit.

11. The verses read:

Para venir a gustarlo todo,
no quieras tener gusto en nada;
para venir a poseerlo todo,
no quieras poseer algo en nada;
para venir a serlo todo,
no quieras ser algo en nada;
para venir a saberlo todo,
no quieras saber algo en nada;
para venir a lo que no gustas,
has de ir por donde no gustas;
para venir a lo que no sabes,
has de ir por donde no sabes;
para venir a lo que no posees,
has de ir por donde no posees;
para venir a lo que no eres,
has de ir por donde no eres.

MODO PARA NO IMPEDIR AL TODO

12. Cuando reparas en algo,
dejas de arrojarte al todo;
porque, para venir del todo al todo,
has de negarte del todo en todo;
y cuando lo vengas del todo a tener,
has de tenerlo sin nada querer;
porque, si quieres tener algo en todo,
no tienes puro en Dios tu tesoro.

13. En esta desnudez halla el alma espiritual su quietud y descanso, porque, no codiciando nada, nada le fatiga hacia arriba y nada le oprime hacia abajo, porque está en el centro de su humildad; porque, cuando algo codicia, en eso mesmo se fatiga.

Libro primero, CAPÍTULO 14

EN EL CUAL DECLARA EL SEGUNDO VERSO DE LA CANCIÓN

Con ansias, en amores inflamada

1. Ya que habemos declarado el primero verso desta canción, que trata de la noche sensitiva, dando a entender qué *Noche* sea esta del sentido y por qué se llama *noche,* y también, habiendo dado el orden y modo que se ha de tener para entrar en ella activamente, síguese ahora por su orden tratar de las propiedades y efectos de ella, que son admirables, los cuales se contienen en los versos siguientes de la dicha

In order finally to enjoy everything,
have no desire to enjoy anything;
   in order finally to possess everything,
have no desire to possess anything at all;
   in order finally to be everything,
have no desire to be anything at all;
   in order finally to know everything,
have no desire to know anything at all;
   in order to attain what you do not enjoy,
you must traverse a place where you have no pleasure;
   in order to attain what you do not know,
you must traverse a place where you have no knowledge;
   in order to obtain what you do not possess,
you must traverse a place where you possess nothing;
   in order to attain what you are not,
you must traverse a place where you have no being.

METHOD TO AVOID OBSTRUCTING THE ALL

12. When you take notice of any one thing,
you cease hurling yourself into the all;
   because, in order to attain the all entirely,
you must deny yourself everything entirely;
   and when you come to possess it entirely,
you must hold onto it with no desire for anything;
   because if you want to possess any one thing in the all,
your treasure is not purely in God.

13. In this nakedness the spiritual soul finds her quietude and repose, because, not coveting anything, she is not fatigued by anything upward or oppressed by anything downward, since she is at the center of her humility; because when she covets anything, she is fatigued by that very act.

Book I, CHAPTER 14

EXPLANATION OF THE SECOND LINE OF THE STANZA

With longings, afire with love

1. Now that I have explained the first verse of this stanza, which refers to the night of the senses, having made clear what night this night of the senses is and why it is called night, and having also supplied the system and method to be followed in order to enter it actively, I now continue by discussing in sequence its properties and effects, which are wonderful, and are contained in the following lines of the aforesaid stanza, which I

canción, los cuales yo apuntaré brevemente en gracia de declarar los dichos versos, como en el prólogo lo prometí, y pasaré luego adelante al Segundo Libro, el cual trata de la otra parte desta *Noche, que es la espiritual.*

2. Dice, pues, el alma, que *con ansias, en amores inflamada,* pasó y salió en esta *Noche oscura del sentido* a la unión del Amado, porque, para vencer todos los apetitos y negar los gustos de todas las cosas—con cuyo amor y afición se suele inflamar la voluntad para gozar de ellos—era menester otra inflamación mayor de otro amor mejor, que es el de su Esposo, para que, teniendo su gusto y fuerza en éste, tuviese valor y constancia para fácilmente negar todos los otros. Y no solamente era menester para vencer la fuerza de los apetitos sensitivos tener amor de su Esposo, sino estar inflamada de amor y con ansias; porque acaece, y así es, que la sensualidad con tantas ansias de apetito es movida y atraída a las cosas sensitivas, que, si la parte espiritual no está inflamada con otras ansias mayores de lo que es espiritual, no podrá vencer el yugo natural ni entrar en esta *Noche del sentido,* ni tendrá ánimo para se quedar a escuras de todas las cosas, privándose del apetito de todas ellas.

3. Y cómo y de cuántas maneras sean estas ansias de amor que las almas tienen en los principios deste camino de unión, y las diligencias y invenciones que hacen para salir de su casa, que es la propia voluntad en la noche de la mortificación de sus sentidos; y cuán fáciles y aun dulces y sabrosos les hacen parecer estas ansias del Esposo todos los trabajos y peligros de esta noche, ni es de decir deste lugar, ni se puede decir; porque es mejor para tenerlo y considerarlo que para escribirlo. Y así, pasaremos a declarar los demás versos en el siguiente capítulo.

Libro primero, CAPÍTULO 15

EN EL CUAL SE DECLARAN LOS DEMÁS VERSOS DE LA DICHA CANCIÓN

¡Oh dichosa ventura!
salí sin ser notada,
estando ya mi casa sosegada.

1. Toma por metáfora el mísero estado del cautiverio, del cual el que se libra tiene por *dichosa ventura,* sin que se lo impida alguno de los carceleros; porque el alma después del pecado original verdaderamente está como cautiva en este cuerpo mortal, sujeta a las pasiones y apetitos naturales, del cerco y sujeción de los cuales tiene ella por

shall comment on briefly with a view to explaining those lines, as I promised in the Prologue; then I shall proceed to Book II, which discusses the other aspect of this night: the spiritual.

2. Well, then, the soul says that "with longings, afire with love" she proceeded and emerged into this dark night of the senses toward union with her Beloved, because to subdue all the appetites and renounce the pleasure of all things—with the love and affection for which the will is customarily set afire in order to enjoy them—another, greater blaze of another, better love was needed: the love for her Bridegroom, so that, having her pleasure and strength in Him, she would have the courage and steadfastness to renounce all other pleasures easily. And to subdue the power of the sensory appetites it was not merely necessary to have the love for her Bridegroom, but also to be afire with love and to feel longings; because it happens (and so it is) that the senses are stirred and attracted to sensory things with such great longings of the appetite that, if the spiritual part is not afire with other, greater longings for that which is spiritual, it will be unable to throw off the yoke of nature or to enter this night of the senses, nor will it be brave enough to be left in the dark without all things, divesting itself of the appetite for all of them.

3. The nature and varied types of these amorous longings which souls have at the outset of this journey to union, and their diligence and contrivances for emerging from their house (which reflect their own will on the night of the mortification of their senses); and the way that those longings for the Bridegroom make all the toils and dangers of this night seem easy and even sweet and delectable—this is not the place to discuss these matters, nor can they be told; because it is more suitable to possess and contemplate them than to write them down. Therefore I shall proceed to explain the remaining lines in the following chapter.

Book I, CHAPTER 15

EXPLANATION OF THE REMAINING LINES IN THE AFORESAID STANZA

> (Oh, happy fortune!),
> I went out without being detected,
> my house being calm now.

1. This uses as a metaphor the wretched state of captivity, release from which is seen as a "happy fortune," not having been hindered by any of the jailers; because after original sin the soul has really become a sort of prisoner in this mortal body, subject to the natural passions and appetites, from whose siege and subjection she considers it a "happy fortune" to

dichosa ventura haber salido *sin ser notada,* esto es, sin ser de ninguno de ellos impedida ni comprehendida.

2. Porque para esto le aprovechó salir en la *noche oscura,* que es en la privación de todos los gustos y mortificación de todos los apetitos, de la manera que habemos dicho. Y esto, *estando ya su casa sosegada;* conviene a saber, la parte sensitiva, que es la casa de todos los apetitos, ya sosegada por el vencimiento y adormecimiento de todos ellos. Porque, hasta que los apetitos se adormezcan por la mortificación en la sensualidad, y la mesma sensualidad esté ya sosegada de ellos de manera que ninguna guerra haga al espíritu, no sale el alma a la verdadera libertad, a gozar de la unión de su Amado.

Libro segundo, CAPÍTULO 1

EN QUE SE DECLARA ESTA CANCIÓN

A escuras y segura
por la secreta escala, disfrazada,
¡oh dichosa ventura!,
a escuras y en celada,
estando ya mi casa sosegada.

1. En esta segunda canción canta el alma *la dichosa ventura* que tuvo en desnudar *el espíritu* de todas las imperfecciones espirituales y apetitos de propiedad en lo espiritual. Lo cual le fue muy mayor ventura, por la mayor dificultad que hay en sosegar esta casa de la parte espiritual y poder entrar en esta escuridad interior, que es la desnudez espiritual de todas las cosas, así sensuales como espirituales, sólo estribando en pura fe y subiendo por ella a Dios. Que por eso la llama aquí *escala* y *secreta,* porque todos los grados y artículos que ella tiene son secretos y escondidos a todo sentido y entendimiento; y así, se quedó ella a oscuras de toda lumbre de sentido y entendimiento, saliendo de todo límite natural y racional para subir por esta divina escala de la fe, que escala y penetra hasta lo profundo de Dios. Por lo cual dice que iba *disfrazada,* porque llevaba el traje y vestido y término natural mudado en divino, subiendo por fe; y así era causa este disfraz de no ser conocida ni detenida de lo temporal ni de lo racional ni del demonio, porque ninguna destas cosas puede dañar al que camina en fe. Y no sólo eso, sino que va el alma tan encubierta y escondida y ajena de todos los engaños del demonio, que verdaderamente camina (como también aquí dice) *a oscuras y en celada,* es a saber, para el demonio, al cual la luz de la fe le es más que tinieblas. Y así el alma que por ella camina le podemos decir que en celada y encubierta al demonio camina, como adelante se verá más claro.

have escaped "without being detected," that is, without being hindered or apprehended by any of them.

2. Because to do this it was to her benefit to go out into the "dark night," which occurs in the divestment of all pleasures and mortification of all appetites, in the way I have described. And this, her "house being calm now"; which is to be understood as the sensory part, which is the house of every appetite, already made calm by the subduing and lulling to sleep of all of them. Because until the appetites fall asleep through the mortification of the senses, and the senses themselves are calm and free of the appetites so that they wage no war on the spirit, the soul does not emerge into true freedom, to enjoy union with her Beloved.

Book II, CHAPTER 1

EXPLANATION OF THIS STANZA

**In the dark, but feeling safe,
by the secret ladder, in disguise
(oh, happy fortune!),
in the dark and in concealment,
my house being calm now.**

1. In this second stanza the soul sings of the "happy fortune" it had in stripping the spirit bare of every spiritual imperfection and appetite for ownership in the spiritual realm. This was much greater good fortune for her, because it is so much harder to calm this house of the spiritual part and to be able to enter into this inner darkness, which is the spiritual divestment of all things, both sensory and spiritual, with the sole support of pure faith, ascending by it to God. Therefore she here calls faith a "ladder" and "secret," because all the rungs and articles that faith possesses are secret and hidden to all the senses and the intellect; thus, she was left in the dark without any light of the senses or the intellect, going beyond all limits of nature and reason to ascend this divine ladder of faith, which scales and penetrates all the way to God's depths. Therefore she says she went "in disguise," because she was wearing garments, clothing, and natural condition that were transformed into the divine, as she ascended by faith; and so, this disguise was the reason for her not being recognized or detained by things of the world or of reason, or by the devil, because none of those things can harm one who journeys in faith. And not only this, but also the soul is traveling in such concealment, hidden from and alien to every deception of the devil, that she is truly journeying (as she also says here) "in the dark and in concealment"; that is, from the devil, to whom the light of faith is more than darkness. And so we can say that the soul journeying by faith is journeying in concealment, hidden from the devil, as will be seen more clearly later.

2. Por eso dice que salió *a oscuras y segura,* porque el que tal ventura tiene que puede caminar por la oscuridad de la fe, tomándola por guía de ciego, saliendo él de todas las fantasmas naturales y razones espirituales, camina muy al seguro, como habemos dicho. Y así dice que también salió por esta *noche* espiritual *estando ya su casa sosegada,* es a saber, la parte espiritual y racional, de la cual, cuando el alma llega a la unión de Dios, tiene sosegadas sus potencias naturales y los ímpetus y ansias sensuales en la parte espiritual. Que, por eso, no dice aquí que salió *con ansias,* como en la primera *Noche del sentido;* porque para ir en la *Noche del sentido* y desnudarse de lo sensible eran menester ansias de amor sensible para acabar de salir, pero para acabar de sosegar *la casa del espíritu* sólo se requiere afirmación de todas las potencias y gustos y apetitos espirituales en pura fe; lo cual hecho, se junta el alma con el Amado en una unión de sencillez y pureza y amor y semejanza.

3. Y es de saber que en la primera Canción, hablando acerca de la parte sensitiva, dice que salió en *noche oscura* y aquí, hablando acerca de la parte espiritual, dice que salió *a oscuras,* por ser muy mayor la tiniebla de la parte espiritual, así como la oscuridad es mayor tiniebla que la de la noche, porque, por oscura que una noche sea, todavía se ve algo, pero en la oscuridad no se ve nada; y así, en la *Noche del sentido* todavía queda alguna luz, porque queda el entendimiento y razón, que no se ciega, pero esta *Noche espiritual,* que es la fe, todo lo priva, ansí en entendimiento como en sentido; y por eso dice el alma en ésta, que iba *a oscuras y segura,* lo cual no lo dijo en la otra, porque cuanto menos el alma obra con habilidad propria va más segura, porque va más en fe. Y esto se irá bien declarando por extenso en este Segundo Libro, en el cual será necesario que el devoto lector vaya con atención, porque en él se han de decir cosas bien importantes para el verdadero espíritu; y, aunque ellas son algo oscuras, de tal manera se abre camino de unas para otras, que entiendo se entenderá todo muy bien.

Libro segundo, CAPÍTULO 2

EN QUE SE COMIENZA A TRATAR DE LA SEGUNDA PARTE O CAUSA DESTA
«NOCHE», QUE ES LA FE.—PRUEBA CON DOS RAZONES COMO ES MÁS
OSCURA QUE LA PRIMERA Y QUE LA TERCERA

1. Síguese ahora tratar de la segunda parte de esta noche, que es la fe, la cual es el admirable medio que decíamos para ir al término, que es Dios, el cual decíamos era también para el alma naturalmente ter-

2. She says she went out "in the dark, but feeling safe" because anyone so fortunate as to be able to travel in the darkness of faith, adopting it as a blind man's guide, and emerging from every image of nature and reasoning of the spirit, travels in great safety, as I have said. And so she says that she also went out into this "night" of the spirit, her "house being calm now"; that is, her spiritual and rational part; when the soul attains union with God, her natural faculties and drives and sensory longings are calmed down in her spiritual part. Therefore, she does not say here that she went out "with longings," as on the first night, that of the senses; because to go into the night of the senses and divest herself of sensory things, she needed longings for sensory love to achieve her exit, whereas to finish calming the house of the spirit all that is needed is the strengthening of every spiritual faculty, pleasure, and appetite in pure faith; having done this, the soul is linked to her Beloved in a union of simplicity, purity, love, and likeness.

3. And one must know that in the first stanza, speaking about her sensory part, she says that she went out into the "dark night," whereas here, speaking about her spiritual part, she says she went out "in the dark," the shadows of the spiritual part being much denser, just as total darkness is blacker than any nocturnal darkness; because, however dark a night may be, one still sees something, but in total blackness one sees nothing; and so in the night of the senses there still remains some light, because there remain the intellect and the reason, which are not blinded, whereas this night of the spirit, which is faith, blacks out everything, in the intellect as well as in the senses; therefore the soul says in this stanza that she was proceeding "in the dark, but feeling safe," which she did not say in the first one, because the less the soul operates by her own skills the more safely she goes, because she goes in faith to a greater extent. And this will be gradually explained at length in this Book II, in which the devout reader will have to pay close attention, because in it I must speak of things very important to the true spirit; and though they are somewhat obscure, each one leads the way to the next in such a manner that I believe everything will finally be very clearly understood.

Book II, CHAPTER 2

BEGINNING OF THE DISCUSSION OF THE SECOND PART OR CAUSE OF THIS
"NIGHT," WHICH IS FAITH. PROOF BY TWO REASONS THAT IT IS DARKER
THAN THE FIRST AND THE THIRD

1. Now I continue to discuss the second part of this night, which is faith, that wonderful above-mentioned means of reaching the goal, which is God, Who, as I also said, is naturally for the soul the third cause or part

cera causa o parte de esta noche. Porque la fe, que es el medio, es comparada a la media noche; y así podemos decir que para el alma es más oscura que la primera y, en cierta manera, que la tercera, porque la primera, que es la del sentido, es comparada a la prima de la noche, que es cuando cesa la vista de todo objeto sensitivo, y así no está tan remota de la luz como la media noche; la tercera parte, que es el antelucano, que es ya lo que está próximo a la luz del día, no es tan oscuro como la media noche, pues ya está inmediata a la ilustración y información de la luz del día, y ésta es comparada a Dios. Porque, aunque es verdad que Dios es para el alma tan oscura noche como la fe hablando naturalmente, pero, porque, acabadas ya estas tres partes de la Noche—que para el alma lo son naturalmente—, ya va Dios ilustrando al alma sobrenaturalmente con el rayo de su divina luz (lo cual es el principio de la perfecta unión que se sigue pasada la tercera noche), se puede decir que es menos oscura.

2. Es también más oscura que la primera, porque ésta pertenece a la parte inferior del hombre, que es la sensitiva y, por consiguiente, más exterior, y esta segunda de la fe pertenece a la parte superior del hombre, que es la racional y, por el consiguiente, más interior y más oscura, porque la priva de la luz racional o, por mejor decir, la ciega; y así, es bien comparada a la media noche, que es lo más adentro y más oscuro de la noche.

3. Pues esta segunda parte de la fe habemos ahora de probar cómo es noche para el espíritu, así como la primera lo es para el sentido; y luego también diremos los contrarios que tiene y cómo se ha de disponer el alma activamente para entrar en ella; porque de lo pasivo, que es lo que Dios hace sin ella para meterla en ella, allá lo diremos en su lugar, que entiendo será el Tercero Libro.

Libro segundo, CAPÍTULO 3

COMO LA FE ES NOCHE OSCURA PARA EL ALMA.—PRUÉBALO CON RAZONES Y AUTORIDADES Y FIGURAS DE LA SAGRADA ESCRITURA

1. La fe dicen los teólogos que es un hábito del alma cierto y oscuro. Y la razón de ser hábito oscuro es porque hace creer verdades reveladas por el mismo Dios, las cuales son sobre toda luz natural y exceden todo humano entendimiento sin alguna proporción. De aquí es que para el alma esta excesiva luz que se le da de fe le es oscura tiniebla, porque lo más priva y vence lo menos, así como la luz del sol

of this night. Because faith, which is the means, may be compared to midnight; and thus we may say that for the soul it is darker than the first night and, in a certain way, than the third, because the first, which is the night of the senses, may be compared to early night, when the sight of every sensory object terminates, and thus it is not as remote from the light as midnight is; the third part, which precedes the dawn, and is already close to the daylight, is not as dark as midnight, because it already verges on the illumination and identification of shapes afforded by daylight, which may be compared to God. Because, though it is true that to the soul God is as dark a night as faith is, speaking according to nature, yet, because after these three parts of the night are over (which are night to the soul according to nature) God proceeds to illumine the soul supernaturally with the beam of His divine light (which is the beginning of the perfect union that follows, once the third night is over), it can be declared that it is less dark.

2. It is also darker than the first because the first pertains to the lower part of man, the sensory part, which is therefore more external; whereas this second night of faith pertains to the higher part of man, the rational part, which is thus more inward and darker because it deprives this part of the light of reason; rather, it blinds it; thus, it may well be compared to midnight, which is the innermost and darkest time of night.

3. So, then, I have now to prove that this second part, that of faith, is night to the spirit, just as the first part is night to the senses; then I shall also state the things that oppose it, and how the soul must prepare herself actively in order to enter it; because the passive aspect, which is what God brings about without her aid in order to place her in the night, I shall discuss later in the proper place, for which I destine Book III.[8]

Book II, CHAPTER 3

SHOWING THAT FAITH IS A DARK NIGHT FOR THE SOUL.—PROOF THEREOF
BY REASONING, AUTHORITIES, AND SYMBOLS DRAWN FROM SCRIPTURE

1. Theologians say that faith is a firm but obscure propensity of the soul. The reason it is an obscure propensity is that it makes us believe truths revealed by God Himself, which go beyond all natural lights and surpass all human understanding enormously. Hence, for the soul this excessive light which she is given by faith is a dark shadow, because the greater prevails over and overcomes the lesser, just as sunlight prevails

---

8. Actually, in the *Noche oscura*.

priva otras cualesquier luces de manera que no parezcan luces cuando ella luce, y vence nuestra potencia visiva de manera que antes la ciega y priva de la vista que se le da, por cuanto su luz es muy desproporcionada y excesiva a la potencia visiva; así la luz de la fe, por su grande exceso, oprime y vence la del entendimiento, la cual sólo se extiende de suyo a la sciencia natural, aunque tiene potencia para lo sobrenatural para cuando nuestro Señor la quisiere poner en acto sobrenatural.

2. De donde ninguna cosa de suyo puede saber sino por vía natural, lo cual es sólo lo que alcanza por los sentidos, para lo cual ha de tener las fantasmas y las figuras de los objetos presentes en sí o en sus semejantes, y de otra manera no; porque, como dicen los filósofos, *ab obiecto et potentia paritur notitia;* esto es, del objeto presente y de la potencia nace en el alma la noticia. De donde, si a uno le dijesen cosas que él nunca alcanzó a conocer ni jamás vio semejanza de ellas, en ninguna manera le quedaría mas luz de ellas que si no se las hubiesen dicho. Pongo ejemplo: Si a uno le dijesen que en cierta isla hay un animal que él nunca vio, si no le dicen de aquel animal alguna semejanza que él haya visto en otros, no le quedará más noticia ni figura de aquel animal que antes, aunque más le estén diciendo dél. Y por otro ejemplo más claro se entenderá mejor: Si a uno que nació ciego (el cual nunca vio color alguno) le estuviesen diciendo cómo es el color blanco o el amarillo, aunque más le dijesen, no entendería más así que así, porque nunca vio los tales colores ni sus semejanzas para poder juzgar de ellos; solamente se le quedaría el nombre dellos, porque aquello púdolo percebir con el oído, mas la forma y figura no, porque nunca la vio.

3. Desta manera es la fe para con el alma, que nos dice cosas que nunca vimos ni entendimos en sí ni en sus semejanzas, pues no la tienen; y así de ella no tenemos luz de sciencia natural, pues a ningún sentido es proporcionado lo que nos dice, pero sabémoslo por el oído, creyendo lo que nos enseña, sujetando y cegando nuestra luz natural, porque, como dice san Pablo, *Fides ex auditu* (Rom 10,17); como si dijera: La fe no es sciencia que entra por ningún sentido, sino sólo es consentimiento del alma de lo que entra por el oído.

4. Y aun la fe excede mucho más de lo que dan a entender los ejemplos dichos, porque no solamente no hace noticia y sciencia, pero, como habemos dicho, priva y ciega de otras cualesquier noticias y sciencia, para que puedan bien juzgar de ella; porque otras sciencias con la luz del entendimiento se alcanzan, mas esta de la fe sin la luz del entendimiento se alcanza (negándola por la fe) y con la luz propria

over all other light sources so that they do not seem to be light while the sun is shining, and it overcomes our faculty of sight so that it blinds it and deprives it of the ability to see which it is normally given, inasmuch as its light is very much out of proportion to the faculty of sight and exceeds it; in the same way, the light of faith, by its great excess, oppresses and overcomes the light of the intellect, which in itself extends merely to natural knowledge, though it possesses a faculty for the supernatural wherever our Lord wishes to activate it supernaturally.

2. Hence the intellect can know nothing on its own except by natural means, learning only what it can attain through the senses; to do this it must have the images and figures of the objects present in themselves or in their likenesses; otherwise it cannot function; because, as the philosophers say, *ab obiecto et potentia paritur notitia;* that is, cognition arises in the soul from the presence of an object and her cognitive faculty. Hence, if someone is told things he never got to know and he has never seen a likeness of them, in no way could he gain more knowledge of them than if he had not been told about them. To give an example: If someone is told that on a certain island there is an animal which he has never seen, if he is not told of some resemblance between that animal and others he has seen, he will not come away with more knowledge or mental picture of that animal than before, however much people keep telling him about it. Another, clearer example will make this better understood: If a man born blind who never saw any color is told what white or yellow looks like, no matter how much people say he will not understand more one way or another, because he never saw such colors or their likenesses to be able to judge of them; he would be left with their mere names because he was able to perceive them with his hearing, but not their form and figure because he never saw them.

3. Faith is like this to the soul, telling us things we never saw or understood in themselves or their likenesses, because they have none; and so from it we do not receive the light of natural knowledge, since what it tells us is out of proportion to any of our senses; but we know it through our hearing, believing what it teaches us, subduing and blinding our natural light, because, as Saint Paul says, "faith cometh by hearing" (Romans 10:17); as if he had said: "Faith is not knowledge that enters by any sense, but merely the soul's consent to what enters by the ear."

4. Yet faith is much greater than these examples lead one to understand, because not only does it effect no cognition or knowledge, but also, as I have said, it deprives one of, and blinds one to, any other cognition and knowledge which would make one able to judge of it; because other knowledge is obtained by the light of the intellect, but this cognition of faith is obtained without the light of the intellect (which is renounced for the sake

se pierde, si no se escurece. Por lo cual dijo Isaías: *Si non credideritis, non intelligetis;* esto es: Si no creyéredes, no entenderéis (7,9). Luego claro está que la fe es noche oscura para el alma, y desta manera la da luz, y cuanto más la oscurece más luz la da de sí; porque cegando la da luz, según este dicho de Isaías: Porque, si no creyéredes, no entenderéis, esto es, no tendréis luz (ib.). Y así fue figurada la fe por aquella nube que dividía a los hijos de Israel y a los egipcios al punto de entrar en el mar Bermejo, de la cual dice la Escritura que *erat nubes tenebrosa, et illuminans noctem* (Ex 14,20). Quiere decir que aquella nube era tenebrosa y alumbradora a la noche.

5. Admirable cosa es que, siendo tenebrosa, alumbrase la noche. Esto era porque la fe, que es nube oscura y tenebrosa para el alma—la cual es también noche, pues en presencia de la fe de su luz natural queda privada y ciega—, con su tiniebla alumbra y da luz a la tiniebla del alma. Porque así convenía que fuese semejante al maestro el discípulo (Lc 6,40), porque el hombre que está en tiniebla no podía convenientemente ser alumbrado sino por otra tiniebla, según nos lo enseña David diciendo: *Dies diei eructat verbum et nox nocti indicat scientiam.* Quiere decir: El día rebosa y respira palabra al día, y la noche muestra sciencia a la noche (Ps 18,3); que, hablando más claro, quiere decir: El día que es Dios en la bienaventuranza, donde ya es de día, a los bienaventurados ángeles y almas que ya son día, les comunica y pronuncia la *Palabra,* que es su Hijo, para que le sepan y le gocen; y la noche que es la fe en la Iglesia militante, donde aún es de noche, muestra sciencia a la Iglesia y, por consiguiente, a cualquiera alma; la cual le es noche, pues está privada de la clara sabiduría beatífica y, en presencia de la fe, de su luz natural está ciega.

6. De manera que lo que de aquí se ha de sacar es que la fe, porque es noche oscura, da luz al alma, que está a oscuras; por que se venga a verificar lo que también dice David a este propósito, diciendo: *Nox illuminatio mea in deliciis meis,* que quiere decir: La noche será mi iluminación en mis deleites (Ps 138,11). Lo cual es tanto como decir: en los deleites de mi pura contemplación y unión con Dios, la noche de la fe será mi guía. En lo cual claramente da a entender que el alma ha de estar en tiniebla para tener luz para este camino.

Libro segundo, CAPÍTULO 5

EN QUE SE DECLARA QUE COSA SEA UNIÓN DEL ALMA CON DIOS.—
PONE UNA COMPARACIÓN

1. Por lo que atrás queda dicho en alguna manera se da a entender

of faith); by one's own light it is lost, if not obscured. Therefore Isaiah said: *Si non credideritis, non intelligetis;* that is, "Unless you believe, you will not understand" ([compare] Isaiah 7:9). It is then clear that faith is a dark night for the soul, giving light to her in this way, and the more it darkens her, the more of its own light it gives her; because it gives her light by blinding her, according to this dictum of Isaiah's: "Because unless you believe, you will not understand"; that is, you will not have light (*ibid.*). And thus faith was symbolized by that cloud which separated the children of Israel from the Egyptians on the point of entering the Red Sea, which Scripture describes saying: *erat nubes tenebrosa, et illuminans noctem* (Exodus 14:20). Which means that that cloud was dark, but lit up the night.

5. It is a marvelous thing that, being dark, it should light up the night. This was so because faith, which is a dark and shadowy cloud to the soul—she is also night, because in the presence of faith she is left shorn of her natural light and blind—illumines by its darkness and gives light to the darkness of the soul. In that way it was fitting for the disciple to be similar to his master (Luke 6:40), because a man in the dark could not be suitably enlightened except by another darkness, as David teaches us when he says: *Dies diei eructat verbum et nox nocti indicat scientiam.* Which means: "The day overflows and breathes word to the day, and the night shows knowledge to the night" ([compare] Psalm 19:2); speaking more clearly, this means: The day, which is God in glory, where it is already daytime, communicates with the blessed angels and souls who are already day, pronouncing the Word, which is His Son, so that they may know and enjoy it; and the night, which is faith in the Church Militant, where it is still night, shows knowledge to the Church and, consequently, to every soul; this knowledge is night to her because she is bereft of clear beatific wisdom and, in the presence of faith, is shorn of her natural light.

6. So that the teaching to be derived from this is that faith, because it is dark night, sheds light on the soul, who is in the dark; which helps to verify another statement David makes on this subject: *Nox illuminatio mea in deliciis meis,* which means: "The night will be my illumination in my delights" ([compare] Psalm 139:11). This is equivalent to saying: in the delights of my pure contemplation of and union with God, the night of faith will be my guide. By which he clearly gives us to understand that the soul must be in darkness in order to receive light for this journey.

Book II, CHAPTER 5

EXPLANATION OF THE SOUL'S UNION WITH GOD. A COMPARISON

1. The discussion above in some manner gives us to understand what

lo que aquí entendemos por unión del alma con Dios, y por eso se entenderá aquí mejor lo que dijéremos de ella. Y no es ahora mi intento tratar de las divisiones de ella ni de sus partes, porque sería nunca acabar si ahora me pusiese a declarar cuál sea la unión del entendimiento, y cuál según la voluntad, y cuál también según la memoria, y cuál la transeúnte, y cuál la permanente en las dichas potencias; y luego cuál sea la total transeúnte y permanente según las dichas potencias juntas. De eso a cada paso iremos tratando en el discurso, ahora de lo uno, ahora de lo otro, pues ahora no hace al caso para dar a entender lo que aquí habemos de decir de ellas, y muy mejor se dará a entender en sus lugares, cuando, yendo tratando de la misma materia, tengamos el ejemplo vivo junto al entendimiento presente, y allí se notará y entenderá cada cosa y se juzgará mejor de ella.

2. Ahora sólo trato de esta unión total y permanente según la sustancia del alma y sus potencias en cuanto al hábito oscuro de unión; porque en cuanto al acto después diremos, con el favor divino, cómo no puede haber unión permanente en las potencias en esta vida, sino transeúnte.

3. Para entender, pues, cuál sea esta unión de que vamos tratando, es de saber que Dios en cualquiera alma, aunque sea la del mayor pecador del mundo, mora y asiste sustancialmente. Y esta manera de unión siempre está hecha entre Dios y las criaturas todas, en la cual les está conservando el ser que tienen; de manera que si de ellas desta manera faltase, luego se aniquilarían y dejarían de ser. Y así, cuando hablamos de unión del alma con Dios, no hablamos de esta sustancial que siempre está hecha, sino de la unión y transformación por amor del alma con Dios, que no está siempre hecha, sino sólo cuando viene a haber semejanza de amor. Y, por tanto, ésta se llamará unión de semejanza, así como aquélla unión esencial o sustancial, aquélla natural, ésta sobrenatural; la cual es cuando las dos voluntades, conviene a saber, la del alma y la de Dios, están en uno conformes, no habiendo en la una cosa que repugne a la otra; y así, cuando el alma quitare de sí totalmente lo que repugna y no conforma con la voluntad divina quedará transformada en Dios por amor.

4. Esto se entiende no sólo lo que repugna según el acto, sino también según el hábito, de manera que no sólo los actos voluntarios de imperfección le han de faltar, mas los hábitos de esas cualesquier imperfecciones ha de anihilar. Y por cuanto toda cualquier criatura y todas las acciones y habilidades de ellas no cuadran ni llegan a lo que es Dios, por eso se ha de desnudar el alma de toda criatura y acciones y habilidades suyas, conviene a saber: de su entender, gustar y sentir,

we mean here by the soul's union with God; therefore in this place what I shall say about it will be better understood. And it is not my intention now to discuss its divisions or parts, because I would never end if I now began to explain the nature of the union by the intellect, the union by the will, as well as by the memory, and the nature of the temporary union and of the permanent union by the aforesaid powers of the soul; next, the nature of the total union, temporary and permanent, in the aforesaid powers taken together. At every step in my disquisition I shall discuss these matters, now one, now another, since it is inopportune now to explain what I shall later say of them, which will be much more comprehensible in the appropriate places when, discussing the topics in detail, we shall have living examples present in our mind; there each item will be mentioned and understood and better evaluated.

2. Now I am merely discussing this total, permanent union in accordance with the soul's substance and powers as regards her obscure propensity for union; because, as regards the very act of union, later, with God's help, I shall explain that there cannot be a permanent union by means of the soul's powers in this life, but only a temporary one.

3. So then, to understand the nature of this union I am discussing, one must know that God substantially dwells, and is present, in every soul, even that of the greatest sinner in the world. And this type of union is always formed between God and all the creatures; in it He maintains for them the type of being that they possess; so that if they should come to lack it, they would immediately be annihilated and cease to exist. And so when I speak of the soul's union with God, I do not mean that substantial one which is always present, but the soul's transformation in God through love, which is not always present, but only when there comes to be a likeness in love. Therefore this will be called the union of likeness, and the aforesaid union will be called essential or substantial, the former being natural, the latter supernatural; which is when the two wills—that is, the soul's and God's—are in conformity, there being in each of them nothing which resists the other; and so, whenever the soul rids herself totally of that which resists, and fails to conform to, the divine will, she will become transformed in God through love.

4. By this I mean not only that which resists with regard to the act, but also with regard to the propensity, so that not only voluntary acts of imperfection must be lacking in her, but she must also destroy the propensities for any of those imperfections. And since no creature whatsoever, nor all its actions and talents, tally with or attain the level of God, the soul of every creature must strip away her actions and talents—that is, her intellect, pleasure, and emotions—so that, once she has cast aside all that is

para que, echado todo lo que es disímil y disconforme a Dios, venga a recibir semejanza de Dios, no quedando en ella cosa que no sea voluntad de Dios; y así se transforma en Dios. De donde, aunque es verdad que, como habemos dicho, está Dios siempre en el alma dándole y conservándole el ser natural de ella con su asistencia, no, empero, siempre la comunica el ser sobrenatural; porque éste no se comunica sino por amor y gracia, en la cual no todas las almas están, y las que están, no en igual grado, porque unas están en más, otras en menos grados de amor. De donde a aquella alma se comunica Dios más que está más aventajada en amor, lo cual es tener más conforme su voluntad con la de Dios, y la que totalmente la tiene conforme y semejante, totalmente está unida y transformada en Dios sobrenaturalmente. Por lo cual, según ya queda dado a entender, cuanto una alma más vestida está de criaturas y habilidades della según el afecto y el hábito, tanto menos disposición tiene para la tal unión, porque no da total lugar a Dios para que la transforme en lo sobrenatural. De manera que el alma no ha menester más que desnudarse destas contrariedades y disimilitúdines naturales para que Dios que se le está comunicando naturalmente por naturaleza, se le comunique sobrenaturalmente por gracia.

5. Y esto es lo que quiso dar a entender san Juan cuando dijo: *Qui non ex sanguinibus, neque ex voluntate carnis, neque ex voluntate viri, sed ex Deo nati sunt* (1,13); como si dijera: Dio poder para que puedan ser hijos de Dios, esto es, se puedan transformar en Dios solamente aquellos que no de las sangres, esto es, que no de las complexiones y composiciones naturales son nacidos, ni tampoco de la voluntad de la carne, esto es, del albedrío de la habilidad y capacidad natural, ni menos de la voluntad del varón (en lo cual se incluye todo modo y manera de arbitrar y comprehender con el entendimiento), no dio poder a ninguno déstos para poder ser hijos de Dios, sino a los que son nacidos de Dios, esto es, a los que, renaciendo por gracia, muriendo primero a todo lo que es hombre viejo, se levantan sobre sí a lo sobrenatural, recibiendo de Dios la tal renacencia y filiación, que es sobre todo lo que se puede pensar. Porque, como el mesmo san Juan dice en otra parte, *Nisi quis renatus fuerit ex aqua et Spiritu Sancto, non potest videre regnum Dei* (3,5). Quiere decir: El que no renaciere en el Espíritu Santo, no podrá ver este reino de Dios, que es el estado de perfección. Y renacer en el Espíritu Santo en esta vida es tener una alma simílima a Dios en pureza, sin tener en sí alguna mezcla de imperfección; y así se puede hacer pura transformación por participación de unión, aunque no esencialmente.

dissimilar to God and out of conformity to Him, she may come to receive the likeness of God, nothing remaining in her that is not God's will; and thus she is transformed in God. Hence, though it is true that, as I have said, God is always present in the soul, bestowing and preserving her natural being by His presence, nevertheless He does not always communicate a supernatural existence to her; because this is communicated solely by love and grace, and not all souls are in grace; those which are, are not so to an equal degree; because some are at higher, others at lower, levels of love. Therefore God communicates more of Himself to that soul who is more outstanding in love, which means having a will more in conformity with God's; the soul whose will is totally in conformity and similar is totally united and transformed in God supernaturally. Therefore, as already explained, the more a soul is clad with creatures and abilities in the way of affection and propensity, the less aptitude she has for such a union, because she does not make total room for God to transform her supernaturally. So that all the soul needs to do is to divest herself of these natural oppositions and dissimilarities in order for God, Who is communicating Himself to her naturally through nature, can communicate Himself to her supernaturally through grace.

5. And this is what Saint John meant when he said: "Which were born, not of blood, nor of the will of the flesh, nor of the will of man, but of God" (John 1:13); which was tantamount to saying: He gave power so that only those might be sons of God—that is, could be transformed in God— who were born not from natural organs and matter, nor from the will of the flesh—that is, from the free will of natural talents and abilities—and least of all from the will of a man (which includes every mode and manner of judging and understanding with the intellect). He gave no power to any of these to be sons of God, but to those born of God; that is, those who, born again through grace, first dying to all that which is the old Adam, rise above themselves to the supernatural, receiving from God such rebirth and kinship, which is beyond all that the mind can conceive. Because, as the same Saint John says elsewhere: *Nisi quis renatus fuerit ex aqua et Spiritu Sancto, non potest videre regnum Dei* (John 3:5). Which means: "Except a man be born of water and of the Spirit, he cannot enter into the kingdom of God," which is the state of perfection. And to be reborn in the Holy Spirit in this life is to have a soul very similar to God in purity, having in oneself no admixture of imperfection; and thus one will be able to achieve a pure transformation by participatory union, though of course not in essence.

6. Y para que se entienda mejor lo uno y lo otro pongamos una comparación: Está el rayo del sol dando en una vidriera. Si la vidriera tiene algunos velos de manchas o nieblas, no la podrá esclarecer y transformar en su luz totalmente como si estuviera limpia de todas aquellas manchas y sencilla; antes tanto menos la esclarecerá cuanto ella estuviere menos desnuda de aquellos velos y manchas, y tanto más cuanto más limpia estuviere. Y no quedará por el rayo, sino por ella; tanto, que, si ella estuviere limpia y pura del todo, de tal manera la transformará y esclarecerá el rayo, que parecerá el mismo rayo y dará la misma luz que el rayo, aunque, a la verdad, la vidriera, aunque se parece al mismo rayo, tiene su naturaleza distinta del mismo rayo; mas podemos decir que aquella vidriera es rayo o luz por participación. Y así el alma es como esta vidriera, en la cual siempre está embistiendo o, por mejor decir, en ella está morando esta divina luz del ser de Dios por naturaleza, que habemos dicho.

7. En dando lugar el alma—que es quitar de sí todo velo y mancha de criatura, lo cual consiste en tener la voluntad perfectamente unida con la de Dios, porque el amar es obrar en despojarse y desnudarse por Dios de todo lo que no es Dios—, luego queda esclarecida y transformada en Dios, y le comunica Dios su ser sobrenatural de tal manera, que parece el mismo Dios y tiene lo que tiene el mismo Dios. Y se hace tal unión cuando Dios hace al alma esta sobrenatural merced, que todas las cosas de Dios y el alma son unas en transformación participante; y el alma más parece Dios que alma, y aun es Dios por participación; aunque es verdad que su ser naturalmente tan distinto se le tiene del de Dios como antes, aunque está transformada; como también la vidriera le tiene distinto del rayo, estando dél clarificada.

8. De aquí queda ahora más claro que la disposición para esta unión, como decíamos, no es el entender del alma, ni gustar, ni sentir, ni imaginar de Dios ni de otra cualquiera cosa, sino la pureza y amor, que es desnudez y resignación perfecta de lo uno y de lo otro sólo por Dios; y cómo no puede haber perfecta transformación si no hay perfecta pureza; y cómo según la proporción de la pureza será la ilustración, iluminación y unión del alma con Dios, en más o en menos; aunque no será perfecta, como digo, si del todo no está perfecta y clara y limpia.

9. Lo cual también se entenderá por esta comparación: Está una imagen muy perfecta con muchos y muy subidos primores y delicados y sutiles esmaltes, y algunos tan primos y tan sutiles, que no se puedan bien acabar de determinar por su delicadez y excelencia; a esta imagen, el que tuviere menos clara y purificada vista, menos primores y

6. For a better understanding of all this, let us make a comparison: The sun's ray is striking a glass window. If the window is obscured by any stains or mildew, the ray will be unable to brighten it and transform it in its light as totally as if it were free of all those stains, and pure; rather, it will brighten it less, the less free it is of those dark spots and stains, and all the more, the cleaner it is. And it will not be the fault of the ray, but of the window; so much so, that if it should be completely clean and pure, the ray will so transform and brighten it that it will seem like the ray itself and will emit the same light as the ray, though in truth, although the window resembles the ray itself, it possesses a nature of its own distinct from that of the ray; but we can say that that window is a ray or light by participation. And thus the soul is like this window, which is constantly being assailed by—or, rather, in which there is dwelling—this divine light of the being of God through nature which I have described.

7. When the soul makes room—by ridding itself of every spot and stain characteristic of creatures, which consists in making her will perfectly in unison with God's, because to love is to strip and divest oneself actively, through God, of all that is not God—she immediately becomes enlightened and transformed in God, and God communicates His supernatural being to her in such a way that she resembles God Himself and possesses what God Himself possesses. And such a union is effected when God bestows upon the soul this supernatural favor: that all the things of God and the soul are one in participatory transformation; and the soul resembles God more than she does a soul, and she even is God by participation; though it is true that naturally her being remains as distinct from God's as before, even though she is transformed; just as the window's being is distinct from the ray's while it is being brightened by it.

8. This now makes it clearer that the prerequisite for this union, as I was saying, is not the soul's intellect, pleasure, or emotion, nor the imagining of God or of anything else, but purity and love, which is nakedness and perfect renunciation of all these things solely through God; and that there cannot be perfect transformation if there is not perfect purity; and that the soul's enlightenment, illumination, and union with God, to a greater or lesser degree, will be in proportion to this purity; though it will not be perfect, as I say, if the soul is not entirely perfect, bright, and clean.

9. This, too, will be made clearer by a comparison: There is a very perfect painting with many very lofty excellences and delicate and subtle coloring, some of these features being so fine and subtle that they cannot fully be made out, so delicate and supreme are they; in this painting a man with less clear, purified sight will discern less excellence and deli-

delicadez echará de ver en la imagen, y el que la tuviere algo más pura echará de ver más primores y perfecciones en ella; y si otro la tuviere aún más pura, verá aún más perfección, y, finalmente, el que más clara y limpia potencia tuviere irá viendo más primores y perfecciones, porque en la imagen hay tanto que ver, que, por mucho que se alcance, queda para poderse mucho más alcanzar della.

10. De la misma manera podemos decir que se han las almas con Dios en esta ilustración o transformación. Porque, aunque es verdad que una alma, según su poca o mucha capacidad, puede haber llegado a unión, pero no en igual grado todas, porque esto es como el Señor quiere dar a cada una. Es a modo de como le ven en el cielo, que unos ven más, otros menos; pero todos ven a Dios y todos están contentos, porque tienen satisfecha su capacidad.

11. De donde, aunque acá en esta vida hallemos algunas almas con igual paz y sosiego en estado de perfección y cada una esté satisfecha, con todo eso, podrá la una dellas estar muchos grados más levantada que la otra y estar igualmente satisfechas, por cuanto tienen satisfecha su capacidad. Pero la que no llega a pureza competente a su capacidad nunca llega a la verdadera paz y satisfacción, pues no ha llegado a tener la desnudez y vacío en sus potencias cual se requiere para la sencilla unión de Dios.

Libro segundo, CAPÍTULO 6

EN QUE SE TRATA COMO LAS TRES VIRTUDES TEOLOGALES SON LAS QUE HAN DE PONER EN PERFECCIÓN LAS TRES POTENCIAS DEL ALMA, Y COMO EN ELLAS HACEN VACÍO Y TINIEBLA LAS DICHAS VIRTUDES

1. Habiendo, pues, de tratar de inducir las tres potencias del alma, entendimiento, memoria y voluntad, en esta noche espiritual, que es el medio de la divina unión, necesario es primero dar a entender en este capítulo cómo las tres virtudes teologales, fe, esperanza y caridad—que tienen respecto a las dichas tres potencias como proprios objetos sobrenaturales, y mediante las cuales el alma se une con Dios según sus potencias—, hacen el mesmo vacío y escuridad cada una en su potencia: la fe en el entendimiento, la esperanza en la memoria y la caridad en la voluntad. Y después iremos tratando cómo se ha de perfeccionar el entendimiento en la tiniebla de la fe, y cómo la memoria en el vacío de la esperanza, y cómo también se ha de enterrar la voluntad en la carencia y desnudez de todo afecto para ir a Dios. Lo cual hecho, se verá claro cuánta necesidad tiene el alma, para ir segura en este camino espiritual, de ir por esta noche oscura arrimada a estas

cacy, whereas a man with somewhat purer sight will discern more excellence and perfections in it; and if another man has even purer sight, he will see even more perfection; and, finally, the man with the clearest and cleanest powers will see the most excellence and perfection, because there is so much to see in the painting that, however much one may achieve, much more remains to be detected in it.

10. We can say that souls relate to God in the same way in this enlightenment or transformation. Because, though it is true that a soul, in accordance with its greater or lesser aptitude, may have achieved union, all souls do not do so to the same degree, because this depends on how much the Lord wishes to bestow upon each. It is just like the sight of Him in heaven: some see more, others less, but everyone sees God and everyone is contented, because their capacity has been filled.

11. Hence, even though here in this life we may find several souls enjoying equal peace and calm in a state of perfection, nevertheless one of them may be raised many degrees higher than another, while they are equally satisfied because their capacity has been filled. But a soul that does not attain purity consonant with her capacity never attains true peace and satisfaction, since she has not reached that state of nakedness and emptiness in her powers which is required for pure union with God.

Book II, CHAPTER 6

THAT IT IS THE THREE THEOLOGICAL VIRTUES WHICH MUST PERFECT THE THREE POWERS OF THE SOUL BY CREATING EMPTINESS AND DARKNESS IN THEM

1. So then, having to discuss how the three powers of the soul—intellect, memory, and will—are to be led into this night of the spirit, which is the means to divine union, it is first necessary to expound in this chapter how the three theological virtues—faith, hope, and charity, which are related to the above three powers as their proper supernatural objects, by means of which the soul unites with God in each of these powers of hers—each create the same void and darkness in its respective power: faith, in the intellect; hope, in the memory; and charity, in the will. Afterward I shall discuss how the intellect must be perfected in the darkness of faith, and the memory in the emptiness of hope; and also how the will must be buried in the lack and divestment of all affection, in order to proceed toward God. When this is done, it will be clearly seen how necessary it is for the soul, in order to proceed safely on this spiritual path, to travel through this dark night with the support of these three virtues,

tres virtudes, que la vacían de todas las cosas y escurecen en ellas. Porque, como habemos dicho, el alma no se une con Dios en esta vida por el entender, ni por el gozar, ni por el imaginar, ni por otro cualquier sentido, sino sólo por la fe según el entendimiento, y por esperanza según la memoria, y por amor según la voluntad.

2. Las cuales tres virtudes todas hacen, como habemos dicho, vacío en las potencias: la fe en el entendimiento, vacío y oscuridad de entender; la esperanza hace en la memoria vacío de toda posesión, y la caridad vacío en la voluntad y desnudez de todo afecto y gozo de todo lo que no es Dios. Porque la fe ya vemos que nos dice lo que no se puede entender con el entendimiento. Por lo cual san Pablo dice de ella *ad Hebraeos* desta manera: *Fides est sperandarum substantia rerum, argumentum non apparentium* (11,1); que a nuestro propósito quiere decir que la fe es sustancia de las cosas que se esperan. Y, aunque el entendimiento con firmeza y certeza consiente en ellas, no son cosas que al entendimiento se le descubren, porque, si se le descubriesen, no sería fe; la cual, aunque le hace cierto al entendimiento, no le hace claro, sino oscuro.

3. Pues de la esperanza no hay duda sino que también pone a la memoria en vacío y tiniebla de lo de acá y de lo de allá; porque la esperanza siempre es de lo que no se posee, porque, si se poseyese, ya no sería esperanza. De donde san Pablo dice *ad Romanos: Spes, quae videtur, non est spes; nam quod videt quis, quid sperat?* Es a saber: La esperanza que se ve, no es esperanza; porque lo que uno ve, esto es, lo que posee, ¿cómo lo espera? (8,24). Luego también hace vacío esta virtud, pues es de lo que no se tiene, y no de lo que se tiene.

4. La caridad, ni más ni menos, hace vacío en la voluntad de todas las cosas, pues nos obliga a amar a Dios sobre todas ellas, lo cual no puede ser sino apartando el afecto de todas ellas, para ponerle entero en Dios. De donde dice Cristo por san Lucas: *Qui non renuntiat omnibus quae possidet, non potest meus esse discipulus;* que quiere decir: el que no renuncia todas las cosas que posee con la voluntad, no puede ser mi discípulo (14,33). Y así, todas estas tres virtudes ponen al alma en escuridad y vacío de todas las cosas.

5. Y aquí debemos notar aquella parábola que nuestro Redentor dijo por san Lucas a los once capítulos (v.5), en que dijo que el amigo había de ir a la media noche a pedir los tres panes a su amigo; los cuales panes significan estas tres virtudes. Y dijo que a la media noche los pedía, para dar a entender que el alma a escuras de todas las cosas según sus potencias ha de adquirir estas tres virtudes, y en esa noche se ha de perfeccionar en ellas. En el capítulo sexto de Isaías (v.2)

which empty her of all things and create darkness in them. Because, as I have said, the soul does not unite with God in this life through the intellect or through enjoyment or through imagination or through any other feeling, but solely through faith with regard to the intellect, hope with regard to the memory, and love with regard to the will.

2. As I have said, all three of these virtues create emptiness in the powers: faith, in the intellect (emptiness and obscurity of understanding); in the memory hope creates the emptiness of all it possesses; and in the will charity creates emptiness and the divestment of all affection and joy for anything else but God. Because we already see that faith tells us what cannot be understood by the intellect. Therefore Saint Paul speaks of it in Hebrews as follows: "Faith is the substance of things hoped for, the evidence of things not seen" (Hebrews 11:1); which for our purpose means that faith is the substance of the things one hopes for. And though the intellect consents to these things with firmness and certitude, they are not things which are revealed to the intellect, because, if they were, this would not be faith, which, though it gives the intellect certitude, makes it not clear, but dark.

3. As for hope, without a doubt it places the memory in a void and darkness as to the matters of this life and the next; because hope is always for something not yet possessed, since, if the thing *were* possessed, we could no longer speak of hope. Hence, Saint Paul says in Romans: "*Spes, quae videtur, non est spes; nam quod videt quis, quid sperat?*" That is: "Hope that is seen is not hope; for what a man seeth, why doth he yet hope for?" (Romans 8:24). So this virtue, too, creates a void, since it pertains to things not possessed, not to things possessed.

4. In the same way charity creates a void in the will for all things, since it obliges us to love God more than all of them, which cannot be effected without diverting one's affection from all of them, in order to place it entirely in God. Hence Christ says through Saint Luke: "*Qui non renuntiat omnibus quae possidet, non potest meus esse discipulus*"; which means: "Whosoever he be of you that forsaketh not all that he hath, he cannot be my disciple" (Luke 14:33). And so all three of these virtues place the soul in darkness and emptiness of all things.

5. And here I must cite that parable which our Redeemer told through Saint Luke in 11:5, saying that the friend had to go at midnight to ask his friend for the three loaves, the loaves signifying these three virtues. He said he requested them at midnight in order to give us to understand that the soul must acquire these three virtues in the darkness of all things with regard to her powers, and that she must perfect herself in them in that night. In Isaiah 6:2 we read that the two seraphim seen by that prophet

leemos que los dos serafines que este profeta vio a los lados de Dios cada uno con seis alas, que con las dos cubrían sus pies, que significaba cegar y apagar los afectos de la voluntad acerca de todas las cosas para con Dios; y con las dos cubrían su rostro, que significaba la tiniebla del entendimiento delante de Dios; y que con las otras dos volaban, para dar a entender el vuelo de la esperanza a las cosas que no se poseen, levantada sobre todo lo que se puede poseer de acá y de allá, fuera de Dios.

6. A estas tres virtudes, pues, habemos de inducir las tres potencias del alma, informando a cada cual en cada una de ellas, desnudándola y poniéndola a escuras de todo lo que no fueren estas tres virtudes. Y ésta es la *Noche espiritual* que arriba llamamos *activa*, porque el alma hace lo que es de su parte para entrar en ella. Y así como en la *Noche sensitiva* damos modo de vaciar las potencias sensitivas de sus objetos visibles según el apetito para que el alma saliese de su término al medio, que es la fe, así en esta *Noche espiritual* daremos, con el favor de Dios, modo como las potencias espirituales se vacíen y purifiquen de todo lo que no es Dios y se queden puestas en la oscuridad destas tres virtudes, que son el medio, como habemos dicho, y disposición para la unión del alma con Dios.

7. En la cual manera se halla toda seguridad contra las astucias del demonio y contra la eficacia del amor propio y sus ramas, que es lo que sutilísimamente suele engañar y impedir el camino a los espirituales, por no saber ellos desnudarse gobernándose según estas tres virtudes, y así, nunca acaban de dar en la sustancia y pureza del bien espiritual, ni van por tan derecho camino y breve como podrían ir.

8. Y hase de tener advertencia que ahora especialmente voy hablando con los que han comenzado a entrar en estado de contemplación, porque con los principiantes algo más anchamente se ha de tratar esto, como notaremos en el Libro Segundo, Dios mediante, cuando tratemos de las propiedades de ellos.

Libro segundo, CAPÍTULO 24

EN QUE SE TRATA DE DOS MANERAS QUE HAY DE VISIONES ESPIRITUALES POR VÍA SOBRENATURAL

1. Hablando ahora propriamente de las que son visiones espirituales sin medio de algún sentido corporal, digo que dos maneras de visiones pueden caer en el entendimiento: unas son de sustancias cor-

at the sides of God each had six wings; with two they covered their feet, which signified the blinding and extinction of the affections of the will for all things in order to be with God; with two they covered their face, which signified the darkness of the intellect before God; they flew with the remaining pair, symbolizing the flight of hope toward the things that are not possessed, upraised above all that can be possessed in this life and the next, except for God.

6. And so we must lead the three powers of the soul to these three virtues, infusing each one into each one, darkening the soul and stripping her bare of everything except these three virtues. And this is the "night of the spirit" that we called "active" above, because the soul acts voluntarily in order to enter it. And just as, in the "night of the senses," we offered a way to rid the sensory powers of their visible objects with regard to the appetite so that the soul could emerge from her condition and attain the means, which is faith, in the same way in this "night of the spirit," with God's help, I shall offer a way for the spiritual powers to be emptied and purified of everything but God and to be left in the darkness of these three virtues, which, as I have said, are the means and prerequisites for the soul's union with God.

7. In this method will be found complete security against the devil's cunning and against the force of self-love and its ramifications, which is what usually deceives spiritual people most subtly, obstructing their path, because they do not know how to strip themselves bare by governing themselves by these three virtues, and thus never completely arrive at the substance and purity of the spiritual good; and they do not proceed by as direct and short a path as they could.

8. And the reader must take note that now above all I am addressing those who have already begun to enter the state of contemplation, because this has to be discussed at somewhat greater length with beginners, as I shall remark in the second part,[9] with God's help, when I discuss their characteristics.

Book II, CHAPTER 24

THE TWO TYPES OF SPIRITUAL VISIONS OF SUPERNATURAL ORIGIN

1. Speaking now specifically about those spiritual visions without the medium of any bodily sense, I say that two types of vision can befall the intellect: one type is the vision of corporeal substances; the other, of detached or incorporeal substances. The corporeal visions relate to all the

---

9. The *Noche oscura.*

póreas, otras de sustancias separadas o incorpóreas. Las de las corpóreas son acerca de todas las cosas materiales que hay en el cielo y
en la tierra, las cuales puede ver el alma (aun estando en el cuerpo)
mediante cierta lumbre sobrenatural derivada de Dios, en la cual
puede ver todas las cosas ausentes del cielo y de la tierra, según
leemos haber visto san Juan en el capítulo 21 del Apocalipsis, donde
cuenta la descripción y excelencia de la celestial Jerusalén que vio en
el cielo; y cual también se lee de san Benito, que en una visión espiritual vio todo el mundo; la cual visión dice santo Tomás en el primero
de sus *Quodlibetos* que fue en la lumbre derivada de arriba, que
habemos dicho.

2. Las otras visiones que son de sustancias incorpóreas, no se
pueden ver mediante esta lumbre derivada que aquí decimos, sino
con otra lumbre más alta que se llama lumbre de gloria. Y así, estas visiones de sustancias incorpóreas, como son ángeles y almas, no son de
esta vida ni se pueden ver en cuerpo mortal; porque si Dios las
quisiese comunicar al alma esencialmente como ellas son, luego sal-
dría de las carnes y se desataría de la vida mortal. Que por eso dijo
Dios a Moisés cuando le rogó le mostrase su esencia: *Non videbit me
homo, et vivet;* esto es: No me verá hombre que pueda quedar vivo
(Ex 33,20). Por lo cual, cuando los hijos de Israel pensaban que habían
de ver a Dios, o que le habían visto, o algún ángel, temían el morir,
según se lee en el Exodo, donde, temiendo los dichos, dijeron: *Non lo-
quatur nobis Dominus; ne forte moriamur;* como si dijeran: No se nos
comunique Dios manifiestamente por que no muramos (20,19). Y
también en los Jueces, pensando Manué, padre de Sansón, que
habían visto esencialmente al ángel que hablaba con él y con su mujer
(el cual les había aparecido en forma de un varón muy hermoso), dijo
a su mujer: *Morte moriemur, quia vidimus Dominum.* Que quiere
decir: Moriremos, porque habemos visto al Señor (13,22).

3. Y así, estas visiones no son desta vida, si no fuese alguna vez por
vía de paso, y esto dispensando Dios o salvando la condición y vida
natural, abstrayendo totalmente al espíritu de ella, y que con su favor
se suplan las veces naturales del alma acerca del cuerpo; que por eso,
cuando se piensa que las vio san Pablo, es a saber, las sustancias separadas en el tercer cielo, dice el mismo santo: *Sive in corpore, sive
extra corpus nescio; Deus scit* (2 Cor 12,2); esto es, que fue arrebatado
a ellas, y lo que vio dice que no sabe si era en el cuerpo o fuera del
cuerpo; que Dios lo sabe; en lo cual se ve claro que se traspuso de la
vida natural, haciendo Dios el cómo. De donde también, cuando se
cree haberle mostrado Dios su esencia a Moisés, se lee que le dijo

material things that exist in heaven and on earth, which the soul (even when within the body) can see by means of a certain supernatural light derived from God; in such a vision she can see all the absent things of heaven and earth, as we read that Saint John saw them in chapter 21 of Revelation, where he describes, and recounts the excellence of, the heavenly Jerusalem he saw in the sky; we read a similar thing about Saint Benedict, that he saw the whole world in a spiritual vision; Saint Thomas Aquinas, in his first *Quodlibetum*, says that this vision was in the light derived from above which I have mentioned.

2. The other type of vision, that of incorporeal substances, cannot be seen by means of this derived light I just spoke of, but by another, loftier light called the light of glory. And so these visions of incorporeal substances, such as angels and souls, do not belong to this life and cannot be seen while in the mortal body; because, if God wished to communicate them to the soul in their true essence, she would immediately come out of the flesh and detach herself from mortal life. Therefore God said to Moses when he asked Him to show him His essence: "*Non videbit me homo, et vivet*"; that is: "There shall no man see me, and live" (Exodus 33:20). Thus, when the children of Israel thought that they were to see God, or that they had seen Him, or some angel, they feared death, as we read in Exodus, where, in fear of the abovesaid, they cried: "Let not God speak with us, lest we die" (Exodus 20:19), which is as much as to say: "Let not God communicate Himself to us manifestly, lest we die." And· also in Judges, when Manoah, father of Samson, thought he and his wife had seen in his essence the angel who had addressed them (he had appeared to them in the shape of a very handsome man), he said to his wife: "*Morte moriemur, quia vidimus Dominum.*" Which means: "We shall surely die, because we have seen God" (Judges 13:22).

3. And so these visions are not of this life, except occasionally and transitorily, when God dispenses them or exempts the viewer from his normal condition of life, totally abstracting the spirit from that condition, and by His favor filling the soul's natural role vis-à-vis the body; therefore, when people think that Saint Paul saw them—that is, the separated substances in the third heaven—the saint himself says: "Whether in the body, I cannot tell; or whether out of the body, I cannot tell: God knoweth" (II Corinthians 12:2); that is, he was torn away up to them, and he says that he does not know whether he saw what he did while in the body or out of it, but that only God knows; whereby it is clearly seen that he was carried out of his natural life, God furnishing the means. Hence, in addition, when people believe that God showed His essence to Moses, we read that

Dios que El le pondría en el horado de la piedra y ampararía cubriéndole con la diestra, y amparándole por que no muriese cuando pasase su gloria (la cual pasada era mostrarse por vía de paso), amparando El con su diestra la vida natural de Moisés (Ex 33,22). Mas estas visiones tan sustanciales, como la de san Pablo y Moisés y nuestro padre Elías cuando cubrió su rostro al silbo suave de Dios, aunque son por vía de paso, rarísimas veces acaecen y casi nunca y a muy pocos, porque lo hace Dios en aquellos que son muy fuertes del espíritu de la Iglesia y ley de Dios, como fueron los tres arriba nombrados.

4. Pero, aunque estas visiones de sustancias espirituales no se pueden desnudar y claramente ver en esta vida con el entendimiento, puédense, empero, sentir en la sustancia del alma con suavísimos toques y juntas, lo cual pertenece a los sentimientos espirituales, de que con el divino favor trataremos después. Porque a éstos se endereza y encamina nuestra pluma, que es la divina junta y unión del alma con la Sustancia divina, lo cual ha de ser cuando tratemos de la inteligencia mística y confusa o oscura que queda por decir, donde habemos de tratar cómo, mediante esta noticia amorosa y oscura, se junta Dios con el alma en alto grado y divino; porque, en alguna manera, esta noticia oscura amorosa, que es la fe, sirve en esta vida para la divina unión, como la lumbre de gloria sirve en la otra de medio para la clara visión de Dios.

5. Por tanto, tratemos ahora de las visiones de corpóreas sustancias que espiritualmente se reciben en el alma, las cuales son a modo de las visiones corporales, porque, así como ven los ojos las cosas corporales mediante la luz natural, así el alma con el entendimiento, mediante la lumbre derivada sobrenaturalmente (que habemos dicho), ve interiormente esas mismas cosas naturales y otras, cuales Dios quiere. Sino que hay diferencia en el modo y en la manera; porque las espirituales y intelectuales mucho más clara y sutilmente acaecen que las corporales; porque, cuando Dios quiere hacer esa merced al alma, comunícala aquella luz sobrenatural que decimos, en que fácilmente y clarísimamente ve las cosas que Dios quiere, ahora del cielo, ahora de la tierra, no haciendo impedimento, ni al caso ausencia ni presencia de ellas. Y es, a veces, como si se le abriese una clarísima puerta, y por ella viese una luz a manera de un relámpago, cuando en una noche oscura súbitamente esclarece las cosas y las hace ver clara y distintamente y luego las deja a escuras, aunque las formas y figuras de ellas se quedan en la fantasía; lo cual en el alma acaece muy más perfectamente, porque de tal manera se quedan en ella impresas aquellas cosas que con el espíritu vio en aquella luz, que cada vez que advierte

God told him He would place him in the cleft of the rock and would protect him by covering him with His right hand; this protection was to save him from dying when His glory passed by (this passing signified the transitory nature of the vision), as with His right hand he protected the natural life of Moses (Exodus 33:22). But these visions, as substantial as those of Saint Paul, Moses, and our father Elijah when he covered his face at God's soft whistling, though only transitory, occur extremely rarely, almost never, and to very few, because God vouchsafes them only to those who are very strong in the spirit of the Church and the law of God, as the three above-mentioned men were.

4. But though these visions of spiritual substances cannot be divested and clearly seen in this life by the intellect, they nevertheless can be felt in the substance of the soul as very gentle contacts and junctures; this pertains to the spiritual sentiments, which I will discuss later, with God's favor, because my pen is heading and proceeding toward them and toward the explanation of the soul's divine juncture and union with the divine Substance. This will be when I discuss the mystical and confused or obscure knowledge that is still to be described when I explain how, by means of this obscure amorous cognition, God unites with the soul in a lofty, divine degree; because in some way this obscure amorous cognition, which is faith, serves in this life for the divine union, just as the light of glory serves in the next life as a means to the clear vision of God.

5. Therefore let us now discuss the visions of corporeal substances that are received spiritually in the soul; these are like bodily viewings because, just as the eyes see corporeal things using natural light, so the soul, with her intellect, by light of supernatural origin (as has been described), sees inwardly those same material things and any others God wishes her to. Except that the mode and manner are different; because the things of the spirit and intellect occur much more clearly and subtly than the corporeal ones, since, when it pleases God to grant this favor to the soul, He communicates to her that supernatural light I have mentioned, in which she readily and very clearly sees whatever God wishes her to, sometimes heavenly things, sometimes earthly things, their absence or presence creating no obstacle nor having any importance. And at times it is as if a very bright door were opened for her, through which she saw a light like a lightning flash, when on a dark night it suddenly illuminates things and allows them to be seen clearly and distinctly, immediately afterward leaving them in the dark, although their forms and figures linger in the mind; in the soul this occurs much more perfectly because those things which she saw with the spirit in that light remain so imprinted on her that every time she recalls them she sees them in herself just as she saw them be-

las ve en sí como las vio antes—bien así como en el espejo se ven las formas que están en él cada vez que en él miren—; y es de manera que ya aquellas formas de las cosas que vio nunca jamás se le quitan del todo del alma, aunque por tiempo se van haciendo algo remotas.

6. El efecto que hacen en el alma estas visiones es quietud, iluminación y alegría a manera de gloria, suavidad, limpieza y amor, humildad y inclinación o elevación del espíritu en Dios, unas veces más, otras menos, unas más en lo uno, otras en lo otro, según el espíritu en que se reciben y como Dios quiere.

7. Puede también el demonio causar estas visiones en el alma mediante alguna lumbre natural, en que por sugestión espiritual aclara al espíritu las cosas, ahora sean presentes, ahora ausentes. De donde, sobre aquel lugar de san Mateo donde dice que el demonio a Cristo *ostendit omnia regna mundi et gloriam eorum,* es a saber: Le mostró todos los reinos del mundo y la gloria de ellos (4,8), dicen algunos doctores que lo hizo por sugestión espiritual, porque con los ojos corporales no era posible hacerle ver tanto, que viese todos los reinos del mundo y su gloria. Pero, de estas visiones que causa el demonio a las que son de parte de Dios, hay mucha diferencia; porque los efectos que éstas hacen en el alma no son como los que hacen las buenas, antes hacen sequedad de espíritu acerca del trato con Dios y inclinación a estimarse y a admitir y tener en algo las dichas visiones, y en ninguna manera causan blandura de humildad y amor de Dios. Ni las formas déstas se quedan impresas en el alma con aquella claridad suave que las otras, ni duran, antes se raen luego del alma, salvo si el alma las estima mucho, que, entonces, la propia estimación hace que se acuerde de ellas naturalmente; mas es muy secamente y sin hacer aquel efecto de amor y humildad que las buenas causan cuando se acuerdan de ellas.

8. Estas visiones, por cuanto son de criaturas con quien Dios ninguna proporción ni conveniencia esencial tiene, no pueden servir al entendimiento de medio próximo para la unión de Dios; y así conviene al alma haberse puramente negativa en ellas (como en las demás que habemos dicho) para ir adelante por el medio próximo, que es la fe. De donde, de aquellas formas de las tales visiones que se quedan en el alma impresas, no ha de hacer archivo ni tesoro el alma, ni ha de querer arrimarse a ellas, porque sería estarse con aquellas formas, imágenes y personajes, que acerca del interior residen embarazada, y no iría por negación de todas las cosas a Dios; porque, dado caso que aquellas formas siempre se presenten allí, no la impedirán mucho si el alma no quisiere hacer caso de ellas, porque, aunque es verdad que la

fore—exactly as when the forms reflected in a mirror are seen each time people look into it—and so those forms of things she has once seen never entirely leave the soul, though with time they grow somewhat remote.

6. The effect that these visions have on the soul is quietude, illumination, happiness like that of being in glory, gentleness, cleanliness, love, humility, and the inclination or elevation of the spirit toward God, sometimes more so, sometimes less so, sometimes more in one way, sometimes more in another, depending on the spirit in which they are received and on God's wishes.

7. The devil, too, can cause these visions in the soul by means of some natural light, in which by spiritual suggestion he illuminates things for the soul, whether they are present or absent. Hence, with reference to that passage where Saint Matthew says that the devil showed Christ *omnia regna mundi et gloriam eorum,* that is "all the kingdoms of the world, and the glory of them" (Matthew 4:8), some theologians say he did it by spiritual suggestion, because with bodily eyes it was impossible to make Him see that much: all the kingdoms of the world and their glory. But there is a great difference between the visions caused by the devil and those which come from God, because the effects of the former on the soul are unlike those produced by the good visions; instead, they produce an aridity of the spirit in its dealings with God and a tendency toward exaggerated self-esteem, as one accepts and prizes those visions; in no way do they produce the meekness of humility and love for God. Nor do their forms remain imprinted on the soul with that sweet clarity of the others, nor do they last; instead, they are immediately erased from the soul, unless the soul prizes them greatly and, consequently, self-esteem makes her remember them naturally—though this will be with great aridity and without that effect of love and humility produced by the good visions when they are remembered.

8. Since these visions are of creatures lacking in any proportion or essential conformity to God, they cannot serve the intellect as a proximate means to union with God; and so it behooves the soul to behave purely negatively toward them (as toward all the others I have described) and to move onward by the proximate means, which is faith. Hence she must not make an archive or treasury of the forms in such visions which remain imprinted on the soul; nor should she try to look to them for support, because that would be to remain encumbered by those forms, images, and persons residing within her, and she would not proceed toward God by renouncing all things; since, even supposing that those forms constantly presented themselves to her, they would not hinder her greatly if she refused to make much of them: though it is true that the memory of them

memoria de ellas incita al alma a algún amor de Dios y contemplación, pero mucho más incita y levanta la pura fe y desnudez a escuras de todo eso, sin saber el alma cómo ni de dónde le viene. Y así, acaecerá que ande el alma inflamada con ansias de amor de Dios muy puro, sin saber de dónde le vienen ni qué fundamento tuvieron, y fue que, así como la fe se arraigó y infundió más en el alma mediante aquel vacío y tiniebla y desnudez de todas cosas, o pobreza espiritual—que todo lo podemos llamar una misma cosa—, también justamente se arraiga e infunde más en el alma la caridad de Dios. De donde, cuanto más el alma se quiere escurecer y anihilar acerca de todas las cosas exteriores e interiores que puede recibir, tanto más se infunde de fe y, por consiguiente, de amor y esperanza en ella, por cuanto estas tres virtudes teologales andan en uno.

9. Pero este amor algunas veces no lo comprende la persona ni lo siente, porque no tiene este amor su asiento en el sentido con ternura, sino en el alma con fortaleza y más ánimo y osadía que antes, aunque algunas veces redunde en el sentido y se muestre tierno y blando. De donde para llegar a aquel amor, alegría y gozo que le hacen y causan las tales visiones al alma, conviénele que tenga fortaleza y mortificación y amor para querer quedarse en vacío y a escuras de todo ello, y fundar aquel amor y gozo en lo que no ve ni siente ni puede ver ni sentir en esta vida, que es Dios, el cual es incomprehensible y sobre todo, y por eso nos conviene ir a El por negación de todo; porque, si no, dado caso que el alma sea tan sagaz, humilde y fuerte, que el demonio no la pueda engañar en ellas ni hacerla caer en alguna presunción, como lo suele hacer, no dejará ir al alma adelante, por cuanto pone obstáculo a la desnudez espiritual y pobreza de espíritu y vacío en fe, que es lo que se requiere para la unión del alma con Dios.

10. Y porque acerca destas visiones sirve también la misma doctrina que en el capítulo 19 y 20 dimos para las visiones y aprehensiones sobrenaturales del sentido, no gastaremos aquí más tiempo en decirlas.

Libro tercero, CAPÍTULO 1

1. Instruida ya la primera potencia del alma, que es el entendimiento, por todas sus aprehensiones en la primera virtud teológica, que es la fe, para que según esta potencia se pueda unir el alma con Dios por medio de pureza de fe, resta ahora hacer lo mismo acerca de las otras dos potencias del alma, que son memoria y voluntad, purificándolas también acerca de sus aprehensiones, para que, según estas dos potencias, el alma se venga a unir con Dios en perfecta es-

incites the soul to some love for God and contemplation, she is incited and uplifted much more by pure faith and nakedness of all such things in darkness, the soul not knowing how or whence this comes to her. And so it will happen that the soul will go about afire with longings of very pure love for God, not knowing whence they reach her or what basis they had; the reason was that, just as faith took root in the soul, and infused itself into her more deeply, by means of that emptiness, darkness, or nakedness of all objects, or spiritual poverty—all names for the same thing—the charity of God also takes root in her at the same time, and infuses itself more deeply into her. Hence, the more the soul tries to grow dark and annihilate herself vis-à-vis all the outward and inward things she may receive, the more she is infused with faith and, consequently, with love and hope, since these three theological virtues go together.

9. But sometimes a person fails to comprehend or feel this love because it is not situated in the senses as tenderness, but in the soul as fortitude and greater courage and daring than ever before, though at times it does overflow into the senses, where it shows itself as tenderness and meekness. Hence, to attain that love, cheerfulness, and joy which such visions produce and cause in the soul, it behooves her to have fortitude and mortification and love so she will want to be left in the dark, in the emptiness of all those things, and to base that love and joy on what she neither sees nor feels, nor can see and feel, in this life: God, Who is incomprehensible and above all. Therefore it behooves us to go to Him through renunciation of everything; because otherwise, unless the soul is so wise, humble, and strong that the devil cannot deceive her in these matters, nor make her fall into some presumption, as he generally does, he will not allow her to move forward, creating some obstacle to the spiritual nakedness, poverty of spirit, and emptiness in faith which the soul requires for her union with God.

10. And because the same teaching is valid for these visions as I expounded in chapters 19 and 20, on the subject of the visions and supernatural perceptions of the senses, I shall not spend more time on them here.

Book III, CHAPTER 1

1. Now that the first power of the soul, the intellect, has been instructed with regard to all its perceptions by the first theological virtue, faith, so that the soul may be able to unite with God vis-à-vis that power through the purity of faith, it now remains to do the same for the other two powers of the soul, memory and will, purifying them, too, with regard to *their* perceptions, so that, in these two powers, as well, the soul can come to unite with God in perfect hope and charity. This will be done

peranza y caridad. Lo cual se hará brevemente en este Tercero Libro, porque habiendo concluido con el entendimiento, que es el receptáculo de todos los demás objetos en su manera (en lo cual está andado mucho camino para lo demás), no es necesario alargarnos tanto acerca destas potencias, porque no es posible que si el espiritual instruyere bien al entendimiento en fe según la doctrina que se le ha dado, no instruya también de camino a las otras dos potencias en las otras dos virtudes, pues las operaciones de las unas dependen de las otras.

2. Pero porque, para cumplir con el estilo que se lleva y también para que se entienda, es necesario hablar en la propria y determinada materia, habremos aquí de poner las proprias aprehensiones de cada potencia, y primero de las de la memoria, haciendo de ellas aquí la distinción que basta para nuestro propósito; la cual podremos sacar de la distinción de sus objetos, que son tres: naturales, imaginarios y espirituales según los cuales también son en tres maneras las noticias de la memoria, es a saber: naturales y sobrenaturales y imaginarias espirituales.

3. De las cuales, mediante el favor divino, iremos aquí tratando, comenzando de las noticias naturales, que son de objeto más exterior; y luego se tratará de las afecciones de la voluntad, con que *se concluirá* este Libro Tercero de la *Noche activa espiritual*.

Libro tercero, CAPÍTULO 4

QUE TRATA DEL SEGUNDO DAÑO QUE PUEDE VENIR AL ALMA DE PARTE DEL DEMONIO POR VÍA DE LAS APREHENSIONES NATURALES DE LA MEMORIA

1. El segundo daño positivo que al alma puede venir por medio de las noticias de la memoria es de parte del *demonio*, el cual tiene gran mano en el alma por este medio, porque puede añadir formas, noticias y discursos, y por medio de ellos afectar el alma con soberbia, avaricia, ira, envidia, etc., y poner odio injusto, amor vano, y engañar de muchas maneras; y, allende desto, suele él dejar las cosas y asentarlas en la fantasía de manera que las que son falsas parezcan verdaderas, y las verdaderas falsas; y, finalmente, todos los más engaños que hace el demonio y males al alma entran por las noticias y discursos de la memoria, la cual, si se oscurece en todas ellas y se aniquila en olvido, cierra totalmente la puerta a este daño del demonio y se libra de todas estas cosas, que es gran bien; porque el demonio no puede nada en el alma si no es mediante las operaciones de las potencias de ella, principalmente por medio de las noticias, porque de ellas dependen casi todas las demás operaciones de las demás poten-

briefly in this Book III, because, having concluded my discussion of the intellect, which is the receptacle of all other objects in its way (and thus having made great headway toward discussing the rest), I do not need to spend as much time on the other two powers, because it is not possible for a spiritual person to instruct his intellect fully in faith by the teachings I have given without simultaneously instructing his other two powers in the other two virtues, their operations being interdependent.

2. But because (in order to comply with the system I am following, and also to ensure the reader's understanding) I must discuss each subject on its own for its own sake, I shall here have to state the perceptions peculiar to each power, beginning with those of the memory, making the distinction between them here which is sufficient for my purpose; this distinction can be derived from the distinction between their objects, of which there are three kinds: natural, imaginative, and spiritual. In accordance with them there are also three types of cognition, or idea, in the memory: natural, supernatural, and spiritual-imaginative.

3. With God's help, I shall be discussing these here, beginning with the natural ideas, which have a more external object; then I shall discuss the affections of the will, with which this Book III, on the active night of the spirit, will conclude.

Book III, CHAPTER 4

ON THE SECOND HARM THE SOUL MAY SUFFER FROM THE DEVIL BY WAY OF THE NATURAL APPREHENSIONS OF THE MEMORY

1. The second positive harm that may come to the soul by way of the ideas of the memory is sent by the devil, who has great control over the soul by this means, because he can add forms, ideas, and arguments and, by means of them, can afflict the soul with pride, avarice, wrath, envy, etc., instilling unjust hatred and vain love in her, and can also deceive her in many ways; besides this, he generally leaves things behind in the mind, lodging them so firmly there that those which are false seem true, and the true false; lastly, all the other deceits and evils the devil inflicts on the soul enter by way of the ideas and arguments of the memory, which, if it becomes dark to them all and annihilates itself in oblivion, locks the door entirely on this harm caused by the devil and frees itself from all these things, which is a great benefit; because the devil has no power over the soul except through the workings of her powers, especially by way of ideas, because nearly all the other workings of the other powers depend on them; hence, if the memory annihilates itself with regard to these

cias; de donde, si la memoria se aniquila en ellas, el demonio no puede nada, porque nada halla de donde asir, y sin nada, nada puede.

2. Yo quisiera que los espirituales acabasen bien de echar de ver cuántos daños les hacen los demonios en las almas por medio de la memoria cuando se dan mucho a usar de ella, cuántas tristezas y aflicciones y gozos malos vanos los hacen tener, así cerca de lo que piensan en Dios como de las cosas del mundo, y cuántas impurezas les dejan arraigadas en el espíritu, haciéndolos también grandemente distraer del sumo recogimiento, que consiste en poner toda el alma, según sus potencias, en sólo el bien incomprehensible y quitarla de todas las cosas aprehensibles, porque no son bien incomprehensibles. Lo cual, aunque no se siguiera tanto bien deste vacío como es ponerse en Dios, por sólo ser causa de librarse de muchas penas, aflicciones y tristezas, allende de las imperfecciones y pecados de que se libra, es grande bien.

Libro tercero, CAPÍTULO 36

EN QUE PROSIGUE DE LAS IMÁGENES Y DICE DE LA IGNORANCIA
QUE ACERCA DE ELLAS TIENEN ALGUNAS PERSONAS

1. Mucho había que decir de la rudeza que muchas personas tienen acerca de las imágenes, porque llega la bobería a tanto, que algunas ponen más confianza en unas imágenes que en otras, entendiendo que les oirá Dios más por ésta que por aquélla, representando ambas una misma cosa, como dos de Cristo o dos de nuestra Señora; y esto es porque tienen más afición a la una hechura que a la otra, en lo cual va envuelta gran rudeza acerca del trato con Dios y culto y honra que se le debe, el cual sólo mira a la fe y pureza del corazón del que ora. Porque el hacer Dios a veces más mercedes por medio de una imagen que de otra de aquel mesmo género, no es porque haya más en una que en otra para ese efecto (aunque en la hechura tenga mucha diferencia), sino porque las personas despiertan más su devoción por medio de una que de otra. Que si la misma devoción tuviese por la una que por la otra (y aun sin la una y sin la otra), las mesmas mercedes recibirían de Dios.

2. De donde la causa por que Dios despierta milagros y hace mercedes por medio de algunas imágenes más que por otras, no es para que estimen más aquéllas que las otras, sino que, para que con aquella novedad se despierte más la devoción y afecto de los fieles a oración; y de aquí es que, como entonces y por medio de aquella imagen se enciende la devoción y se continúa la oración (que lo uno y lo

things, the devil can do nothing because he finds nothing to grasp, and without anything he cannot do anything.

2. I would be glad if spiritual people finally came to see how much harm the demons do them in their souls by way of the memory when they make much use of it, how much sadness, affliction, and vain, evil joy they make them suffer, as much with regard to their thoughts of God as to worldly things, and how many impurities they leave rooted in their spirit, also distracting them enormously from that deepest concentration which consists of directing their whole soul and her powers solely to the quite incomprehensible One, and diverting her from all things that can be perceived, because they are not fully incomprehensible. This, even if they fail to derive as much benefit from this self-emptying as they would by placing themselves in God, is still a great good, if only as the cause of their freeing themselves from much grief, affection, and sadness, not to mention the imperfections and sins they get rid of.

Book III, CHAPTER 36

MORE ABOUT RELIGIOUS IMAGES AND THE IGNORANCE
OF SOME PEOPLE ON THAT SUBJECT

1. Much could be said about the crude notions about images that many people have, their folly extending so far that some of them place greater trust in some images than in others, thinking that God will hear them more clearly through the power of this one than of that one, when both depict the same person, such as two images of Christ or two of Our Lady; this is because they are fonder of the workmanship of one than of the other, which bespeaks great crudeness in their dealings with God and the worship and honor due to Him, for He regards only the faith and purity of heart of the person praying. Since, if God sometimes grants more favors by way of one image than another of the same person, it is not because one possesses greater power to sway Him than the other (despite the fact that their workmanship is very different), but because people kindle their piety by one more than the other. For if they had the same devotion for one and the other (and even without either of them), they would receive the same favors from God.

2. Hence, the reason God awakens more miracles and grants more favors by way of some images than of others is not so that the former should be more highly regarded than the latter, but so that this novelty will more greatly kindle the devotion and affection of the faithful for prayer; and so it is that, just as, at that time and by way of that image, devotion is kindled and prayer is continued (for both of these are the means by which

otro es medio para que oiga Dios y conceda lo que se le pide), entonces y por medio de aquella imagen, por la oración y afecto continúa Dios las mercedes y milagros en aquella imagen; que cierto está que no los hace Dios por la imagen, pues en sí no es más que pintura, sino por la devoción y fe que se tiene con el santo que representa. Y así, si la misma devoción tuvieses tú y fe en nuestra Señora delante de esta su imagen que delante de aquella que representa la mesma (y aun sin ella, como habemos dicho), las mesmas mercedes recebirías; que, aun por experiencia se ve que, si Dios hace algunas mercedes y obras milagrosas, ordinariamente los hace por medio de algunas imágenes no muy bien talladas ni curiosamente pintadas o figuradas, por que los fieles no atribuyan algo desto a la figura o pintura.

3. Y muchas veces suele nuestro Señor obrar estas mercedes por medio de aquellas imágenes que están más apartadas y solitarias; lo uno, porque con aquel movimiento de ir a ellas crezca más el afecto y sea más intenso el acto; lo otro, porque se aparten del ruido y gente a orar, como lo hacía el Señor (Mt 14,23; Lc 6,12). Por lo cual, el que hace la romería, hace bien de hacerla cuando no va otra gente, aunque sea tiempo extraordinario; y, cuando va mucha turba, nunca yo se lo aconsejaría, porque, ordinariamente, vuelven más distraídos que fueron; y muchos las toman y hacen más por recreación que por devoción. De manera que, como haya devoción y fe, cualquiera imagen bastará, mas, si no la hay, ninguna bastará; que harto viva imagen era nuestro Salvador en el mundo y, con todo, los que no tenían fe, aunque más andaban con él y veían sus obras maravillosas, no se aprovechaban. Y ésa era la causa por que en su tierra no hacía muchas virtudes, como dice el evangelista (Mt 13,58; Lc 4,24).

4. También quiero aquí decir algunos efectos sobrenaturales que causan a veces algunas imágenes en personas particulares, y es que a algunas imágenes da Dios espíritu particular en ellas, de manera que queda fijada en la mente la figura de la imagen y devoción que causó, trayéndola como presente, y cuando de repente della se acuerda le hace el mismo espíritu que cuando la vio, a veces menos y aun a veces más; y en otra imagen, aunque sea de más perfecta hechura, no hallará aquel espíritu.

5. También muchas personas tienen devoción más en una hechura que en otras, y en algunas no será más que afición y gusto natural, así como a uno contentará más un rostro de una persona que de otra, y se aficionará más a ella naturalmente, y la traerá más presente en su imaginación, aunque no sea tan hermosa como las otras, porque se inclina su natural a aquella manera de forma y figura; y así, pensarán al-

God hears us and grants our requests), at that time and by way of that image, because of our devotion and affection God continues the favors and miracles associated with that image; for the truth is that God does not do this for the sake of the image, which in itself is nothing but paint, but because of the devotion to and faith in the saint it depicts. And so, if you should have the same devotion to and faith in Our Lady in front of one image of her as in front of another one also depicting her (or even without an image, as I said), you would receive the same favors; it is seen even by experience that, if God grants some favors and performs some miracles, He generally does so by way of some images that are not very well carved or elegantly painted or fashioned, so that the faithful will not attribute any of this to the carving or painting.

3. And many times our Lord is accustomed to grant these favors by way of those images that are more remote and in lonelier places; for one thing, so that the necessity of traveling to them will increase the affection and the prayer will be more intense; for another, so that people will avoid noise and crowds when they pray, as the Lord did (Matthew 14:23, Luke 6:12). Therefore, a man who goes on a pilgrimage will do well to perform it when no other people go, even at an out-of-the-ordinary time; when a big mob goes, I would never advise him to do so, because usually they come back more distracted than when they went; and many people look on pilgrimages as vacations, and perform more in the way of recreation than of devotion. So that, if devotion and faith are present, any image will do; if they are absent, none will do; because our Savior was a sufficiently vivid image in the world and nevertheless those without faith, even though they journeyed in His close company and witnessed His miraculous works, were not benefited. This is why He did not perform many wonders in His own land, as the Evangelists say (Matthew 13:58, Luke 4:24).

4. I also wish to mention here some supernatural effects sometimes made on particular people by some images; this is because God grants a particular spirit to some images, so that the form of the images and the devotion they aroused remain fixed in the mind, which carries them along as if still present, and when it suddenly recalls them they produce the same spiritual effect as when they were seen, lesser or greater at different times; and in another image, though it be more perfectly crafted, the person will not find the same spiritual effect.

5. In addition, many people have greater devotion for one rendering than for others; in some cases this will be merely natural inclination and liking, just as a man will take more pleasure in the face of one person than another's, and will feel more natural inclination toward it, and will carry it along in his imagination with greater presence, even though it is not as

gunas personas que la afición que tienen a tal o tal imagen es devoción, y no será quizá más que afición y gusto natural. Otras veces acaece que, mirando una imagen, la vean moverse, o hacer semblantes y muestras, y dar a entender cosas, o hablar. Esta manera y la de los afectos sobrenaturales que aquí decimos de las imágenes, aunque es verdad que muchas veces son verdaderos afectos y buenos, causando Dios aquello, o para aumentar la devoción, o para que el alma tenga algún arrimo a que ande asida por ser algo flaca y no se distraiga, muchas veces lo hace el demonio para engañar y dañar; por tanto, para todo daremos doctrina en el capítulo siguiente.

beautiful as others, because his nature is inclined toward that kind of form and figure; and so, some people probably think that their inclination toward such or such an image is devotion, whereas it is possibly merely inclination and natural liking. At other times it happens that people looking at an image see it move or change its facial expression or make gestures, and communicate things, or speak. Though it is true that often this phenomenon, and that of the above-mentioned supernatural effects of images, are true and good ones, caused by God, either to enhance devotion or to lend the soul some support, something to cling to in her relative weakness to avoid losing concentration, yet many times this is caused by the devil, to deceive or harm; therefore, I shall offer teachings on all this in the next chapter.

Noche oscura

En una noche obscura,
con ansias, en amores inflamada,
oh dichosa ventura!,
salí sin ser notada,
estando ya mi casa sosegada.

DECLARACIÓN

1. Cuenta el alma en esta primera canción el modo y manera que tuvo en salir según el afección de sí y de todas las cosas, muriendo por verdadera mortificación a todas ellas y a sí misma, para venir a vivir vida de amor dulce y sabrosa con Dios. Y dice que este salir de sí y de todas las cosas fue en una *noche oscura,* que aquí entiende por la contemplación purgativa (como después se dirá), la cual *pasivamente* causa en el alma la dicha negación de sí misma y de todas las cosas.

2. Y esta salida dice ella aquí que pudo hacer con la fuerza y calor que para ello le dio el amor de su Esposo en la dicha contemplación oscura; en lo cual encarece la buena dicha que tuvo en encaminar a Dios por esta *noche* con tan próspero suceso, que ninguno de los tres enemigos, que son mundo, demonio y carne (que son los que siempre contrarían este camino), se lo pudiese impedir, por cuanto la dicha *noche* de contemplación purificativa hizo adormecer y amortiguar en la casa de su sensualidad todas las pasiones y apetitos según sus apetitos y movimientos contrarios. Dice, pues, el verso: "En una noche escura."

Libro primero, CAPÍTULO 1

PONE EL PRIMER VERSO Y COMIENZA A TRATAR DE LAS IMPERFECCIONES
DE LOS PRINCIPIANTES

1. En esta noche escura comienzan a entrar las almas cuando Dios las va sacando de estado de *principiantes,* que es de los que meditan en el camino espiritual, y las comienza a poner en el de los *aprovechantes,* que es ya el de los contemplativos, para que, pasando por

Dark Night

On a dark night,
with longings, afire with love
(oh, happy fortune!),
I went out without being detected,
my house being calm now.

EXPLANATION

1. In this first stanza the soul sings of the way in which she emerged from love of self and of all created things, dying to all of them and to herself through true mortification, to come to live a sweet and delectable life of love with God. And she says that this emergence from self and from all things took place on a "dark night," here understood as purificatory contemplation (as I shall explain later), which *passively* gives rise in the soul to the aforesaid denial of herself and all things.

2. And she here says that she was able to make this going forth by the strength and warmth given her for that purpose by love for her Bridegroom in the aforesaid dark contemplation; saying this, she extols the good fortune she had in setting out toward God on this "night" with such good success, without any of the three enemies, the world, the devil, and the flesh (which are those which always oppose this journey), being able to hinder her, because the aforesaid "night" of purificatory contemplation lulled to sleep and deadened in the house of her senses all passions and appetites which could have bestirred themselves against it. Thus she speaks the line: "On a dark night."

Book I, CHAPTER 1

THE FIRST LINE OF THE POEM. THE START OF THE DESCRIPTION OF THE IMPERFECTIONS OF BEGINNERS.

1. Souls begin to enter this dark night when God removes them from the state of "beginners," those who meditate on the spiritual path, and starts to place them in the state of "proficients," which is already that of contemplatives, so that, passing through it, they can attain the state of the

aquí, lleguen al estado de los *perfectos,* que es el de la divina unión del alma con Dios. Por tanto, para entender y declarar mejor qué noche sea esta por que el alma pasa, y por qué causa la pone Dios en ella, primero convendrá tocar aquí algunas propiedades de los principiantes. Lo cual, aunque será con la brevedad que pudiere, no dejará también de servir a los mismos principiantes, para que, entendiendo la flaqueza del estado que llevan, se animen y deseen que los ponga Dios en esta noche, donde se fortalece y confirma el alma en las virtudes y pasa a los inestimables deleites del amor de Dios. Y, aunque nos detengamos un poco, no será más de lo que basta para tratar luego de esta noche oscura.

2. Es, pues, de saber que el alma, después que determinadamente se convierte a servir a Dios, ordinariamente la va Dios criando en espíritu y regalando, al modo que la amorosa madre hace al niño tierno, al cual al calor de sus pechos le calienta, y con leche sabrosa y manjar blando y dulce le cría, y en sus brazos le trae y le regala; pero, a la medida que va creciendo, le va la madre quitando el regalo y, escondiendo el tierno amor, pónele el amargo acíbar en el dulce pecho y, abajándole de los brazos, le hace andar por su pie, por que, perdiendo las propiedades de niño, se dé a cosas más grandes y sustanciales. La amorosa madre de la gracia de Dios (Sap 16,25), luego que por nuevo calor y hervor de servir a Dios reengendra al alma, eso mismo hace con ella, porque la hace hallar dulce y sabrosa la leche espiritual sin algún trabajo suyo en todas las cosas de Dios, y en los exercicios espirituales gran gusto, porque le da Dios aquí su pecho de amor tierno, bien así como a niño tierno (1.ª Petr 2,2–3).

3. Por tanto, su deleite halla pasarse grandes ratos en oración, y por ventura las noches enteras, sus gustos son las penitencias, sus contentos los ayunos, y sus consuelos usar de los sacramentos y comunicar en la cosas divinas; las cuales cosas, aunque con gran eficacia y porfía asisten a ellas y las usan y tratan con gran cuidado los espirituales, hablando espiritualmente, comúnmente se han muy flaca e imperfectamente en ellas, porque, como son movidos a estas cosas y exercicios espirituales por el consuelo y gusto que allí hallan y como también ellos no están habilitados por exercicios de fuerte lucha en las virtudes, acerca de estas sus obras espirituales tienen muchas faltas e imperfecciones; porque, al fin, cada uno obra conforme al hábito de perfección que tiene, y, como éstos no han tenido lugar de adquirir los dichos hábitos fuertes, de necesidad han de obrar, como flacos niños, flacamente. Lo cual, para que más claramente se vea, y cuán faltos van estos principiantes en las virtudes acerca de lo que con el dicho gusto

"perfected," which is that of the soul's divine union with God. Therefore, the better to understand and explain what this night is through which the soul passes, and for what reason God places her in it, it will first be fitting here to mention a few characteristics of beginners. Though this will be done as briefly as I can, yet it will not fail to be useful to the beginners themselves, so that, understanding the weakness of the state they are in, they can take heart and desire God to place them in this night in which the soul is strengthened and confirmed in virtues and moves along to the inestimable delights of God's love. And though I may linger a bit, I shall say only enough to be able to discuss this dark night afterward.

2. So, then, one must know that, after the soul has deliberately turned herself to the service of God, He generally nurtures her gradually in spirit and caresses her, just as a loving mother does with her tender babe, whom she warms with the warmth of her breasts, nurturing him with tasty milk and soft, sweet foods, carrying him in her arms and caressing him; but, as he grows, his mother gradually leaves off caressing him and, concealing her tender love, smears bitter aloes on her sweet breast and, lowering him from her arms, makes him walk on his own, so that, losing the characteristics of an infant, he can devote himself to greater, more substantial things. The loving mother which is the grace of God (Wisdom of Solomon 16:25), after reengendering the soul by new warmth and fervor to serve God, does the same thing with her: she makes her find the spiritual milk sweet and tasty, without any toil of her own, in all the things of God, and makes her take great pleasure in spiritual exercises, because here God gives her His tenderly loving breast, as if to a tender babe (I Peter 2:2–3).

3. Therefore, she finds her delight in spending long periods in prayer, entire nights perhaps; her pleasures are penitences, her contentments are fasts, and her comfort is partaking of the sacraments and participating in divine matters; though spiritual people may attend to such things with great effectiveness and perseverance and partake of them and join in them with great care, speaking spiritually, generally their behavior in this regard is very weak and imperfect because, incited to these things and spiritual exercises by the comfort and pleasure they find in them, and at the same time not being trained in the virtues by extremely difficult exercises, they have many faults and imperfections in these spiritual works of theirs; since, after all, every man works in proportion to the propensity for perfection that he possesses, and, these beginners not having had the opportunity to acquire the aforesaid strong habits, by necessity they must act like weak children, weakly. For this to be seen more clearly, and to indicate how lacking these beginners are in the virtues, as shown by their readiness to perform their works for the aforesaid pleasure, I shall indi-

con facilidad obran, irémoslo notando por los *siete vicios capitales,* diciendo algunas de las muchas imperfecciones que cada uno dellos tienen, en que se verá claro cuán de niños es el obrar que éstos obran. Y veráse también cuántos bienes trae consigo la noche oscura de que luego habemos de tratar, pues de todas estas imperfecciones limpia al alma y la purifica.

Libro primero, CAPÍTULO 9

DE LAS SEÑALES EN QUE SE CONOCERÁ QUE EL ESPIRITUAL VA POR EL CAMINO DESTA NOCHE Y PURGACIÓN SENSITIVA

1. Pero, porque estas sequedades podrían proceder muchas veces, no de la dicha noche y purgación del apetito sensitivo, sino de pecados e imperfecciones, o de flojedad y tibieza, o de algún mal humor o indisposición corporal, pondré aquí algunas señales en que se conoce si es la tal sequedad de la dicha purgación, o si nace de alguno de los dichos vicios. Para lo cual hallo que hay tres señales principales.

2. La primera es si, así como no halla gusto ni consuelo en las cosas de Dios, tampoco le halla en alguna de las cosas criadas, porque, como pone Dios al alma en esta oscura noche a fin de enjugarle y purgarle el apetito sensitivo, en ninguna cosa le deja engolosinarse ni hallar sabor. Y en esto se conoce muy probablemente que esta sequedad y sinsabor no proviene ni de pecados ni de imperfecciones nuevamente cometidos, porque, si esto fuese, sentirse hía en el natural alguna inclinación o gana de gustar de otra alguna cosa que de las de Dios, porque, cuando quiera que se relaja el apetito en alguna imperfección, luego se siente quedar inclinado a ella poco o mocho, según el gusto y afición que allí aplicó. Pero, porque este no gustar ni de cosa de arriba ni de abajo podría provenir de alguna indisposición o humor melancólico, el cual muchas veces no deja hallar gusto en nada, es menester la segunda señal y condición.

3. La segunda señal para que se crea ser la dicha purgación, es que ordinariamente trae la memoria en Dios con solicitud y cuidado penoso, pensando que no sirve a Dios, sino que vuelve atrás, como se ve con aquel sinsabor en las cosas de Dios. Y en esto se ve que no sale de flojedad y tibieza este sinsabor y sequedad; porque de razón de la tibieza es no se dar mucho ni tener solicitud interior por las cosas de Dios. De donde entre la sequedad y tibieza hay mucha diferencia, porque la que es tibieza tiene mucha flojedad y remisión en la voluntad y en el ánimo, sin solicitud de servir a Dios; la que sólo es sequedad purgativa tiene consigo ordinaria solicitud con cuidado y pena

cate this by making pedagogical use of the seven deadly sins, mentioning some of the many imperfections associated with each of these; hereby it will be seen clearly how infantile are the works that such beginners perform. And it will also be seen how many benefits are conferred by the dark night which I shall later discuss, because it cleanses the soul of all these imperfections and purifies her.

Book I, CHAPTER 9

THE SIGNS BY WHICH IT WILL BE KNOWN THAT THE SPIRITUAL MAN
IS FOLLOWING THE PATH OF THIS NIGHT OF SENSORY PURIFICATION

1. But because this aridity may often result, not from the aforesaid night and the purification of the sensory appetite, but from sins and imperfections, or from laxity and lukewarmness, or from some adverse humor or bodily indisposition, I shall here give a few signs by which to tell whether this aridity is caused by the aforesaid purification, or whether it springs from any of the aforesaid vices. For this, I find that there are three chief signs.

2. The first is that, just as the person finds no pleasure or comfort in the things of God, he finds none in any of the created things, either; because, since God places the soul in this dark night in order to dry her and purge away her sensory appetite, He does not allow her to become fond of, or find a taste in, anything. And hereby one can tell with great probability that this dryness and displeasure arise neither from sins nor from imperfections newly committed, because, if that were the case, the soul would feel in her nature some inclination or yearning to enjoy something else which was not of the things of God (since, when the appetite is indulged in some imperfection, it immediately feels itself drawn to it to a greater or lesser degree, depending on the liking and inclination it showed for it). But, because this failure to enjoy anything, whether heavenly or earthly, might be the result of some indisposition or melancholy humor, which often prevents one from enjoying anything, the second sign or condition is necessary.

3. The second sign by which one may believe that the aforesaid purification is in question is when the person usually fixes his memory on God with solicitude and painful cares, thinking that he is not serving God but is retrogressing, as is seen in that dislike for the things of God. And hereby one can see that this dislike and aridity do not result from laxity and lukewarmness; because it pertains to the nature of lukewarmness that it does not much care about or feel inner solicitude for the things of God. Hence, there is a great difference between aridity and lukewarmness, because lukewarmness is very lax and remiss in will and mind and has no solicitude to serve God; mere purificatory aridity usually entails careworn

(como digo) de que no sirve a Dios. Y ésta, aunque algunas veces sea
ayudada de la melancolía u otro humor (como muchas veces lo es), no
por eso deja de hacer su efecto purgativo del apetito, pues de todo
gusto está privado y sólo su cuidado trae en Dios; porque cuando es
puro humor sólo se va en disgusto y estrago del natural, sin estos deseos de servir a Dios que tiene la sequedad purgativa, con la cual,
aunque la parte sensitiva está muy caída y floja y flaca para obrar por
el poco gusto que halla, el espíritu, empero, está pronto y fuerte.

4. Porque la causa de esta sequedad es porque muda Dios los bienes y fuerza del sentido a el espíritu, de los cuales, por no ser capaz el
sentido y fuerza natural, se queda ayuno, seco y vacío, porque la parte
sensitiva no tiene habilidad para lo que es puro espíritu, y así, gus-
tando el espíritu, se desabre la carne y se afloja para obrar. Mas el espíritu que va recibiendo el manjar, anda fuerte y más alerto y solícito
que antes en el cuidado de no faltar a Dios; el cual, si no siente luego
al principio el sabor y deleite espiritual, sino la sequedad y sinsabor, es
por la novedad del trueque, porque, habiendo tenido el paladar hecho
a estotros gustos sensibles (y todavía tiene los ojos puestos en ellos) y
porque también el paladar espiritual no está acomodado ni purgado
para tan sutil gusto, hasta que sucesivamente se vaya disponiendo por
medio desta seca y oscura noche no puede sentir el gusto y bien espiritual, sino la sequedad y sinsabor, a falta del gusto que antes con
tanta facilidad gustaba.

5. Porque estos que comienza Dios a llevar por estas soledades del
desierto son semejantes a los hijos de Israel, que luego que en el desierto les comenzó Dios a dar *el manjar del cielo,* que de suyo tenía
todos los sabores y, como allí se dice, *se convertía al sabor que cada
uno quería* (Sap. 16,20–21), con todo, sentían más la falta de los gustos y sabores de las carnes y cebollas que comían antes en Egipto—
por haber tenido el paladar hecho y engolosinado en ellas—que la
dulzura delicada del maná angélico, y lloraban y gemían por las carnes
entre los manjares del cielo (Num 11,4–6); que a tanto llega la bajeza
de nuestro apetito, que nos hace desear nuestras miserias y fastidiar el
bien incomunicable del cielo.

6. Pero, como digo, cuando estas sequedades provienen de la vía
purgativa del apetito sensible, aunque el espíritu no siente al principio el sabor por las causas que acabamos de decir, siente la fortaleza y
brío para obrar en la sustancia que le da el manjar interior, el cual
manjar es principio de oscura y seca contemplación para el sentido; la
cual contemplación, que es oculta y secreta para el mismo que la
tiene, ordinariamente, junto con la sequedad y vacío que hace al sen-

solicitude and sorrow (as I say) for not being of service to God. And though this aridity is sometimes enhanced by melancholy or some other humor (as it frequently is), it does not therefore fail to produce its purging effect on the appetite, since it is bereft of all pleasure and its cares are for God alone; because the humor on its own merely results in dislike and damage to nature, without these desires to serve God which the purificatory aridity possesses. In the case of the aridity, even though the sensory part of the soul is very dejected, lax, and weak in action because it finds so little pleasure in it, nevertheless the spirit is alert and strong.

4. The answer is that this aridity results from God's transfer of benefits and strength from the senses to the spirit; since the senses and natural strength do not have the capacity for these good things, they are left deprived, dry, and empty, because the sensory part of the soul has no aptitude for that which is pure spirit, so that, when the spirit is enjoying, the flesh becomes insipid and slack in its works. But the spirit, which is receiving the food, is strong and more alert and solicitous than before in its care not to fail God. If the spirit does not at the very outset feel any spiritual pleasure and delight, but aridity and dislike, this is due to the novelty of the transfer, because, having had a palate attuned to those other sensory tastes (which it still has its eyes on), and, also, the spiritual palate not being adapted by purification to so subtle a taste, until it gradually adjusts by means of this dry, dark night it cannot feel the spiritual taste and good, but aridity and dislike, for want of the pleasure it formerly tasted so readily.

5. This is because those whom God begins to lead through these desert wildernesses are like the children of Israel, who, as soon as God began to give them the food from heaven, which contained all flavors in itself and, as Scripture says, changed to the flavor each man desired (Wisdom of Solomon 16:20–21), nevertheless felt more strongly the lack of the tastes and flavors of the meats and onions they used to eat in Egypt—because their palate had been attuned to and tempted by them—than they felt the delicate sweetness of the angelic manna, and they wept and groaned for meat in the midst of heavenly nourishment (Numbers 11:4–6); for the lowness of our appetite reaches such a point that it makes us desire our wretchedness and spurn heaven's incommunicable good.

6. But, as I say, when these periods of aridity result from the path that purifies the sensory appetite, even if the spirit does not at the outset feel that taste for things which I have just mentioned, it feels the fortitude and vigor to work upon the substance supplied to it by the inner food, which is the principle of dark, dry contemplation for the senses; this contemplation (which is secret and hidden to the very man who has it) usually, together with the aridity and void it creates in the senses, gives the soul

tido, da al alma inclinación y gana de estarse a solas y en quietud, sin poder pensar en cosa particular ni tener gana de pensarla y entonces, si a los que esto acaece se supiesen quietar, descuidando de cualquiera obra interior y exterior sin solicitud de hacer allí nada, luego en aquel descuido y ocio sentirán delicadamente aquella refección interior; la cual es tan delicada, que ordinariamente, si tiene gana o cuidado en sentirla, no la siente, porque, como digo, ella obra en el mayor ocio y descuido del alma; que es como el aire, que, en queriendo cerrar el puño, se sale.

7. Y a este propósito podemos entender lo que a la Esposa dijo el Esposo en los Cantares: *Aparta tus ojos de mí, porque ellos me hacen volar* (6,4); porque de tal manera pone Dios al alma en este estado y en tan diferente camino la lleva, que, si ella quiere obrar con sus potencias, antes estorba la obra que Dios en ella va haciendo que ayuda; lo cual antes era muy al revés. La causa es porque ya en este estado de contemplación, que es cuando sale del discurso y entra en el estado de aprovechados, ya Dios es el que obra en el ánima, porque por eso la ata las potencias interiores, no dejándole arrimo en el entendimiento, ni jugo en la voluntad, ni discurso en la memoria; porque en este tiempo, lo que de suyo puede obrar el alma no sirve sino (como habemos dicho) de estorbar la paz interior y la obra que en aquella sequedad del sentido hace Dios en el espíritu; la cual, como es espiritual y delicada, hace obra quieta, delicada, solitaria, satisfactoria y pacífica, muy ajena de todos esotros gustos primeros que eran muy palpables y sensibles; porque es la paz esta que dice David que *habla Dios en el alma para hacerla espiritual* (Ps 84,9). Y de aquí es la tercera.

8. La tercera señal que hay para que se conozca esta purgación del sentido es el no poder ya meditar ni discurrir en el sentido de la imaginación como solía, aunque más haga de su parte; porque, como aquí comienza Dios a comunicársele, no ya por el sentido, como antes hacía por medio del discurso que componía y dividía las noticias, sino por el espíritu puro, en que no cae discurso sucesivamente, comunicándosele con acto de sencilla contemplación—la cual no alcanzan los sentidos de la parte inferior exteriores ni interiores—, de aquí es que la imaginativa y fantasía no pueden hacer arrimo en alguna consideración ni hallar en ella pie ya de ahí adelante.

9. En esta tercera señal se ha de tener que este empacho de las potencias y de el gusto de ellas no proviene de algún mal humor, porque cuando de aquí nace, en acabándose aquel humor (porque nunca permanece en un ser), luego, con algún cuidado que ponga el alma,

the inclination and desire to remain alone and in quietude, without being able to think about any given thing or feel the desire to think about it; then, if those whom this befalls know how to quiet themselves, taking no care for any inward or outward work, without the solicitude of doing anything of that sort, they will immediately, in that idleness and freedom from care, delicately feel that inner restoration, which is so delicate that usually the man who has the desire or care to feel it will not feel it, since, as I say, it operates during the greatest idleness and nonchalance of the soul; for it is like air that escapes when you try to close your fist on it.

7. And on this subject we can understand what the Bridegroom said to the bride in the Song of Songs: "Turn your eyes away from me, because they make me fly" ([compare] Song of Solomon 6:5); because God puts the soul in this state in such a way, leading her onto so different a path that, if she wishes to operate with her own powers, she will rather hinder than aid the work which God is performing in her; which formerly was just the opposite. The reason is that, now that she is in this state of contemplation, having emerged from the discursive mode (of meditation) and entered the state of the proficients, it is God Who works within her, binding her inner powers for that purpose and leaving her without the support of the intellect, the savor of the will, or discourse in the memory; because at such times that which the soul can do on her own (as I have said) is of no effect except to disturb her inner peace and the work God is performing in the spirit during that aridity of the senses; this peace, being spiritual and delicate, performs quiet, delicate, solitary, satisfying, and pacific work, quite alien to all those other primary pleasures which were very palpable and sensory; because it is this peace which David says God speaks to the soul to make her spiritual ([compare] Psalm 85:8). And from here the third sign comes.

8. The third sign that exists for recognizing this purification of the senses is the inability any longer to meditate or discourse with the senses of the imagination, as formerly, despite all efforts; because, since God is here beginning to communicate Himself to the soul, no longer through the senses as He did previously, by means of the discourse which arranged and classified the ideas, but through pure spirit, in which consecutive discourse has no place—now that He is communicating Himself to her in an act of unmixed contemplation, unattainable by either the outer or inner senses of her lower part—as a result, the imagination and fancy cannot have the support of any consideration or find a foothold in it any longer.

9. In this third sign it is to be understood that this disturbance of the soul's powers, and of her pleasure in them, is not the result of any adverse bodily humor, because whenever it *is*, when that humor ceases (they are never permanently the same) the soul immediately, if she just takes a little

vuelve a poder lo que antes, y hallan sus arrimos las potencias; lo cual en la purgación del apetito no es así, porque, en comenzando a entrar en ella, siempre va delante el no poder discurrir con las potencias. Que, aunque es verdad que a los principios en algunos, a veces, no entra con tanta continuación, de manera que algunas veces dejen de llevar sus gustos y discursos sensibles—porque, por ventura, por su flaqueza no convendría destetarlos tan de un golpe—, con todo, van siempre entrando más en ella y acabando con la obra sensitiva, si es que han de ir adelante. Porque los que no van por camino de contemplación, muy diferente modo llevan, porque esta noche de sequedades no suele ser en ellos continua en el sentido, porque, aunque algunas veces las tienen, otras veces no, y, aunque algunas no pueden discurrir, otras pueden, porque, como sólo les mete Dios en esta noche a éstos para exercitarlos y humillarlos y reformarles el apetito, por que no vayan criando golosina viciosa en las cosas espirituales, y no para llevarlos a la vida del espíritu que es la contemplación—que no todos los que se exercitan de propósito en el camino del espíritu lleva Dios a contemplación, ni aun a la mitad; el porqué El se lo sabe—, de aquí es que a éstos nunca les acaba de hecho de desarrimar el sentido de los pechos de las consideraciones y discursos, sino algunos ratos a temporadas, como habemos dicho.

Libro segundo, CAPÍTULO 4

PÓNESE LA PRIMERA CANCIÓN Y SU DECLARACIÓN

> **En una noche obscura,**
> **con ansias, en amores inflamada**
> **¡oh dichosa ventura!,**
> **salí sin ser notada,**
> **estando ya mi casa sosegada.**

DECLARACIÓN

1. Entendiendo ahora esta canción a propósito de la purgación contemplativa o desnudez y pobreza de espíritu (que todo aquí casi es una misma cosa), podémosla declarar en esta manera, y que dice el alma así: En pobreza, desamparo y desarrimo de todas las aprehensiones de mi alma, esto es, en oscuridad de mi entendimiento y aprieto de mi voluntad, en aflicción y angustia acerca de la memoria, dejándome a escuras en pura fe, la cual es *noche oscura* para las dichas potencias naturales, sólo la voluntad tocada de dolor y aflicciones y *ansias de amor* de Dios, *salí* de mí misma, esto es, de mi bajo modo de entender, y de mi flaca suerte de amar, y de mi pobre y escasa manera de gustar de Dios, sin que la sensualidad ni el demonio me lo estorben.

trouble, regains her former ability, and her powers find their footholds; whereas in the purification of the appetite this is not so, because, when the soul begins to enter it, her inability to discourse by means of her powers becomes steadily greater. For, though it is true that, for some people just starting out, this inability is sometimes not so continual that they cease to feel sensory pleasures or engage in sensory discourses (perhaps because, in view of their weakness, it would be inadvisable to wean them so abruptly), nevertheless they constantly enter more deeply onto this path and do away with the work of the senses, if they are to make progress. Because those who do not follow the path of contemplation behave very differently: this night of aridity of the senses is usually not continual in them; though they feel this aridity at some times, at others they do not, and, though at times they are unable to discourse, at others they can, because (God placing them in this night solely to train them, humble them, and reform their appetite, so that they will not go on nurturing a sinful sweet tooth in spiritual matters, but not to raise them to that life of the spirit which is contemplation, for God does not raise to contemplation all who purposely train themselves in the path of spirit, not even half of them, He alone knows why) in these cases He never completely and actually frees them from the support of the senses, from the "breasts" of considerations and discourses; He does so only a few times for a short while, as I have said.

Book II, CHAPTER 4

THE FIRST STANZA AND ITS EXPLANATION

> **On a dark night,**
> **with longings, afire with love**
> **(oh, happy fortune!),**
> **I went out without being detected,**
> **my house being calm now.**

EXPLANATION

1. Now, understanding this stanza in the light of contemplative purification or nakedness and poverty of spirit (all meaning practically the same in this case), I can explain it as follows. The soul says: "In poverty and abandonment, and without the support of any of my perceptions—that is, in the darkness of my intellect and the difficulties of my will, in the affliction and anguish of my memory, left in the dark in pure faith, which is a 'dark night' for my above-mentioned natural powers, with my will affected solely by sorrow, afflictions, and 'longings' for the love of God, I 'went out' of myself—that is, out of my low way of understanding, my feeble kind of loving, and my poor, skimpy manner of enjoying God, and neither my senses nor the devil hindered me.

2. La cual fue grande *dicha* y buena *ventura* para mí, porque en acabándose de aniquilarse y sosegarse las potencias, pasiones, apetitos y afecciones de mi alma, con que bajamente sentía y gustaba de Dios, salí del trato y operación humana mía a operación y trato de Dios; es a saber: mi entendimiento salió de sí, volviéndose de humano y natural en divino, porque, uniéndose por medio de esta purgación con Dios, ya no entiende por su vigor y luz natural, sino por la divina Sabiduría con que se unió. Y mi voluntad salió de sí, haciéndose divina, porque, unida con el divino amor, ya no ama bajamente con su fuerza natural, sino *con fuerza y pureza del Espíritu Santo*, y así, la voluntad acerca de Dios no obra humanamente; y, ni más ni menos, la memoria se ha trocado en aprehensiones eternas de gloria. Y, finalmente, *todas las fuerzas* y afectos del alma, por medio de esta noche y purgación del viejo hombre, todas se renuevan en temples y deleites divinos. Síguese el verso: "En una noche oscura."

Libro segundo, CAPÍTULO 5

PÓNESE EL PRIMER VERSO Y COMIENZA A DECLARAR CÓMO ESTA
CONTEMPLACIÓN ESCURA NO SOLO ES NOCHE PARA EL ALMA,
SINO TAMBIÉN PENA Y TORMENTO

1. Esta *Noche oscura* es una influencia de Dios en el alma que la purga de sus ignorancias e imperfecciones habituales, naturales y espirituales, que llaman los contemplativos contemplación infusa, o MÍSTICA TEOLOGÍA, en que de secreto enseña Dios a el alma y la instruye en perfección de amor, sin ella hacer nada ni entender cómo. Esta contemplación infusa, por cuanto es sabiduría de Dios amorosa, hace dos principales efectos en el alma, porque la dispone *purgándola* e *iluminándola* para la unión de amor de Dios; de donde la misma sabiduría amorosa que purga los espíritus bienaventurados, ilustrándolos, es la que aquí purga al alma y la ilumina.

2. Pero es la duda: ¿por qué pues es lumbre divina—que, como decimos, ilumina y purga el alma de sus ignorancias—, la llama aquí el alma *noche oscura*? A lo cual se responde que por dos cosas es esta divina Sabiduría, no sólo Noche y tiniebla para el alma, mas también le es pena y tormento: la primera, es por la alteza de la Sabiduría divina, que excede al talento del alma, y en esta manera le es tiniebla; la segunda, por la bajeza e impureza della, y desta manera le es penosa y aflictiva, y también oscura.

3. Para probar la primera, conviene suponer cierta doctrina del

2. "This was a most 'happy fortune' for me because, when my powers, passions, appetites, and affections, with which I had felt and enjoyed God in a vulgar fashion, were finally annihilated and stilled, I emerged from my human dealings and functions into working and dealing with God. That is, my intellect went out of itself, changing from human and natural into divine, because, uniting with God by means of this purification, it no longer understands through its natural vigor and light, but through the divine Wisdom with which it has united. And my will went out of itself, becoming divine, because, united with divine love, it no longer loves vulgarly with its natural strength, but with the strength and purity of the Holy Spirit, so that my will does not function humanly with regard to God. And, in the same way, my memory has been converted into eternal perceptions of glory. Lastly, all my forces and affections, by means of this night and the purging away of the old Adam, are renewed into divine energy and delights." There follows the verse: "On a dark night."

Book II, CHAPTER 5

THE FIRST LINE OF THE POEM. BEGINNING OF THE EXPLANATION
THAT THIS DARK CONTEMPLATION IS NOT ONLY NIGHT FOR THE SOUL,
BUT ALSO PAIN AND TORMENT

1. This dark night is an influence of God on the soul which purifies her of her ignorance and imperfections, habitual, natural, and spiritual; contemplatives call this "infused contemplation" or "mystical theology," in which God secretly teaches the soul, instructing her in the perfection of love (she neither contributes to this, nor understands how it comes about). Because this infused contemplation is the loving wisdom of God, it has two main effects on the soul: it prepares her, by purging her and illuminating her, for her loving union with God; hence, the same loving wisdom that purifies and illuminates the spirits in bliss is the one that here purifies and illuminates the soul.

2. But there is a question. Why, if it is a divine light (which, as I said, illuminates the soul and purges her of her ignorance), does the soul here call it a "dark night"? The answer is that, for two reasons, this divine Wisdom is not only night and darkness for the soul, but also causes her pain and torment. The first is that the loftiness of divine Wisdom surpasses the soul's capacity, and in this way is darkness to her; the second is that she is low and impure, so that it is painful and afflicting for her, as well as dark.

3. To prove the first reason, it is fitting to affirm a certain teaching of

Filósofo, que dice que cuanto las cosas divinas son en sí más claras y manifiestas, tanto más son al alma de oscuras y ocultas naturalmente; así como de la luz, cuanto más clara es, tanto más se ciega y oscurece la pupila de la lechuza; y cuanto el sol se mira más de llano, más tinieblas causa a la potencia visiva y la priva, excediéndola por su flaqueza. De donde, cuando esta divina luz de contemplación embiste en el alma que aún no está ilustrada totalmente, le hace tinieblas espirituales, porque no sólo la excede, pero también la priva y escurece el acto de su inteligencia natural. Que por esta causa san Dionisio y otros místicos teólogos llaman a esta contemplación infusa *rayo de tiniebla*—conviene a saber, para el alma no ilustrada y purgada—, porque de su gran luz sobrenatural es vencida la fuerza natural intelectiva y privada. Por lo cual David también dijo que *cerca de Dios y en rededor de Él está oscuridad y nube* (Ps 96,2), no porque en sí ello sea ansí, sino para nuestros entendimientos flacos, que en tan inmensa luz se oscurecen y quedan frustrados, no alcanzando; que, por eso, el mismo David lo declaró luego, diciendo: *Por el gran resplandor de su presencia se atravesaron nubes* (Ps 17,13), es a saber, entre Dios y nuestro entendimiento. Esta es la causa por que, en derivando de sí Dios al alma que aún no está transformada este esclarecido rayo de su sabiduría secreta, le hace tinieblas oscuras en el entendimiento.

4. Y que esta oscura contemplación también le sea al alma penosa a estos principios está claro, porque, como esta divina contemplación infusa tiene muchas excelencias en extremo buenas, y el alma que las recibe, por no estar purgada, tiene muchas miserias también en extremo malas, de aquí es que, no pudiendo caber dos contrarios en el sujeto del alma, de necesidad haya de penar y padecer el alma, siendo ella el sujeto en que contra sí se exercitan estos dos contrarios haciendo los unos contra los otros, por razón de la purgación que de las imperfecciones del alma por esta contemplación se hace. Lo cual probaremos por inducción en esta manera:

5. Cuanto a lo primero, porque la luz y sabiduría de esta contemplación es muy clara y pura, y el alma en que ella embiste está oscura e impura; de aquí es que pena mucho el alma recibiéndola en sí, como cuando los ojos están de mal humor, impuros y enfermos, del embestimiento de la clara luz reciben pena. Y esta pena en el alma a causa de su impureza es inmensa cuando de veras es embestida de esta divina luz, porque embistiendo en el alma esta luz pura, a fin de expeler la impureza del alma, siéntese el alma tan impura y miserable, que le

the Philosopher,[10] who says that the clearer and more manifest divine matters are in themselves, the darker and more secret they naturally are to the soul. So it is with light: the brighter it is, the more the pupils of the owl are blinded and darkened; and the more fixedly the sun is stared at, the more darkness it causes in the faculty of sight, dimming it with its excess, since it is so weak. Hence, when this divine light of contemplation strikes a soul that has not yet been totally illumined, it causes spiritual darkness in her, because it not only surpasses her capacity, but also dims her and darkens the actions of her natural cognition. And for that reason Saint Dionysius[11] and other mystical theologians call this infused contemplation "a ray of darkness" (that is, for the unillumined, unpurified soul), because her natural cognitive power is overcome and dimmed by its great supernatural light. Therefore David also said: "Clouds and darkness are round about him" (Psalm 97:2), not because it is essentially so, but because our weak intellects, darkened and frustrated by such immense light, cannot deal with it; therefore the same David explained it at once, saying: "At the brightness that was before him his thick clouds passed" (Psalm 18:12); that is, passed between God and our intellect. This is the reason that, when God deflects this bright ray of His secret wisdom away from Himself onto a soul not yet transformed, He causes dark shadows in her intellect.

4. And it is clear that this dark contemplation is also painful for the soul at these early stages because this divine infused contemplation contains numerous extremely fine excellences, and the soul who receives them, not being purified, suffers numerous miseries, also extremely harsh; therefore, since two contraries cannot be contained in the soul as a single subject, she must of necessity feel pain and suffering, she being the subject in which these two contraries clash, one working against the other, because of the purgation of the soul's impurities caused by this contemplation. I shall prove this inductively as follows:

5. In the first place, because the light and wisdom of this contemplation are very bright and pure, and the soul whom it strikes is dark and impure, the soul suffers greatly on receiving it, just as eyes that are suffering from a bad humor, and are impure and ailing, are pained when struck by bright light. And this pain in the soul due to her impurity is immense when she is truly struck by this divine light, because when this pure light strikes the soul in order to expel her impurity, she feels so impure and miserable that she thinks God is against her and that she has come into

---

10. Aristotle.   11. Pseudo-Dionysius Areopagita.

parece estar Dios contra ella, y que ella está hecha contraria a Dios. Lo cual es de tanto sentimiento y pena para el alma, porque le parece aquí que la ha Dios arrojado, que uno de los mayores trabajos que sentía Job cuando Dios le tenía en este exercicio era éste, diciendo: *¿Por qué me has puesto contrario a ti y soy grave y pesado para mí mismo?* (7,20); porque viendo el alma claramente aquí por medio desta pura luz (aunque a escuras) su impureza, conoce claro que no es digna de Dios ni de criatura alguna; y lo que más le pena es que piensa que nunca lo será, y que ya se le acabaron sus bienes. Esto le causa la profunda inmersión que tiene de la mente en el conocimiento y el sentimiento de sus males y miserias, porque aquí se las muestra todas al ojo esta divina y oscura luz, y que vea claro cómo de suyo no podrá tener ya otra cosa. Podemos entender a este sentido aquella autoridad de David, que dice: *Por la iniquidad corregiste el hombre e hiciste deshacer y contabescer su alma, como la araña se desentraña* (Ps 38,12).

6. La segunda manera en que pena el alma es a causa de su flaqueza natural moral y espiritual, porque, como esta divina contemplación embiste en el alma con alguna fuerza al fin de la ir fortaleciendo y domando, de tal manera pena en su flaqueza, que poco menos desfallece, particularmente algunas veces cuando con alguna más fuerza embiste, porque el sentido y espíritu, ansí como si estuviese debajo de una inmensa y oscura carga, está penando y agonizando tanto, que tomaría por alivio y partido el morir. Lo cual habiendo experimentado el profeta Job, decía: *No quiero que trate conmigo con mucha fortaleza, por que no me oprima con el peso de su grandeza* (23,6).

7. En la fuerza de esta opresión y peso se siente el alma tan ajena de ser favorecida, que le parece, y así es, que aun en lo que solía hallar algún arrimo se acabó con lo demás, y que no hay quien se compadezca della. A cuyo propósito dice también Job: *Compadeceos de mí a lo menos vosotros, mis amigos, porque me ha tocado la mano del Señor* (19,21). Cosa de grande maravilla y lástima que sea aquí tanta la flaqueza e impureza de el alma, que, siendo la mano de Dios de suyo tan blanda y suave, la sienta el alma aquí tan grave y contraria con no cargar ni asentar, sino solamente tocando, y eso misericordiosamente, pues lo hace a fin de hacer mercedes al alma y no de castigarla.

Libro segundo, CAPÍTULO 8

DE OTRAS PENAS QUE AFLIGEN AL ALMA EN ESTE ESTADO

1. Pero hay aquí otra cosa que al alma aqueja y desconsuela mucho, y es que, como esta oscura noche la tiene impedidas las potencias y

opposition with God. This causes the soul all that regret and pain, because she now thinks that God has cast her off; thus one of the greatest griefs Job felt when God gave him those trials was this, when he said: "Why hast thou set me as a mark against thee, so that I am a burden to myself?" (Job 7:20). Because, now that the soul clearly sees her impurity by means of this pure light (though it is still dark to her), she recognizes clearly that she is not worthy of God or of any creature; and what pains her most is her belief that she never will be, and that her good days are now over. This produces in her that deep immersion of her mind in the awareness and feeling of her woes and miseries, because now this divine, dark light shows them all to her eyes, so she may see clearly that things can no longer improve for her by her own efforts. We can understand in this sense that passage of David's saying: "When thou with rebukes dost correct man for iniquity, thou makest his beauty to consume away like a moth" (Psalm 39:11).

6. The second way the soul suffers is through her natural weakness, moral and spiritual, because, since this divine contemplation strikes the soul with some force in order to go on strengthening and subduing her, she suffers so in her weakness that she all but swoons away, particularly at times when it strikes her with somewhat greater force, because her senses and spirit, as if beneath an immense, dark load, are suffering and agonizing so greatly that she would take death as a relief and a blessing. The prophet Job, having experienced this, said: "I do not want Him to deal with me with much strength, so that He does not crush me with the weight of His greatness" ([compare] Job 23:6).

7. Under the force of this oppressive weight the soul feels so far from being favored that she believes (and it is so) that even those things in which she once found some support have vanished with all the rest, and that there is no one to take pity on her. On this subject, Job also says: "Have pity upon me, O ye my friends; for the hand of God hath touched me" (Job 19:21). It is a matter of great wonder and pity that the soul is now so weak and impure that, God's hand being in itself so soft and gentle, the soul feels it to be so heavy and contrary, though it is not burdening her or pressing down hard, but merely touching her, and mercifully at that, since He is doing this to grant favors to the soul and not to chastise her.

Book II, CHAPTER 8

OTHER PAINS THAT AFFLICT THE SOUL IN THIS STATE

1. But here there is something else that causes the soul much lamenting and disconsolation: since this dark night hampers her powers and af-

afecciones, ni puede levantar afecto ni mente a Dios, ni le puede rogar, pareciéndole lo que a Jeremías, que ha puesto Dios *una nube delante por que no pase la oración* (Thren 3,44); porque esto quiere decir lo que en la autoridad alegada dice, es a saber: *Atrancó y cerró mis vías con piedras cuadradas* (ibid., 3,9). Y si algunas veces ruega, es tan sin fuerza y sin jugo, que le parece que ni lo oye Dios ni hace caso dello, como también este profeta lo da a entender en la misma autoridad, diciendo: *Cuando clamare y rogare, ha excluido mi oración* (ibid., 3,8). A la verdad, no es éste tiempo de hablar con Dios, sino de *poner,* como dice Jeremías, *su boca en el polvo, si por ventura le viniese alguna actual esperanza* (ibid., 3,29), sufriendo con paciencia su purgación. Dios es el que anda aquí haciendo pasivamente la obra en el alma; por eso ella no puede nada; de donde ni rezar ni asistir con advertencia a las cosas divinas puede, ni menos en las demás cosas y tratos temporales. Tiene no sólo esto, sino también muchas veces tales enajenamientos y tan profundos olvidos en la memoria, que se le pasan muchos ratos sin saber lo que se hizo ni qué pensó, ni qué es lo que hace ni qué va a hacer, ni puede advertir, aunque quiera, a nada de aquello en que está.

2. Que, por cuanto aquí no sólo se purga el entendimiento de su lumbre y la voluntad de sus afecciones, sino también la memoria de sus discursos y noticias, conviene también aniquilarla acerca de todas ellas; para que se cumpla lo que de sí dice David en esta purgación, es a saber: *Fui yo aniquilado y no supe* (Ps 72,22). El cual *no saber* se refiere aquí a estas insipiencias y olvidos de la memoria, las cuales enajenaciones y olvidos son causados del interior recogimiento en que esta contemplación absorbe al alma; porque, para que el alma quede dispuesta y templada a lo divino con sus potencias para la divina unión de amor, convenía que primero fuese absorta con todas ellas en esta divina y oscura luz espiritual de contemplación, y así fuese abstraída de todas las afecciones y aprehensiones de criatura, lo cual singularmente dura según es la intensión. Y ansí, cuanto esta divina luz embiste más sencilla y pura en el alma, tanto más la oscurece, vacía y aniquila de la pasión acerca de sus aprehensiones y afecciones particulares, así de cosas de arriba como de abajo; y también, cuanto menos sencilla y pura embiste al alma, tanto menos la priva y menos oscura le es. Que es cosa que parece increíble decir que la luz sobrenatural y divina tanto más oscurece al alma cuanto ella tiene más de claridad y pureza, y cuanto menos, le sea menos oscura. Lo cual, si consideramos lo que arriba queda probado, con la sentencia del Filósofo conviene: que las cosas sobrenaturales tanto son a nuestro entendimiento más oscuras, cuanto ellas en sí son más claras y manifiestas.

fections, she cannot raise her love or her mind to God, or pray to Him, believing, as Jeremiah did, that God has covered Himself "with a cloud, that our prayer should not pass through" (Lamentations 3:44); because this means what he says in another passage from the same book: "He hath inclosed my ways with hewn stone" (Lamentations 3:9). And if she sometimes prays, it is with so little strength and vigor that she believes God does not hear or heed her, just as this prophet gives us to understand in the same book, when he says: "Also when I cry and shout, he shutteth out my prayer" (Lamentations 3:8). Actually this is not the time for a man to speak with God, but, as Jeremiah says, to put "his mouth in the dust; if so be there may be hope" (Lamentations 3:29), suffering his purification patiently. It is God who now does His work in the passive soul; therefore she can do nothing; hence, she can neither pray nor attend closely to divine matters, let alone all other matters and worldly dealings. She is affected not only by this, but also frequently by such derangements and such deep lapses of memory that many a time she does not know what she has done or thought, nor what she is currently doing or is going to do, nor can she attend to any matter before her, as hard as she may try.

2. Since now not only is the intellect purged of its light, and the will of its affections, but also the memory of its discourses and ideas, it is also fitting to annihilate all these powers of the soul, so that what David says about himself in this purification may be accomplished: "I was annihilated and had no knowledge" ([compare] Psalm 73:21). This lack of knowledge refers here to these lapses and gaps in the memory; these derangements and forgetful moments are caused by the inner concentration into which this contemplation immerses the soul; because, to make the soul prepared and attuned to the divine, along with her powers, for the divine union of love, she first had to be immersed, with all of them, in this divine, dark spiritual light of contemplation, and thus freed from all of a creature's affections and perceptions; this lasts in each case in proportion to the intensity. And so, the more unmixed and pure the divine light that strikes the soul, the more it darkens, empties, and annihilates her, freeing her from passion as to her individual perceptions and affections, from heavenly as well as from earthly matters; similarly, the less unmixed and pure the light that strikes the soul, the less it deprives her and the less dark it is to her. It seems an incredible thing to say: that the supernatural, divine light darkens the soul the more thoroughly the brighter and purer it is, and that the less so it is the less dark it is to her. But, if we consider what was proved above, this agrees with the Philosopher's dictum that supernatural things are the more obscure to our intellect the more clear and manifest they are in themselves.

3. Y, para que más claramente se entienda, pondremos aquí una semejanza de la luz natural y común. Vemos que el rayo del sol que entra por la ventana, cuanto más limpio y puro es de átomos, tanto menos claramente se ve, y cuanto más de átomos y motas tiene el aire, tanto parece más claro al ojo. La causa es porque la luz no es la que por sí misma se ve, sino el medio con que se ven las demás cosas que embiste; y entonces ella, por la reverberación que hace en ellas, también se ve; y si no diese en ellas, ni ellas ni ella se verían, de tal manera que, si el rayo del sol entrase por la ventana de un aposento y pasase por otra de la otra parte por medio del aposento, como no topase en alguna cosa ni hubiese en el aire átomos en qué reverberar, no tendría el aposento más luz que antes ni el rayo se echaría de ver; antes, si bien se mirase, entonces hay más oscuridad por donde está el rayo, porque priva y oscurece algo de la otra luz y él no se ve, porque, como habemos dicho, no hay objetos visibles en que pueda reverberar.

4. Pues ni más ni menos hace este divino rayo de contemplación en el alma, que embistiendo en ella con su lumbre divina, excede la natural del alma, y en esto la oscurece y priva de todas las aprehensiones y afecciones naturales que antes, mediante la luz natural, aprehendía; y así, no sólo la deja oscura, sino también vacía según las potencias y apetitos, así espirituales como naturales, y, dejándola así, vacía y a escuras, la purga e ilumina con divina luz espiritual, sin pensar el alma que la tiene, sino que está en tinieblas, como habemos dicho del rayo, que, aunque está en medio del aposento, sí está puro y no tiene en qué topar, no se ve. Pero en esta oscura luz espiritual de que está embestida el alma, cuando tiene en qué reverberar, esto es, cuando se ofrece alguna cosa que entender espiritual y de perfección o de imperfección—por mínimo átomo que sea, o juicio de lo que es falso o verdadero—, luego la ve y entiende mucho más claramente que antes que estuviese en estas oscuridades y, ni más ni menos, conoce la luz que tiene espiritual para conocer con facilidad la imperfección que se le ofrece; así como cuando el rayo que habemos dicho está oscuro en el aposento, aunque él no se ve, si se ofrece pasar por él una mano o cualquier cosa, luego se ve la mano y se conoce que estaba allí aquella luz del sol.

5. Donde, por ser esta luz espiritual tan sencilla, pura y general, no afectada ni particularizada a ningún particular inteligible natural ni divino—pues acerca de todas estas aprehensiones tiene las potencias del alma vacías y aniquiladas—, de aquí es que con grande generalidad y facilidad conoce y penetra el alma cualquier cosa de arriba o de

3. To make this more readily understood, I shall here make a comparison with natural, everyday light. We observe that the brighter and freer from dust a sunbeam is when it comes through a window, the less clearly it is seen; whereas the more specks and motes there are in the air, the more clearly the beam appears to the eye. The reason is that it is not the light in itself that is seen, but the medium by which we see the other things it strikes; then the light, by the reflection it produces in those things, is also seen; but if it did not touch them, neither it nor they would be seen; so that, if the sunbeam entered through one window of a room, and exited through another on the opposite side after crossing the room, but did not encounter anything, and the air contained no particles to reflect it, the room would be no brighter than before, nor would the sunbeam be seen; on the contrary, if you were to look closely, you would find greater darkness where the beam is, because it darkens and removes some of the other light, while itself remaining unseen, because, as I said, there are no visible objects to reflect it.

4. Well, in the same way does this divine ray of contemplation act on the soul; striking her with its divine light, it surpasses the soul's capacity, thereby darkening her and robbing her of all the natural perceptions and affections she formerly perceived by means of the natural light. And so it leaves her not only dark, but also empty of her powers and appetites, spiritual as well as natural; and, leaving her thus empty and in the dark, it purifies and illumines her with divine spiritual light, while the soul does not think that she has it, but thinks she is in shadow, just as I said apropos of the sunbeam that, though it is in the middle of the room, if it is pure and finds nothing to encounter, it is not seen. But when this dark spiritual light by which the soul is struck finds something to reflect it—that is, when something spiritual, whether perfect or imperfect, is offered to the intellect, be it the tiniest speck, or a judgment whether something is true or false—the soul immediately sees it and understands things much more clearly than before she was in that darkness; in the same way, she recognizes the spiritual light she possesses to discern readily the imperfection offered to her view; just as when the aforesaid sunbeam is dark in the room, though it is unseen, if a hand or anything else happens to pass through it, the hand is immediately seen and one realizes that that sunbeam was present.

5. Hence, because this spiritual light is so unmixed, pure, and general, not concerned or associated with any individual intelligible thing, either natural or divine—since it has rendered the powers of the soul empty and annihilated vis-à-vis all these perceptions—therefore the soul, with great generality and readiness, recognizes and penetrates any heavenly or

abajo que se ofrece; que por eso dijo el Apóstol que el espiritual *todas las cosas penetra, hasta los profundos de Dios* (1 Cor 2,10); porque desta sabiduría general y sencilla se entiende lo que por el Sabio dice el Espíritu Santo, es a saber: *Que toca hasta doquiera por su pureza* (Sap 7,24); es a saber, porque no se particulariza a ningún particular inteligible ni afección. Y ésta es la propiedad de el espíritu purgado y aniquilado acerca de todas particulares afecciones e inteligencias que, en este no gustar nada ni entender nada en particular, morando en su vacío y tiniebla, lo abraza todo con grande disposición, para que se verifique en él lo de san Pablo: *Nihil habentes, et omnia possidentes* (2 Cor 6,10); porque tal bienaventuranza se debe a tal pobreza de espíritu.

Libro segundo, CAPÍTULO 15

PÓNESE LA SEGUNDA CANCIÓN Y SU DECLARACIÓN

A escuras y segura
por la secreta escala, disfrazada,
¡oh dichosa ventura!,
a escuras y en celada,
estando ya mi casa sosegada.

DECLARACIÓN

1. Va el alma cantando en esta canción todavía algunas propiedades de la oscuridad de esta noche, repitiendo la buena dicha que le vino con ellas. Dícelas, respondiendo a cierta objeción tácita, diciendo que no se piense que por haber en esta noche y oscuridad pasado por tanta tormenta de angustias, dudas, recelos y horrores, como se ha dicho, corría por eso más peligro de perderse, porque antes en la oscuridad desta noche se ganó; porque en ella se libraba y escapaba sutilmente de sus contrarios, que le impedían siempre el paso, porque en la oscuridad de la noche iba mudado el traje, y disfrazada con tres libreas y colores que después diremos; y por una *escala* muy *secreta,* que ninguno de casa la sabía, que (como también en su lugar notaremos) es la viva fe, por la cual salió tan encubierta y *en celada* para poder bien hacer su hecho, que no podía dejar de ir muy *segura,* mayormente estando ya en esta noche purgativa los apetitos, afecciones y pasiones, etc., de su ánima adormidos, mortificados y apagados, que son los que estando despiertos y vivos no se lo consintieron. Sigue, pues, el verso, y dice así: "A escuras y segura."

earthly matter that comes before her. This is why the Apostle said that the spiritual man "searches all things, yea, the deep things of God" (I Corinthians 2:10); because it is this general, unmixed wisdom which is meant when the Holy Spirit says, through the lips of the sage, that it touches wherever it wishes because of its purity (Wisdom of Solomon 7:24); that is, because it is not associated with any individual intelligible thing or affection. And this is the characteristic of the spirit purged and annihilated vis-à-vis all individual affections and knowledge: while not enjoying or understanding anything in particular, dwelling in its emptiness and darkness, it embraces all things most readily, so that it may confirm Saint Paul's statement: "Having nothing, and yet possessing all things" (II Corinthians 6:10); because such bliss is owed to such poverty of spirit.

Book II, CHAPTER 15

THE SECOND STANZA AND ITS EXPLANATION

In the dark, but feeling safe,
by the secret ladder, in disguise
(oh, happy fortune!),
in the dark and in concealment,
my house being calm now.

EXPLANATION

1. In this stanza the soul is still singing of some characteristics of the darkness of this night, mentioning again the good fortune that came to her with them. She states them in response to a certain unspoken objection, saying that no one should think that, just because, in this night and darkness, she had passed through such a storm of anguish, doubts, fears, and horrors (as I have said), she was therefore running a greater risk of becoming lost; since, on the contrary, in the darkness of this night she found herself; because in it she was freeing herself and escaping subtly from her opponents, who were always blocking her way, since in the darkness of the night she was wearing different clothes and was disguised by three liveries and colors which I shall speak of later; and she used a very "secret ladder," no one at home knowing this; this ladder (as I shall also state at the proper time) is living faith, by which she sallied forth so disguised and "in concealment," in order to perform her deed properly, that she could not help feeling very "safe" as she went, especially since, already being in this purificatory night, her appetites, affections, passions, etc., were lulled to sleep, mortified, and extinguished—those appetites which, when awake and lively, did not allow her to go. Then the first line follows, saying: "In the dark, but feeling safe."

Libro segundo, CAPÍTULO 25

EN QUE BREVEMENTE SE DECLARA LA TERCERA CANCIÓN

En la noche dichosa,
en secreto, que naide me veía,
ni yo miraba cosa,
sin otra luz y guía
sino la que en el corazón ardía.

DECLARACIÓN

1. Continuando todavía el alma la metáfora y semejanza de la noche temporal en esta suya espiritual, va todavía contando y engrandeciendo las buenas propiedades que hay en ella, y que por medio della halló y llevó, para que breve y seguramente consiguiese su deseado fin; de las cuales aquí pone tres:

2. La primera dice que en esta dichosa noche de contemplación lleva Dios el alma por tan solitario y secreto modo de contemplación, y tan remoto y ajeno del sentido, que cosa ninguna perteneciente a él ni toque de criatura alcanza a llegarle al alma, de manera que la estorbase y detuviese en el camino de la unión de amor.

3. La segunda propiedad que dice es por causa de las tinieblas espirituales desta noche, es que todas las potencias de la parte superior del alma están a escuras; no mirando el alma ni pudiendo mirar en nada, no se detiene en nada fuera de Dios para ir a El, por cuanto va libre de los obstáculos de formas y figuras y de las aprehensiones naturales, que son las que suelen empachar el alma para no se unir en el siempre ser de Dios.

4. La tercera es que, aunque ni va arrimada a alguna particular luz interior del entendimiento ni a alguna guía exterior para recebir satisfacción de ella en este alto camino, teniéndola privada de todo esto estas escuras tinieblas, pero el amor solo que en este tiempo arde, solicitando el corazón por el Amado, es el que guía y mueve al alma entonces y la hace volar a su Dios por el camino de la soledad, sin ella saber cómo ni de qué manera.

Síguese el verso "En la noche dichosa."

Book II, CHAPTER 25

BRIEF EXPLANATION OF THE THIRD STANZA

**In the happy night,
secretly, with no one seeing me
and I looking at nothing,
with no other guiding light
than the one burning in my heart.**

EXPLANATION

1. The soul, still continuing the metaphor and simile of the worldly dark night in this spiritual one she is in, is still narrating and magnifying its good qualities, which by means of that night she found and brought away, so that she could quickly and safely attain the end she desired; here she states three of these qualities:

2. The first: in this fortunate night of contemplation God leads the soul through such a solitary and secret mode of contemplation, so remote from and alien to the senses, that nothing pertaining to them, nor any contact with a created thing, succeeds in reaching the soul so as to disturb her or detain her on her path to loving union.

3. The second quality she mentions is the spiritual shadows of this night, in which all the powers of the higher part of the soul are in the dark; since the soul does not behold anything (nor can she), she is detained by nothing that is not God, on her way to Him, because she is free of the obstacles of forms and figures and of natural perceptions, those which generally impede her and keep her from merging with the eternal being of God.

4. The third: although she is unsupported by either any particular inner light of the intellect or any outward guide from which she might receive satisfaction on this lofty path (since these dark shadows keep her bereft of all of that), it is solely the love burning at this time, and attracting her heart to her Beloved, which now guides and incites her, making her fly to her God along the path of solitude, though she does not know how or in what way this occurs.

There follows the first line: "In the happy night."[12]

---

12. The *Noche oscura* breaks off here.

Cántico espiritual

Prólogo

1. Por cuanto estas canciones, religiosa Madre, parecen ser escritas con algún fervor de amor de Dios, cuya sabiduría y amor es tan inmenso, que, como se dice en el libro de la Sabiduría, *toca desde un fin hasta otro fin* (8,1), y el alma que de él es informada y movida en alguna manera esa misma abundancia e ímpetu lleva en el su decir, no pienso yo ahora declarar toda la anchura y copia que el espíritu fecundo de el amor en ellas lleva; antes sería ignorancia pensar que los dichos de amor en inteligencia mística, cuales son los de las presentes Canciones, con alguna manera de palabras se puedan bien explicar; porque el Espíritu del Señor que *ayuda nuestra flaqueza,* como dice san Pablo (Rom 8,26), morando en nosotros, *pide por nosotros con gemidos inefables,* lo que nosotros no podemos bien entender ni comprehender para lo manifestar. Porque ¿quién podrá escrebir lo que a las almas amorosas donde El mora hace entender?, ¿y quién podrá manifestar con palabras lo que las hace sentir?, ¿y quién, finalmente, lo que las hace desear? Cierto, nadie lo puede; cierto, ni ellas mesmas por quien pasa lo pueden; porque ésta es la causa por que con figuras, comparaciones y semejanzas, antes rebosan algo de lo que sienten y de la abundancia de el espíritu vierten secretos y misterios que con razones lo declaran. Las cuales semejanzas, no leídas con la sencillez del espíritu de amor e inteligencia que ellas llevan, antes parecen dislates que dichos puestos en razón, según es de ver en los divinos Cantares de Salomón y en otros libros de la Escritura divina, donde, no pudiendo el Espíritu Santo dar a entender la abundancia de su sentido por términos vulgares y usados, habla misterios en extrañas figuras y semejanzas. De donde se sigue que los santos doctores, aunque mucho dicen y más digan, nunca pueden acabar de declararlo por palabras, así como tampoco por palabras se pudo ello decir; y así, lo que dello se declara ordinariamente es lo menos que contiene en sí.

Spiritual Canticle

Prologue

1. Because, Reverend Mother, this poem seems to be written with some fervor of love for God, Whose wisdom and love are so immense that, as is said in the book of Wisdom, they reach from one end of the world to the other ([compare] Wisdom of Solomon 8:1), and because the soul that is guided and moved by this love brings that same abundance and drive to her utterances to some extent, I do not now intend to explain all of the amplitude and fullness that a spirit fertile in love expresses in the poem; rather, it would be ignorance to imagine that the sayings of love during mystical communication, such as the sayings in the present poem, can be properly explained by words of any kind; because the Spirit of the Lord, which "helpeth our infirmities," as Saint Paul says (Romans 8:26), dwelling in us, "maketh intercession for us with groanings which cannot be uttered"; this we cannot understand or grasp, to make it manifest. Because who can set down what He communicates to the loving souls in which He dwells? And who can make manifest in words what He makes them feel? And, lastly, who can say what He makes them desire? Surely, no one can; surely, not even the souls who experience it can; this is the reason that, with the use of figures, comparisons, and similes, something of what they feel flows over, and from their abundance of spirit they pour forth secrets and mysteries which explain it in rational terms. These similes, if not read with the simplicity of the spirit of love and intelligence inherent in them, resemble absurdities rather than rational discourse, as can be seen in the divine Song of Solomon and other books of Holy Scriptures, in which the Holy Spirit, unable to make known the abundance of His meaning in commonplace, hackneyed terms, speaks mysteries in strange figures and similes. Hence it follows that saintly theologians, though they say much, and however much they say, can never fully explain this in words, just as it was not capable of being expressed in words in the first place; and so the usual explanation of such matters covers only the least part of their content.

2. Por haberse, pues, estas Canciones compuesto en amor de abundante inteligencia mística, no se podrán declarar al justo, ni mi intento será tal, sino sólo dar alguna luz general, pues V. R. así lo ha querido. Y esto tengo por mejor, porque los dichos de amor es mejor declararlos en su anchura, para que cada uno de ellos se aproveche según su modo y caudal de espíritu, que abreviarlos a un sentido a que no se acomode todo paladar; y así, aunque en alguna manera se declaran, no hay para qué atarse a la declaración, porque la sabiduría mística, la cual es por amor (de que las presentes Canciones tratan), no ha menester distintamente entenderse para hacer efecto de amor y afición en el alma, porque es a modo de la fe, en la cual amamos a Dios sin entenderle.

3. Por tanto, seré bien breve; aunque no podrá ser menos de alargarme en algunas partes donde lo pidiere la materia y donde se ofreciere ocasión de tratar y declarar algunos puntos y efectos de oración, que, por tocarse en las Canciones muchos, no podrá ser menos de tratar algunos; pero, dejando los más comunes, trataré brevemente los más extraordinarios que pasan por los que han pasado, con el favor de Dios, de principiantes; y esto por dos cosas: la una, porque para los principiantes hay muchas cosas escritas; la otra, porque en ello hablo con V. R. por su mandado, a la cual nuestro Señor ha hecho merced de haberle sacado de esos principios y llevádole más adentro al seno de su amor divino; y así espero que, aunque se escriban aquí algunos de teología escolástica cerca de el trato interior del alma con su Dios, no será en vano haber hablado algo a lo puro de el espíritu en tal manera, pues, aunque a V. R. le falte el ejercicio de teología escolástica con que se entienden las verdades divinas, no le falta el de la mística, que se sabe por amor en que, no solamente se saben, mas juntamente se gustan.

4. Y porque lo que dijere—lo cual quiero sujetar al mejor juicio y totalmente a el de la santa Madre Iglesia—haga más fe, no pienso afirmar cosa de mío fiándome de experiencia que por mí haya pasado, ni de lo que en otras personas espirituales haya conocido o de ellas oído (aunque de lo uno y de lo otro me pienso aprovechar), sin que con autoridades de la Escritura divina vaya confirmado y declarado, a lo menos en lo que pareciere más dificultoso de entender. En las cuales llevaré este estilo: que primero las pondré las sentencias de su latín y luego las declararé al propósito de lo que se trajeren; y pondré primero juntas todas las canciones, y luego por su orden iré poniendo cada una de por sí para haberla de declarar; de las cuales declararé cada verso, poniéndole al principio de su declaración, etcétera.

2. Thus, this poem, having been composed in the love of abundant mystical communication, cannot be explained fully, nor is that my intention; I merely wish to shed some general light, since Your Reverence has so requested. And I consider this best, because it is better to explain the utterances of love broadly, so that each of them will be found useful in accordance with its mode and wealth of spirit, rather than boil them down to one interpretation that may not please every palate; and so, even if they are explained in some manner, there is no need to be bound by that explanation, because mystical wisdom, wisdom through love (which the present poem treats of), does not need to be understood distinctly to produce an effect of love and inclination in the soul, since it resembles faith, through which we love God without understanding Him.

3. Therefore, I shall be very brief, though I cannot avoid dwelling on some parts where the subject matter demands it and where an opportunity is offered to treat and explain some points and effects of prayer. Since there are many such references in the poem, I shall be unable to avoid discussing some, but, omitting the most commonplace ones, I shall briefly discuss only the most unusual instances experienced by those who, with God's aid, have progressed beyond the state of beginners. And this for two reasons: first, because many things have already been written for beginners; second, because thereby I shall address Your Reverence in accordance with your command; to you Our Lord has granted the favor of being promoted from these early stages and led more deeply into the bosom of His divine love; and thus I hope that, even though this treatise will contain some trace of scholastic theology concerning the soul's inner dealings with her God, it will not be in vain to have addressed some words to the purity of the spirit in this way, since, though Your Reverence lacks the training in scholastic theology whereby the divine truths are fully understood, you do not lack training in mysticism, which is learned through love, and by which those truths are not only learned, but also savored at the same time.

4. And, so that what I shall say (which I wish to submit to the best judgments, and totally to that of our holy mother the Church) may be better believed, I do not intend to affirm anything of my own or rely on any experience I may have had or observed or heard about in other spiritual people (though I intend to make some use of all this) without confirming and explaining it by the authority of Scripture, at least for those matters which seem hardest to understand. In these passages I shall follow this system: I shall first set them down in Latin and then explain the matter contained in them; also, I shall first set down the entire poem, then each stanza in sequence with its explanation, then each line, repeating it just before it is explained, etc.[13]

---

13. Here follows poem 2, pages 4–14.

Argumento

1. El orden que llevan estas canciones es desde que un alma comienza a servir a Dios hasta que llega a el último estado de perfección, que es matrimonio espiritual; y así, en ellas se tocan los tres estados o vías de exercicio espiritual por las cuales pasa el alma hasta llegar al dicho estado, que son: purgativa, iluminativa y unitiva, y se declaran acerca de cada una algunas propiedades y efectos della.

2. El principio dellas trata de los principiantes, que es la vía purgativa. Las de más adelante tratan de los aprovechados, donde se hace el desposorio espiritual; y ésta es la vía iluminativa. Después déstas, las que se siguen tratan de la vía unitiva, que es la de los perfectos, donde se hace el matrimonio espiritual; la cual vía unitiva y de perfectos se sigue a la iluminativa, que es de los aprovechados. Y las últimas canciones tratan del estado beatífico, que sólo ya el alma en aquel estado perfecto pretende.

Anotación

1. Cayendo el alma en la cuenta de lo que está obligada a hacer; viendo que *la vida es breve* (Iob 14,5), *la senda de la vida eterna estrecha* (Mt 7,14), que *el justo apenas se salva* (1 Petr 4,18), que las cosas del mundo son vanas y engañosas (Eccl 1,2), que *todo se acaba y falta como el agua que corre* (2 Reg 14,14), el tiempo incierto, la cuenta estrecha, la perdición muy fácil, la salvación muy dificultosa; conociendo, por otra parte, la gran deuda que a Dios debe en haberle criado solamente para sí, por lo cual le debe el servicio de toda su vida, y en haberla redimido solamente por sí mismo, por lo cual le debe todo el resto y respondencia del amor de su voluntad, y otros mil beneficios en que se ve y se conoce obligada a Dios desde antes que naciese, y que gran parte de su vida se ha ido en el aire, y que de todo esto ha de haber cuenta y razón, así de lo primero como de lo postrero, *hasta el último cuadrante* (Mt 5,26), *cuando escudriñará Dios a Jerusalén con candelas encendidas* (Soph 1,12), y que *ya es tarde y por ventura lo postrero del día* (Mt 20,6) para remediar tanto mal y daño, mayormente sintiendo a Dios muy enojado y escondido por haberse ella querido olvidar tanto de El entre las criaturas; tocada ella de pavor y dolor de corazón interior sobre tanta perdición y peligro, renunciando todas las cosas, dando de mano a todo negocio, sin dilatar un día ni una hora, con ansia y gemido salido del corazón herido ya del amor de Dios, comienza a invocar a su Amado y dice:

ARGUMENT

1. The sequence of this poem is from a soul beginning to serve God until she attains the final state of perfection, which is spiritual matrimony; thus it touches upon the three states or avenues of spiritual training through which the soul passes before reaching that final state: the purgative, illuminative, and unitive ways; some of the characteristics and effects of each of them are explained.

2. The beginning of the poem concerns beginners; this is the purgative way. The stanzas later on concern proficients; here the spiritual betrothal takes place; this is the illuminative way. After that, the stanzas that follow concern the unitive way, that of the perfected, whereby the spiritual marriage takes place; this unitive way of the perfected follows after the illuminative way of the proficients. And the final stanzas concern the state of bliss, which can be sought only by the soul in that state.

COMMENTARY

1. When the soul realizes what she is obliged to do, seeing that life is short ([compare] Job 14:5), that the path to eternal life is narrow ([compare] Matthew 7:14), that even the righteous are scarcely saved ([compare] I Peter 4:18), that worldly things are vain and deceitful ([compare] Ecclesiastes 1:2), that everything ends and passes like flowing water ([compare] II Kings 14:14 [??]), that the times are unsure, the account strictly observed, perdition all too easy, salvation very difficult; on the other hand, recognizing the great debt she owes God for having created her for Himself only, for which she owes Him the service of her whole life, and for having redeemed her by Himself only, for which she owes Him all the remaining requital that her will can lovingly give, and a thousand other benefits to her for which she recognizes her obligation to God even before she was born; and seeing that a great part of her life has been frittered away, and that she must give an account of all these things, the first and the last, to the last farthing ([compare] Matthew 5:26), when God will scrutinize Jerusalem with burning candles ([compare] Wisdom of Solomon 1:12), and seeing that it is already late and perhaps the end of the day ([compare] Matthew 20:6): in order to remedy so much evil and harm (especially sensing that God is very angry and hidden because she has wished to forget Him so thoroughly out of love for mere created things), while smitten with fear and inward pain of heart over such great perdition and danger, she renounces all worldly things and abandons all her business, without delaying for a day or even an hour; with longing and with a moan issuing from her heart, which is already wounded by love for God, she begins to invoke her Beloved, saying:

Canción 1

¿Adónde te escondiste,
Amado, y me dejaste con gemido?
Como el ciervo huiste,
habiéndome herido;
salí tras ti clamando, y eras ido.

Declaración

2. En esta primera canción el alma, enamorada del Verbo Hijo de Dios, su Esposo, deseando unirse con él por clara y esencial visión, propone sus ansias de amor querellándose a él de la ausencia, mayormente que, habiéndola él herido de su amor, por el cual ha salido de todas las cosas criadas y de sí misma, todavía haya de padecer la ausencia de su Amado, no desatándola ya de la carne mortal para poderle gozar en gloria de eternidad; y así, dice: "¿Adónde te escondiste?"

3. Y es como si dijera: Verbo, Esposo mío, muéstrame el lugar donde estás escondido; en lo cual le pide la manifestación de su divina esencia, porque el lugar donde está escondido el Hijo de Dios es, como dice san Juan, *el seno del Padre* (1,18), que es la esencia divina, la cual es ajena de todo ojo mortal y escondida de todo humano entendimiento; que por eso Isaías, hablando con Dios, dijo: *Verdaderamente tú eres Dios escondido* (45,15). De donde es de notar que, por grandes comunicaciones y presencias y altas subidas noticias de Dios que un alma en esta vida tenga, no es aquello esencialmente Dios ni tiene que ver con El, porque todavía, a la verdad, le está al alma escondido, y por eso siempre le conviene al alma sobre todas esas grandezas tenerle por escondido y buscarle escondido, diciendo: *¿Adónde te escondiste?*; porque ni la alta comunicación ni presencia sensible es cierto testimonio de su graciosa presencia, ni la sequedad y carencia de todo eso en el alma lo es de su ausencia en ella; por lo cual el profeta Job dice: *Si viniere a mí, no le veré, y si se fuere, no le entenderé* (9,11).

4. En lo cual se ha de entender que, si el alma sintiere gran comunicación o sentimiento o noticia espiritual, no por eso se ha de persuadir a que aquello que siente es poseer o ver clara y esencialmente a Dios, o que aquello sea tener más a Dios o estar más en Dios, aunque más ello sea; y que, si todas esas comunicaciones sensibles y espirituales faltaren quedando ella en sequedad, tiniebla y desamparo, no por eso ha de pensar que la falta Dios más así que así, pues que realmente ni por lo uno puede saber de cierto estar en su gracia, ni por lo otro estar fuera della, diciendo el Sabio: *Ninguno sabe si es*

Stanza 1

Where have You hidden Yourself,
Beloved, leaving me moaning?
Like a stag You fled
after wounding me;
I sallied forth after You, calling out, but You were gone.

EXPLANATION

2. In this first stanza the soul, in love with the Word, Son of God, her Bridegroom, and desirous of uniting with Him in a clear, essential vision, declares her amorous longings, complaining to Him of His absence, especially because He has wounded her with love for Him, so that she has gone out from all created things and from herself, but must still suffer the absence of her Beloved, Who has not yet released her from her mortal flesh to let her enjoy Him in the glory of eternity; so that she says: "Where have You hidden Yourself?"

3. Which is as if to say: "Word, my Bridegroom, show me the place where You are hidden!" Thereby she asks Him to make His divine essence manifest, because the place where the Son of God is hidden is, as Saint John says, "the bosom of the Father" (John 1:18), which is the divine essence, removed from every mortal eye and concealed from all human understanding, for which reason Isaiah, addressing God, said: "Verily thou art a God that hidest thyself" (Isaiah 45:15). Hence it is to be noted that, however great the communications, acts of presence, and lofty messages that a soul may receive from God in this life, none of them is God in His essence or has anything to do with Him per se, because in truth He is still hidden from the soul, and therefore it behooves her to consider Him hidden despite all these great things and to seek Him as one hidden, saying: "Where have You hidden Yourself?" Because neither the lofty communication nor the felt presence is a sure testimony to His gracious presence, nor are the aridity and lack of all this in the soul a sign of His absence from her; for that reason the prophet Job says: "Lo, he goeth by me, and I see him not: he passeth on also, but I perceive him not" (Job 9:11).

4. By this it is to be understood that, if the soul should sense a great communication or feeling or spiritual message, she should not therefore persuade herself that what she feels signifies the possession, or clear and essential sight, of God, or that it means having more of God or being more in God, however true that may be; or that, if all those sensory and spiritual communications cease and she remains arid, dark, and abandoned, she should therefore imagine that she lacks God in one way more than another, because, in reality, in the first situation she cannot be sure

digno de amor o de aborrecimiento delante de Dios (Eccl 9,11). De manera que el intento principal del alma en este verso no es sólo pedir la devoción afectiva y sensible, en que no hay certeza ni claridad de la posesión del Esposo en esta vida, sino principalmente la clara presencia y visión de su esencia en que desea estar certificada y satisfecha en la otra.

5. Esto mismo quiso decir la esposa en los Cantares divinos cuando, deseando unirse con la divinidad del Verbo Esposo suyo, la pidió al Padre, diciendo: *Muéstrame dónde te apacientas y dónde te recuestas al mediodía* (1,6); porque en pedir le mostrase *dónde se apacentaba* era pedir le mostrase la esencia del Verbo divino, su Hijo, porque el Padre no se apacienta en otra cosa que en su único Hijo, pues es la gloria del Padre y en pedir le mostrase el lugar donde *se recostaba* era pedirle lo mismo, porque el Hijo sólo es el deleite del Padre, el cual no se recuesta en otro lugar ni cabe en otra cosa que en su amado Hijo, en el cual todo él se recuesta comunicándole toda su esencia *al mediodía,* que es la eternidad donde siempre le engendra y le tiene engendrado. Este pasto, pues, de el Verbo Esposo, donde el Padre se apacienta en infinita gloria, y este pecho florido, donde con infinito deleite de amor se recuesta escondido profundamente de todo ojo mortal y de toda criatura, pide aquí el alma esposa cuando dice: *¿Adónde te escondiste?*

6. Y para que esta sedienta alma venga a hallar a su Esposo y unirse con él por unión de amor en esta vida según puede, y entretenga su sed con esta gota que de él se puede gustar en esta vida, bueno será (pues lo pide a su Esposo, tomando la mano por él) le respondamos mostrándole el lugar más cierto donde está escondido, para que allí lo halle a lo cierto con la perfección y sabor que puede en esta vida, y así no comience a vaguear en vano tras las pisadas de las compañías. Para lo cual es de notar que el Verbo Hijo de Dios, juntamente con el Padre y el Espíritu Santo, esencial y presencialmente está escondido en el íntimo ser del alma; por tanto, el alma que le ha de hallar conviene salir de todas las cosas según la afección y voluntad y entrarse en sumo recogimiento dentro de sí misma, siéndole todas las cosas como si no fuesen; que por eso san Agustín, hablando en los *Soliloquios* con Dios, decía: *No te hallaba, Señor, de fuera, porque mal te buscaba fuera, que estabas dentro.* Está, pues, Dios en el alma escondido, y ahí le ha de buscar con amor el buen contemplativo, diciendo: *¿Adónde te escondiste?*

she is in His grace, or out of it in the second, the sage having said: "No one knows whether he is worthy of love or of loathing in the face of God" ([compare] Ecclesiastes 9:1). So that the soul's chief intention in this line is not only to ask for loving, sensory devotion, which brings no certitude or clarity as to the possession of the Bridegroom in this life, but above all for the clear presence and sight of His essence, in which she desires to be confirmed and contented in the next life.

5. This was also the meaning of the bride in the Song of Solomon when, desiring union with the divinity of the Word, her Bridegroom, she asked this of the Father: "Show me where You graze and where you recline at noon" ([compare] Song of Solomon 1:7); to ask to be shown where He grazed was to ask to be shown the essence of the divine Word, His Son, because the Father feeds on nothing else than His only Son, since He is the glory of the Father; and to ask to be shown the place where He reclined was to make the same request, because the Son alone is the delight of His Father, Who reclines nowhere else, nor is contained in anything else, than in His beloved Son, on Whom he reclines completely, communicating all His essence to Him, at noon, which is the eternity in which He always begets Him and has begotten Him. And so, this pasture of the Word and Bridegroom, where His Father feeds in infinite glory, and that flowery bosom on which He reclines with infinite loving delight, deeply hidden from every mortal eye and every creature, are what the soul-bride is requesting here when she asks: "Where have You hidden Yourself?"

6. And in order that this thirsting soul may come to find her Bridegroom and join with him in a loving union in this life to the extent possible, and stave off her thirst with this drop of Him that can be tasted in this life, it will be a good thing (since she asks this of her Bridegroom, and begins her activities with Him) if we were to answer her, showing her the most sure place where He is hidden, so that she can find Him there with surety to the degree of perfection and savor possible in this life, and thus will not begin to roam about vainly, following her companions' footsteps. For this purpose it is to be noted that the Word, Son of God, together with the Father and the Holy Spirit, is in essence and presence hidden in the soul's inmost being; therefore the soul who is to find Him must abandon all things in her affections and her will, and enter into deep seclusion within herself, all things being as if nonexistent to her; this is why Saint Augustine, addressing God in his *Soliloquies,* said: "I did not find You outside, Lord, because I was wrong to seek You outside: You were within." And so, God is hidden in the soul, and it is there that He must be lovingly sought by a good contemplative, asking: "Where have You hidden Yourself?"

7. ¡Oh, pues, alma hermosísima entre todas las criaturas, que tanto deseas saber el lugar donde está tu Amado para buscarle y unirte con él!, ya se te dice que tú misma eres el aposento donde él mora y el retrete y escondrijo donde está escondido; que es cosa de grande contentamiento y alegría para ti ver que todo tu bien y esperanza está tan cerca de ti que esté en ti, o, por mejor decir, tú no puedas estar sin él. *Catá*—dice el Esposo—*que el reino de Dios está dentro de vosotros* (Lc 17,21); y su siervo el apóstol san Pablo: *Vosotros*—dice—*sois templo de Dios* (2 Cor 6,16).

8. Grande contento es para el alma entender que nunca Dios falta del alma, aunque esté en pecado mortal, cuanto menos de la que está en gracia. ¿Qué más quieres, ¡oh alma!, y qué más buscas fuera de ti, pues dentro de ti tienes tus riquezas, tus deleites, tu satisfacción, tu hartura y tu reino, que es tu Amado, a quien desea y busca tu alma? Gózate y alégrate en tu interior recogimiento con él, pues le tienes tan cerca. Ahí le desea, ahí le adora y no le vayas a buscar fuera de ti, porque te distraerás y cansarás y no le hallarás ni gozarás más cierto, ni más presto, ni más cerca que dentro de ti. Sólo hay una cosa, es a saber, que, aunque está dentro de ti, está escondido. Pero gran cosa es saber el lugar donde está escondido para buscarle allí a lo cierto. Y esto es lo que tú también aquí, alma, pides cuando con afecto de amor dices: *¿Adónde te escondiste?*

8. Pero todavía dices: Pues está en mí el que ama mi alma, ¿cómo no le hallo ni le siento? La causa es porque está escondido, y tú no te escondes también para hallarle y sentirle; porque el que ha de hallar una cosa escondida tan a lo escondido y hasta lo escondido donde ella está ha de entrar, y cuando la halla él también está escondido como ella. Como quiera, pues, que tu Esposo amado es *el tesoro escondido en el campo* de tu alma, *por el cual el sabio mercader dio todas sus cosas* (Mt 13,44), convendrá que para que tú le halles, olvidadas todas las tuyas y alejándote de todas las criaturas, *te escondas en tu retrete interior del espíritu y, cerrando la puerta sobre ti,* es a saber, tu voluntad a todas las cosas, *ores a tu Padre en escondido* (Mt 6,6); y así, quedando escondida con Él, entonces le sentirás en escondido y le amarás y gozarás en escondido y te deleitarás en escondido con Él, es a saber, sobre todo lo que alcanza la lengua y sentido.

10. ¡Ea, pues, alma hermosa!, pues ya sabes que en tu seno tu deseado Amado mora escondido, procura estar con Él bien escondida, y en tu seno le abrazarás y sentirás con afección de amor, y mira que a ese escondrijo te llama El por Isaías diciendo: *Anda, entra en tus re-*

7. Oh, then, soul, loveliest of all creatures, you that so desire to know the location of your Beloved in order to seek Him and unite with Him: now you have been told that you yourself are the chamber he lives in and the inner room and hiding place where He is concealed; for it is a matter of great contentment and cheer for you to see that all your good and your hope are so close to you that they are in you, or, to express it better, that you cannot be anywhere without Him. "Behold," says the Bridegroom, "the kingdom of God is within you" (Luke 17:21); and His servant the apostle Saint Paul says: "Ye are the temple of the living God" (II Corinthians 6:16).

8. It gives great contentment to the soul to learn that God is never absent from her, even when she is in mortal sin, let alone when she is in a state of grace. What more do you want, O soul? And what else do you seek outside yourself, since within you you have your riches, your delights, your contentment, your plentitude, and your kingdom, which is your Beloved, Whom you desire and seek? Rejoice and be of good cheer in your inward seclusion with Him, since He is so near to you. Desire Him there, worship Him there, and do not go seeking Him outside yourself, because you will go astray and become weary, nor will you find Him or enjoy Him more surely, more swiftly, or at closer range than within yourself. There is only one drawback: though He is within you, He is hidden. But it is a great achievement to know the place where He is hidden, so you can seek Him there with certainty. And this is also what you request here, soul, when you lovingly ask: "Where have You hidden Yourself?"

9. But you still ask: "If the One I love is within me, why do I not find Him or feel Him?" The reason is that He is hidden but you do not hide yourself as well, so that you can find and feel Him; because a man who must find a hidden thing must be in hiding to enter the spot where it is concealed, all the way to its hiding place, and when he finds it he, too, is hidden like it. So, since your beloved Bridegroom is "the treasure hidden in the field" of your soul, "for which the wise merchant gave all that he had" ([compare] Matthew 13:44), it is necessary, if you are to find Him, to forget everything you have, distance yourself from all created things, and "hide in the inner chamber of your spirit, lock the door behind you" (that is, shut your will to all things), and "pray to your Father in hiding" ([compare] Matthew 6:6). Thus, being hidden with Him, you will then feel Him in your hiding place and you will love and enjoy Him in hiding and will take delight in hiding with Him; that is, beyond all that the tongue and the senses can reach.

10. So, then, lovely soul, since you now know that your longed-for Beloved dwells hidden in your bosom, try to be well hidden with Him, and in your bosom you will embrace Him and feel Him with loving affection; observe that He summons you to that hiding place by Isaiah's words: "Come, my peo-

tretes, cierra tus puertas sobre ti, esto es, todas tus potencias a todas
las criaturas, *escóndete un poco hasta un momento* (26,20), esto es, por
este momento de vida temporal; porque, *si en esta brevedad de vida
guardares,* ¡oh alma!, *con toda guarda tu corazón,* como dice el Sabio
(Prov 4,23), sin duda ninguna te dará Dios lo que adelante dice Dios
también por Isaías diciendo: *Daréte los tesoros escondidos, y des-
cubrirte he la sustancia y misterios de los secretos* (45,3). La cual sustancia de los secretos es el mismo Dios, porque Dios es la sustancia de
la fe y el concepto della, y la fe es el secreto y el misterio, y cuando se
revelare y manifestare esto que nos tiene secreto y encubierto la fe,
que es *lo perfecto de Dios,* como dice san Pablo (1 Cor 13,10), entonces se descubrirán al alma la sustancia y misterios de los secretos.
Pero en esta vida mortal, aunque no llegará el alma tan a lo puro dellos como en la otra por más que se esconda, todavía, si se escondiere
como Moisés *en la caverna de la piedra,* que es en la verdadera imi-
tación de la perfección de la vida del Hijo de Dios, Esposo del alma,
amparándola Dios con su diestra, merecerá que le *muestren las es-
paldas de Dios* (Ex 33,22–23), que es llegar en esta vida a tanta perfección, que se una y transforme por amor en el dicho Hijo de Dios,
su Esposo, de manera que se sienta tan junta con El y tan instruida y
sabia en sus misterios, que cuanto a lo que toca a conocerle en esta
vida no tenga necesidad de decir: *¿Adónde te escondiste?*

11. Dicho queda, ¡oh alma!, el modo que te conviene tener para
hallar a el Esposo en tu escondrijo. Pero, si lo quieres volver a oír, oye
una palabra llena de sustancia y verdad inaccesible: es buscarle en fe
y en amor, sin querer satisfacerte de cosa, ni gustarla ni entenderla
más de lo que debes saber, que esos dos son los mozos del ciego que
te guiarán por donde no sabes, allá a lo escondido de Dios; porque la
fe, que es el secreto que habemos dicho, son los pies con que el alma
va a Dios, y el amor es la guía que la encamina y, andando ella
tratando y manoseando estos misterios y secretos de fe, merecerá que
el amor la descubra lo que en sí encierra la fe, que es el Esposo que
ella desea en esta vida por gracia especial—divina unión con Dios—,
como habemos dicho, y en la otra por gloria esencial, gozándole cara
a cara ya de ninguna manera escondido. Pero, entre tanto, aunque el
alma llegue a esta dicha unión, que es el más alto estado a que se
puede llegar en esta vida, por cuanto todavía a el alma le está escondido en el seno del Padre, como habemos dicho, que es como y donde
ella le desea gozar en la otra, siempre dice: *¿Adónde te escondiste?*

ple, enter thou into thy chambers, and shut thy doors about thee" (that is, shut all your powers to all creatures); "hide thyself as it were for a little moment" (Isaiah 26:20); that is, for this moment of earthly life; because "if in the brevity of this life," O soul, "you keep your heart diligently," as the sage declares ([compare] Proverbs 4:23), without any doubt God will give you what He further states in Isaiah's words: "I will give thee the treasures of darkness, and [the substance and] hidden riches of secret places" (Isaiah 45:3). This substance of secrets is God Himself, because God is the substance of faith and its very notion, while faith is the secret and mystery; when that which faith, which is "God's perfection" ([compare] I Corinthians 13:10), keeps secret and hidden from us is revealed and made manifest, then the substance and mysteries of the secrets will be uncovered for the soul. But in this mortal life, even if the soul will not arrive at their purity as much as she will in the next life, no matter how well she hides herself, yet, if she were to hide like Moses in the cleft of the rock (that is, in the true imitation of the perfection of the life of the Son of God, Bridegroom of the soul) and God protected her with His right hand, she would deserve to be shown God's back ([compare] Exodus 33:22–23), which means arriving in this life at such perfection that she will unite with the aforesaid Son of God and transform herself in Him, her Bridegroom, through love, so that she feels so close to Him and so instructed and wise in His mysteries that, as regards knowing Him in this life, she will not need to ask: "Where have You hidden Yourself?"

11. Now, O soul, I have stated the path you are to follow to find your Bridegroom in your hiding place. But if you wish to hear it again, hear a word that is full of substance and inaccessible truth: seek Him in faith and love, without wishing to content yourself with anything, or to enjoy it, or understand it beyond your proper knowledge, for these two, faith and love, are the blind-man's boys who will guide you through places where you have no knowledge, beyond, to the hidden places of God. Faith, which is the secret I have described, lends the feet with which the soul ascends to God, and love is the guide who sets her on the path; as she goes along, handling and touching these mysteries and secrets of faith, she will deserve to have love reveal to her what faith encloses in itself, which is the Bridegroom Whom she desires in this life through special grace (divine union with God), as I said, and in the other life through essential glory, enjoying Him face to face when He is no longer hidden in any way. But meanwhile, though the soul attains that union, which is the loftiest condition attainable in this life, inasmuch as He is still hidden from the soul in the bosom of His Father, as I have said, which is the way and the place where she longs to enjoy Him in the next life, she continues to ask: "Where have You hidden Yourself?"

12. Muy bien haces, ¡oh alma!, en buscarle siempre escondido, porque mucho ensalzas a Dios y mucho te llegas a El teniéndole por más alto y profundo que todo cuanto puedes alcanzar; y, por tanto, no repares en parte ni en todo lo que tus potencias pueden comprehender; quiero decir que nunca te quieras satisfacer en lo que entendieres de Dios, sino en lo que no entendieres dél, y nunca pares en amarle y deleitarte en eso que entendieres o sintieres de Dios, sino ama y deléitate en lo que no puedes entender y sentir de El, que eso es, como habemos dicho, buscarle en fe; que, pues es Dios inaccesible y escondido, como también habemos dicho, aunque más te parezca que le hallas y le sientes y le entiendes, siempre le has de tener por escondido y le has de servir escondido en escondido. Y no seas como muchos insipientes que piensan bajamente de Dios, entendiendo que cuando no le entienden o le gustan o sienten, está Dios más lejos y más escondido, siendo más verdad lo contrario, que cuanto menos distintamente le entienden, más se llegan a él, pues, como dice el profeta David, *puso su escondrijo en las tinieblas* (Ps 17,12); así, llegando cerca de El, por fuerza has de sentir tinieblas en la flaqueza de tu ojo. Bien haces, pues, en todo tiempo, ahora de adversidad, ahora de prosperidad espiritual o temporal, tener a Dios por escondido, y así clamar a El diciendo: ¿*Adónde te escondiste*, "Amado, y me dejaste con gemido?"

13. Llámale *Amado* para más moverle e inclinarle a su ruego, porque, cuando Dios es amado, con grande facilidad acude a las peticiones de su amante; y así lo dice El por san Juan diciendo: *Si permaneciéredes en mí, todo lo que quisiéredes pediréis, y hacerse ha* (15,7). De donde entonces le puede el alma de verdad llamar *Amado*, cuando ella está entera con El, no teniendo su corazón asido a alguna cosa fuera de El, y así, de ordinario trae su pensamiento en El; que por falta de esto dijo Dalila a Sansón que *cómo podía él decir que la amaba, pues su ánimo no estaba con ella* (Iud 16,15); en el cual ánimo se incluye el pensamiento y la afección. De donde algunos llaman a el Esposo *Amado* y no es amado de veras, porque no tienen entero con El su corazón, y así su petición no es en la presencia de Dios de tanto valor, por lo cual no alcanzan luego su petición, hasta que, continuando la oración, vengan a tener su ánimo más continuo con Dios y el corazón con El más entero con afección de amor, porque de Dios no se alcanza nada si no es por amor.

14. En lo que dice luego: *y me dejaste con gemido*, es de notar que la ausencia de el Amado causa contino gemir en el amante, porque, como fuera dél nada ama, en nada descansa ni recibe alivio. De donde en esto se conocerá el que de veras a Dios ama, si con ninguna cosa

12. It is a very good thing you do, O soul, to seek Him while He is still hidden, because you greatly exalt God and you come very close to Him when you consider Him loftier and deeper than anything you can reach; therefore, pay no heed, partially or entirely, to what your powers can grasp; I mean, never try to be contented with what you may understand about God, but with what you do not understand about Him, and never merely love Him and take delight in what you understand or feel about God, but love and take delight in what you cannot understand and feel about Him, which amounts, as I have said, to seeking Him in faith; for, since God is inaccessible and hidden, as I have also said, even if you really believe that you find, feel, and understand Him, you must always consider Him to be hidden and serve him as one hidden thing in another. And do not be like many fools who have a low opinion of God, imagining that, when they fail to understand, enjoy, or feel Him, He is more distant and more deeply hidden. The opposite is truer: the less clearly they understand Him the closer they come to Him, since, as the prophet David says, "he made darkness his secret place" (Psalm 18:11); thus, coming near Him, you must of necessity feel darkness in the weakness of your eye. So you do well at all times, whether of adversity or of spiritual or worldly prosperity, to consider God hidden, and so call to Him, asking: "Where have You hidden Yourself, Beloved, leaving me moaning?"

13. She calls Him Beloved in order to stir and bend Him more to her prayer, because when God is loved, He very readily lends an ear to His lover's requests; He says so through Saint John's lips: "If you abide in me . . . ye shall ask what ye will, and it shall be done unto you" (John 15:7). Hence, the soul can then truly call Him Beloved when she is with Him entirely, and her heart is not attached to anything outside of Him, and she thus customarily has Him in her thoughts. It was for lack of this that Delilah asked Samson how he could say he loved her if his heart was not with her ([compare] Judges 16:15); this "heart" includes thoughts and affections. Hence, some call the Bridegroom their Beloved, but He is not truly loved, because their whole hearts are not in Him, and so their request is not as meritorious in God's eyes, and they are not immediately granted their request, but only when, continuing their prayer, they come to have their mind more steadily with God and their heart more entirely immersed in love for Him, since nothing is obtained from God except through love.

14. In her following words, "leaving me moaning," it is to be noted that the absence of the Beloved causes the lover to moan constantly, because, loving nothing outside of Him, she cannot find repose or relief in anything. Hence, you may recognize that a man truly loves God when he is con-

menos que El se contenta; mas ¿qué digo se contenta?, pues, aunque
todas juntas las posea, no estará contento, antes cuantas más tuviere,
estará menos satisfecho, porque la satisfacción del corazón no se halla
en la posesión de las cosas, sino en la desnudez de todas ellas y pobreza de espíritu; que, por consistir en ésta la perfección de amor en
que se posee Dios con muy junta y particular gracia, vive el alma en
esta vida cuando ha llegado a ella con alguna satisfacción, aunque no
con hartura, pues que David con toda su perfección la esperaba en el
cielo, diciendo: *Cuando pareciere tu gloria, me hartaré* (Ps 16,15); y
así, no le basta la paz y tranquilidad y satisfacción de corazón a que
puede llegar el alma en esta vida para que deje de tener dentro de sí
gemido (aunque pacífico y no penoso) en la esperanza de lo que la
falta, porque el gemido es anejo a la esperanza, como el que decía el
Apóstol que tenía él y los demás (aunque perfectos), diciendo:
*Nosotros mismos, que tenemos las primicias del espíritu, dentro de
nosotros mismos gemimos, esperando la adopción de hijos de Dios*
(Rom 8,23). Este gemido, pues, tiene aquí el alma dentro de sí en el
corazón enamorado, porque donde hiere el amor, allí está el gemido
de la herida clamando siempre en el sentimiento de la ausencia, mayormente cuando, habiendo ella gustado alguna dulce y sabrosa
comunicación del Esposo, ausentándose, se quedó sola y seca de
repente; que por eso dice luego: "Como el ciervo huiste."

15. Donde es de notar que en los Cantares compara la esposa al
Esposo al ciervo y a la cabra montesa, diciendo: *Semejante es mi
Amado a la cabra y al hijo de los ciervos* (2,9); y esto, no sólo por ser
extraño y solitario y huir de las compañas como el ciervo, sino también
por la presteza del esconderse y mostrarse, cual suele hacer en las visitas que hace a las devotas almas para regalarlas y animarlas, y en los
desvíos y ausencias que las hace sentir después de las tales visitas para
probarlas y humillarlas y enseñarlas; por lo cual las hace sentir con
mayor dolor la ausencia, según ahora da aquí a entender en lo que se
sigue, diciendo: "habiéndome herido."

16. Que es como si dijera: No sólo me bastaba la pena y el dolor que
ordinariamente padezco en tu ausencia, sino que, hiriéndome más de
amor con tu flecha y aumentando la pasión y apetito de tu vista, huyes
con ligereza de ciervo y no te dejas comprehender algún tanto.

17. Para más declaración deste verso es de saber que, allende de
otras muchas diferencias de visitas que Dios hace al alma con que la
llaga y levanta en amor, suele hacer unos encendidos toques de amor

tented with nothing less than Him. But what do I mean, "contented"?! Even if he possesses all things together, he will not be contented; rather, the more he has the less satisfied he will be, because the heart's satisfaction does not lie in the possession of things, but in the privation of all of them and in poverty of spirit; for, since it is in the latter that that perfection of love exists in which God is possessed with very deep-lying and particular grace, after the soul has attained this she lives in this life with some contentment, though not with entire satisfaction, seeing that, with all his perfection, David was still awaiting it in heaven, saying: "When your glory appears, I shall be fully satisfied" ([compare] Psalm 17:15); thus, the peace, tranquillity, and contentment of heart that the soul can attain in this life are not sufficient to keep her from having moans within her (even if they are peaceful and not painful ones) in her expectation of what she lacks, because her moaning is linked to her hope, like the moaning which the apostle said that he and everyone else had (though they were perfected): "Ourselves also, which have the firstfruits of the Spirit, even we ourselves groan within ourselves, waiting for the adoption [as children of God]" (Romans 8:23). So then, the soul here has this moaning within her in her enamored heart, because where love wounds, there the moaning caused by the wound calls out constantly in the soul's sensation of absence, especially when, after she has enjoyed some sweet, delicious communication with her Bridegroom, He absents Himself and she is left suddenly alone and arid. This is why she then says: "Like a stag You fled."

15. Hence it is to be noted that in the Song of Solomon the bride compares her Bridegroom to a deer and a wild goat, saying: "My Beloved is like the goat and the son of the deer" ([compare] Song of Solomon 2:9), not merely because He is aloof and solitary and shuns company like a deer, but also because of His swiftness to hide and reveal Himself, as He generally does on His visits to devout souls to caress and encourage them, and because of the periods of coldness and absence which He makes them feel after such visits, in order to test, humble, and instruct them; therefore He makes them feel His absence with greater sorrow, as the soul now gives us to understand in what follows, saying: "after wounding me."

16. Which is as if she had said: "The pain and sorrow I normally suffer in Your absence were not enough for me; no, wounding me more deeply with love with Your arrow, and increasing my passion and appetite for the sight of You, you flee with the speed of a deer and do not allow Yourself to be grasped even a little."

17. To explain this line further, one must know that, besides many other differences in God's visits to the soul, with which He wounds her and uplifts her in love, He often gives her burning touches of love which, like a

que, a manera de saeta de fuego, hieren y traspasan el alma y la dejan toda cauterizada con fuego de amor; y éstas propiamente se llaman heridas de amor, de las cuales habla aquí el alma. Inflaman éstas tanto la voluntad en afición, que se está el alma abrasando en fuego y llama de amor; tanto, que parece consumirse en aquella llama, y la hace salir fuera de sí y renovar toda y pasar a nueva manera de ser, así como el ave fénix, que se quema y renace de nuevo. De lo cual hablando David, dice: *Fue inflamado mi corazón, y las renes se mudaron, y yo me resolví en nada, y no supe* (Ps 72,21–22).

18. Los apetitos y afectos (que aquí entiende el profeta por renes) todos se conmueven y mudan en divinos en aquella inflamación del corazón, y el alma por amor se resuelve en nada, nada sabiendo sino amor. Y a este tiempo es la conmutación destas renes en grande manera de tormento y ansia por ver a Dios; tanto, que le parece al alma intolerable rigor de que con ella usa el amor, no porque la hubo herido (porque antes tiene ella las tales heridas por salud), sino porque la dejó así penando en amor y no la hirió más valerosamente, acabándola de matar para verse y juntarse con El en vida de amor perfecto.

19. Por tanto, encareciendo o declarando ella su dolor, dice: *habiéndome herido,* es a saber, dejándome así herida, muriendo con heridas de amor de ti, te escondiste con tanta ligereza como ciervo. Este sentimiento acaece así tan grande, porque en aquella herida de amor que hace Dios a el alma levántase el afecto de la voluntad con súbita presteza a la posesión del Amado, cuyo toque sintió, y con esa misma presteza siente la ausencia y el no poderle poseer aquí como desea, y así, luego allí juntamente siente el gemido de la tal ausencia, porque estas visitas tales no son como otras en que Dios recrea y satisface al alma, porque éstas sólo las hace más para herir que para sanar y más para lastimar que para satisfacer, pues sirven para avivar la noticia y aumentar el apetito y, por consiguiente, el dolor y ansia de ver a Dios. Estas se llaman heridas espirituales de amor, las cuales son al alma sabrosísimas y deseables, por lo cual querría ella estar siempre muriendo mil muertes a estas lanzadas, porque la hacen salir de sí y entrar en Dios; lo cual da ella a entender en el verso siguiente, diciendo: "salí tras ti clamando, y eras ido."

20. En las heridas de amor no puede haber medicina sino de parte del que hirió, y por eso esta herida alma salió, en la fuerza del fuego que causó la herida, tras de su Amado que la había herido, clamando a El para que la sanase. Es de saber que este salir espiritualmente se

fiery arrow, wound and pierce her, leaving her totally cauterized with the fire of love; and these are properly called love wounds, which the soul speaks of here. These set the will so afire with inclination that the soul is ablaze in the fire and flame of love; so much so, that she seems to be consumed in that flame, and He makes her come out of herself, totally renewed, and change to a new mode of being, just like the phoenix, which burns up and is reborn. Speaking of this, David says: "My heart was on fire, and my kidneys changed, and I dissolved into nothingness, and I had no knowledge" ([compare] Psalm 73:21–22).

18. All the appetites and affections (which are what the prophet here calls the kidneys) are shaken up and changed into divine ones in that conflagration of the heart, and through love the soul is dissolved into nothingness, knowing nothing but love. And at that time the conversion of these kidneys takes place in a severe kind of torture and a longing to see God; so much so, that the soul believes she is being treated by love with intolerable rigor, not because it has wounded her (because, on the contrary, she considers such wounds to be good health), but because it has left her that way, suffering from love, instead of striking her more boldly and achieving her death, so she could find herself united with Him in the life of perfect love.

19. Therefore, emphasizing or explaining her sorrow, she says: "after wounding me"; that is, leaving me wounded this way, dying of wounds of love for You, You hid with the swiftness of a deer. This feeling is so strong in this instance because in that loving wound which God inflicts on the soul, the affection of her will is uplifted with sudden speed to the possession of the Beloved, Whose touch she has felt, and with that same speed she feels His absence and her inability to possess Him here as she desires; and so, immediately, and at the same time, she feels the moaning for that absence, because this type of visit is unlike others, in which God refreshes and satisfies the soul; these visits He only makes more to wound her than to heal her, more to grieve her than to content her, since they serve to enliven her mind and increase her appetite and, consequently, her sorrow and longing to see God. These are called spiritual wounds of love, and are most delightful and desirable to the soul, so that she would like to be always dying a thousand deaths from these spear thrusts, because they make her go out of herself and enter into God; she declares this in the next line when she says: "I sallied forth after You, calling out, but You were gone."

20. For the wounds of love, healing can come only from the Wounder, and therefore this wounded soul sallied forth, with the strength of the fire caused by the wound, after her Beloved, Who had wounded her, calling out to Him to heal her. One must know that this spiritual sallying forth

entiende aquí de dos maneras para ir tras Dios: la una, saliendo de todas las cosas, lo cual se hace por aborrecimiento y desprecio de ellas; la otra, saliendo de sí misma por olvido de sí, lo cual se hace por el amor de Dios, porque, cuando éste toca al alma con las veras que se va diciendo aquí, de tal manera la levanta, que no sólo la hace salir de sí misma por olvido de sí, pero aun de sus quicios y modos e inclinaciones naturales la saca clamando por Dios; y así, es como si dijera: Esposo mío, en aquel toque tuyo y herida de amor sacaste mi alma no sólo de todas las cosas, mas también la sacaste e hiciste salir de sí (porque, a la verdad, y aun de las carnes parece la saca), y levantástela a ti, clamando por ti, ya desasida de todo para asirse a ti, *y eras ido.*

21. Como si dijera: Al tiempo que quise comprehender tu presencia no te hallé, y quedéme desasida de lo uno y sin asir lo otro, penando en los aires de amor sin arrimo de ti y de mí. Esto que aquí llama el alma *salir* para ir a buscar el Amado llama la esposa en los Cantares *levantar* diciendo: *Levantarme he y buscaré al que ama mi alma, rodeando la ciudad por los arrabales y las plazas. Busquéle—*dice*—y no le hallé, y llagáronme* (3,2 y 5,7). Levantarse el alma esposa se entiende allí, hablando espiritualmente, de lo bajo a lo alto, que es lo mismo que aquí dice el alma *salir,* esto es, de su modo y amor bajo al alto amor de Dios; pero dice allí la esposa que quedó llagada porque no le halló, y aquí el alma también dice que está herida de amor y la dejó así. Por eso el enamorado vive siempre penado en la ausencia, porque él está ya entregado al que ama esperando la paga de la entrega que ha hecho, y es la entrega del Amado a él y todavía no se le da y, estando ya perdido a todas las cosas y a sí mismo por el Amado, no ha hallado la ganancia de su pérdida, pues carece de la posesión del que ama su alma.

22. Esta pena y sentimiento de la ausencia de Dios suele ser tan grande a los que van llegando a el estado de perfección al tiempo de estas divinas heridas, que, si no proveyese el Señor, morirían, porque, como tienen el paladar de la voluntad sano y el espíritu limpio y bien dispuesto para Dios y en lo que está dicho se les da a gustar algo de la dulzura del amor divino que ellos sobre todo modo apetecen, padecen sobre todo modo; porque, como por resquicios se les muestra un inmenso bien y no se les concede, así es inefable la pena y el tormento.

after God is to be understood here in two ways: one is the emergence from all worldly things, which is undertaken out of loathing and contempt for them; the other is the emergence from self through self-forgetfulness, which is undertaken out of love for God; because, when that touches the soul as genuinely as described here, it uplifts her so, that it not only makes her come out of herself through self-forgetfulness, but also lifts her out of her natural framework, ways, and inclinations, calling out for God; and so, it is as if she were saying: "My Bridegroom, with that touch and loving wound of Yours You not merely released me from all worldly things but also released me and brought me out of myself (because, in truth, she even feels released from the flesh) and raised me up to You, calling out for You, no longer clinging to anything else so that I may cling to you—but You were gone."

21. As if she were saying: "When I wanted to grasp Your presence I did not find You, and I was left with one thing fallen from my grasp while I had not yet grasped the other, suffering in the winds of love without the support of You or myself." What the soul here calls sallying forth to go and seek her Beloved is what the bride in the Song of Solomon calls "rising": "I will rise now, and go about the city in the streets, and in the broad ways I will seek him whom my soul loveth: I sought him, but I found him not" (3:2) and "they smote me" (5:7). The rising of the soul-bride, spiritually speaking, here means movement from low to high, which is the same as what the soul here calls sallying forth; that is, from her low ways and love to the sublime love for God; there, the bride says she was wounded because she did not find Him, and here the soul also says that she is smitten with love and has been deserted in that condition. Therefore the man in love always lives in suffering for that absence, because he is already committed to the One he loves, awaiting the reward for the commitment he has made, which is the Beloved's commitment to him, but the Beloved does not yet give Himself to him, and now lost to all things and to himself for the Beloved's sake, he has not found any gain to make up his loss, since he lacks the possession of the One his soul loves.

22. This pain and this feeling of God's absence are generally so strong in those who are reaching the state of perfection at the time of these divine wounds that, if the Lord did not look after them, they would die, because, since the palate of their will is healthy, and their spirit clean and well prepared for God, and in the above-mentioned way He gives them some taste of the sweetness of divine love that they long for exceedingly, they suffer exceedingly. The reason is that, since they are allowed to see an immense good merely through cracks, while it is not granted to them, their pain and torment are unspeakable.

ANOTACIÓN PARA LA SIGUIENTE CANCIÓN

1. Pero, por cuanto el alma en este estado de matrimonio espiritual que aquí tratamos no deja de saber algo de *aquello,* pues, por estar transformada en Dios pasa por ella algo de ello, no quiere dejar de decir algo de *aquello* cuyas prendas y rastros siente ya en sí, porque, como se dice en el profeta Job, *¿quién podrá contener la palabra que en sí tiene concebida, sin decirla?* (4,2). Y así, en la siguiente canción se emplea en decir algo de aquella fruición que entonces gozará en la beatífica vista, declarando ella, en cuanto le es posible, qué sea y cómo sea *aquello* que allí será.

Canción 39

> El aspirar del aire,
> el canto de la dulce filomena,
> el soto y su donaire
> en la noche serena,
> con llama que consume y no da pena.

DECLARACIÓN

2. En esta canción dice el alma y declara *aquello* que dice le ha de dar el Esposo en aquella beatífica transformación, declarándolo con cinco términos: el primero dice que es la aspiración del Espíritu Santo de Dios a ella y de ella a Dios; el segundo, la jubilación a Dios en la fruición de Dios; el tercero, el conocimiento de las criaturas y de la ordenación de ellas; el cuarto, pura y clara contemplación de la esencia divina; el quinto, transformación total en el inmenso amor de Dios. Dice, pues, el verso: "El aspirar del aire."

3. Este *aspirar del aire* es una habilidad que el alma dice que le dará Dios allí en la comunicación de el Espíritu Santo, el cual, a manera de aspirar, con aquella su aspiración divina muy subidamente levanta el alma y la informa y habilita para que ella aspire en Dios la misma aspiración de amor que el Padre aspira en el Hijo y el Hijo en el Padre, que es el mismo Espíritu Santo que a ella la aspira en el Padre y el Hijo en la dicha transformación, para unirla consigo; porque no sería verdadera y total transformación si no se transformase el alma en las tres Personas de la Santísima Trinidad en revelado y manifiesto grado. Y esta tal aspiración de el Espíritu Santo en el alma con que Dios la transforma en sí le es a ella de tan subido y delicado y profundo

COMMENTARY ON THE FOLLOWING STANZA [39]

1. But, because, in this state of spiritual marriage we are discussing here, the soul does not fail to know something about "that,"[14] since in her transformation in God she experiences something of it, she does want to omit some mention here of "that" of which she already feels some tokens and traces in herself; because, as it is said in the book of the prophet Job: "Who can withhold himself from speaking?" (Job 4:2). And so, in the stanza that follows she occupies herself with saying something about that fruition which she will then enjoy in the beatific vision, explaining as best she can what it is and what "that" will be like there.

Stanza 39

The breathing of the air,
the song of the sweet nightingale,
the grove and its elegance
in the serene night,
with flame that consumes but causes no pain.

EXPLANATION

2. In this stanza the soul states and explains "that" which she says her Bridegroom will give her at the time of her blissful transformation, explaining it in five ways: first, she says it is the breathing or wafting of the Holy Spirit from God to her and from her to God; second, the jubilation to God in the fruition of God; third, the knowledge of the creatures and of their classification; fourth, the pure and clear contemplation of the divine essence; and fifth, the total transformation in God's immense love. So she speaks the line: "The breathing of the air."

3. This "breathing of the air" is an ability which the soul says God will give her there in the communication of the Holy Spirit, Who, like respiration, raises the soul very high with His divine breath, shaping her and enabling her to breathe in God the same breath of love that the Father breathes in the Son and the Son in the Father, which is none other than the Holy Spirit, wafting it to her in the Father and the Son in the aforesaid transformation, to unite her with Them; because it would not be a genuine and total transformation if the soul were not transformed in the three Persons of the Holy Trinity to a revealed, manifest degree. And this breathing of the Holy Spirit in the soul, by which God transforms her in Himself, is such a lofty, delicate, and profound delight to her that it can-

---

14. Referring to the "that" in the last line of stanza 38, interpreted as a foretaste of heavenly bliss.

deleite, que no hay decirlo por lengua mortal, ni el entendimiento humano en cuanto tal puede alcanzar algo de ello; porque aun lo que en esta transformación temporal pasa cerca de esta comunicación en el alma no se puede hablar, porque el alma, unida y transformada en Dios, aspira en Dios a Dios la misma aspiración divina que Dios—estando ella en El transformada—aspira en sí mismo a ella.

4. Y en la transformación que el alma tiene en esta vida pasa esta misma aspiración de Dios al alma y del alma a Dios con mucha frecuencia, con subidísimo deleite de amor en el alma, aunque no en revelado y manifiesto grado como en la otra vida, porque esto es lo que entiendo quiso decir san Pablo cuando dijo: *Por cuanto sois hijos de Dios, envió Dios en vuestros corazones el espíritu de su Hijo, clamando al Padre* (Gal 4,6); lo cual en los beatíficos de la otra vida y en los perfectos de ésta es en las dichas maneras. Y no hay que tener por imposible que el alma pueda una cosa tan alta, que el alma aspire en Dios como Dios aspira en ella por modo participado, porque, dado que Dios le haga merced de unirla en la Santísima Trinidad, en que el alma se hace deiforme y Dios por participación, ¿qué increíble cosa es que obre ella también su obra de entendimiento, noticia y amor, o, por mejor decir, la tenga obrada en la Trinidad juntamente con ella como la misma Trinidad, pero por modo comunicado y participado, obrándolo Dios en la misma alma? Porque esto es estar transformada en las tres Personas en potencia y sabiduría y amor, y en esto es semejante el alma a Dios, y para que pudiese venir a esto la crió a su imagen y semejanza (Gen 1,26).

5. Y cómo esto sea no hay más saber ni poder para decirlo, sino dar a entender cómo el Hijo de Dios nos alcanzó este alto estado y nos mereció este subido puesto de *poder ser hijos de Dios,* como dice san Juan (1,12), y así lo pidió al Padre por el mismo san Juan, diciendo: *Padre, quiero que los que me has dado, que donde yo estoy también ellos estén conmigo, para que vean la claridad que me diste* (17,24); es a saber, que hagan por participación en nosotros la misma obra que yo por naturaleza, que es aspirar el Espíritu Santo. Y dice más: *No ruego, Padre, solamente por estos presentes, sino también por aquellos que han de creer por su doctrina en mí; que todos ellos sean una misma cosa de la manera que tú, Padre, estás en mí y yo en ti, así ellos en nosotros sean una misma cosa. Y yo la claridad que me has dado he dado a ellos, para que sean una misma cosa, como nosotros somos una misma cosa, yo en ellos y tú en mí; por que sean perfectos en uno, por que conozca el mundo que tú me enviaste y los amaste como me amaste a mí* (17,20–23), que es comunicándoles el mesmo amor que al Hijo,

not be expressed by mortal tongue, nor can the human intellect as such attain any of it; since one cannot even speak of what occurs during this earthly transformation with regard to that communication in the soul, because the soul, united and transformed in God, wafts in God to God the same divine breath that God (she being transformed in Him) breathes in Himself to her.

4. And in the transformation experienced by the soul in this life, this same breath passes from God to the soul and from the soul to God with great frequency, to her most sublime, loving delight, though not to a revealed, manifest degree as in the next life, because this is what I take Saint Paul to have meant when he said: "And because ye are sons, God hath sent forth the Spirit of his Son into your hearts, crying, Abba, Father" (Galatians 4:6); which befalls the blessed in the next life and the perfected in this life in the aforesaid ways. Nor should it be considered impossible for the soul to attain so lofty a thing as to breathe in God as God breathes in her, in a participatory mode, because, if God grants her the favor of uniting her with the Holy Trinity, whereby the soul becomes Godlike, and God by participation, why is it incredible that she should also perform the functions of her intellect, cognition, and love (or, rather, have them performed) in the Persons of the Trinity, together with Them, just as those Persons do, only in a communicated, participatory mode, God working this in the soul herself? Because this is what it means to be transformed in the three Persons in power, wisdom, and love; it is herein that the soul resembles God, and it was so that she could attain this that He created her in His image and likeness (Genesis 1:26).

5. We have no further knowledge or ability to say how this can be, but merely to indicate that it was the Son of God Who obtained this high state for us and earned for us that lofty position of "the power to become the sons of God," as stated by Saint John (John 1:12), who also tells us that He requested this of His Father: "Father, I will that they also, whom thou hast given me, be with me where I am; that they may behold my glory, which thou hast given me" (John 17:24); that is, that they may perform by participation in Us the same work that I do by nature, which is breathing the Holy Spirit. And He also says: "Neither pray I for these alone, but for them also which shall believe in me through their word; That they all may be one; as thou, Father, art in me, and I in thee, that they also may be one in us . . . And the glory which thou gavest me I have given them; that they may be one, even as we are one: I in them, and thou in me, that they may be made perfect in one; and that the world may know that thou hast sent me, and hast loved them, as thou hast loved me" (John 17:20–23)—by communicating to them the same love as to the Son, though not naturally

aunque no naturalmente como al Hijo, sino, como habemos dicho, por unidad y transformación de amor; como tampoco se entiende aquí quiere decir el Hijo al Padre que sean los santos una cosa esencial y naturalmente como lo son el Padre y el Hijo, sino que lo sean por unión de amor, como el Padre y el Hijo están en unidad de amor.

6. De donde las almas esos mesmos bienes poseen por participación que El por naturaleza; por lo cual verdaderamente son dioses por participación, iguales y compañeros suyos de Dios. De donde san Pedro dijo: *Gracia y paz sea cumplida y perfecta en vosotros en el conocimiento de Dios y de Jesucristo nuestro Señor, de la manera que nos son dadas todas las cosas de su divina virtud para la vida y la piedad, por el conocimiento de aquel que nos llamó con su propria gloria y virtud, por el cual muy grandes y preciosas promesas nos dio, para que por estas cosas seamos hechos compañeros de la divina naturaleza* (2.ª 1,2–4). Hasta aquí son palabras de san Pedro, en las cuales da claramente a entender que el alma participará al mismo Dios, que será obrando en él acompañadamente con él la obra de la Santísima Trinidad, de la manera que habemos dicho, por causa de la unión sustancial y por amor entre el alma y Dios. Lo cual, aunque se cumple perfectamente en la otra vida, todavía en ésta, cuando se llega a el estado perfecto como decimos ha llegado aquí el alma, se alcanza gran rastro y sabor de ella, al modo que vamos diciendo, aunque (como habemos dicho) no se puede decir.

7. ¡Oh almas criadas para estas grandezas y para ellas llamadas!, ¿qué hacéis, en qué os entretenéis? Vuestras pretensiones son bajezas y vuestras posesiones miserias. ¡Oh miserable ceguera de los ojos de vuestra alma, pues para tanta luz estáis ciegos y para tan grandes voces sordos, no viendo que, en tanto que buscáis grandezas y glorias, os quedáis miserables y bajos, de tantos bienes hechos ignorantes e indignos! Síguese lo segundo que el alma dice para dar a entender *aquello*, es a saber: "el canto de la dulce filomena."

8. Lo que nace en el alma de aquel *aspirar del aire* es la dulce voz de su Amado a ella, en la cual ella hace a él su sabrosa jubilación; y lo uno y lo otro llama aquí *canto de filomena;* porque, así como el canto de filomena, que es el ruiseñor, se oye en la primavera, pasados ya los fríos, lluvias y variedades de el invierno, y hace melodía al oído y al espíritu recreación, así en esta actual comunicación y transformación de amor que tiene ya la esposa en esta vida, amparada ya y libre de todas las turbaciones y variedades temporales, y desnuda y purgada de las imperfecciones, penalidades y nieblas así del sentido como de el espíritu, siente nueva primavera en libertad y anchura y alegría de es-

as He does to His Son, but, as I have said, through unity and loving transformation; just as it is not to be understood here that the Son is telling His Father that the saints are changed into the essence and nature of the Father and Son, but merely partake of them through loving union, just as Father and Son are united in love.

6. Hence, the souls possess those same benefits by participation which He does by nature; therefore they are really Gods by participation, equals of God, and His companions. Hence, Saint Peter said: "Grace and peace be multiplied unto you through the knowledge of God, and of Jesus our Lord, According as his divine power hath given unto us all things that pertain unto life and godliness, through the knowledge of him that hath called us to glory and virtue: whereby are given unto us exceeding great and precious promises: that by these ye might be partakers of the divine nature" (II Peter 1:2–4). Up to here they are words of Saint Peter's, in which he indicates clearly that the soul will partake in God Himself, performing in Him and in association with Him the work of the Holy Trinity, in the above-mentioned way, because of their substantial union and the love between the soul and God. Though this is perfectly achieved only in the next life, yet in this life, when the soul reaches the perfect state, as I say she has here, she obtains a large trace and flavor of it, in the way I am describing, although (as I said) this cannot really be described.

7. O souls, created for such grandeurs and summoned to enjoy them, what are you doing? On what are you wasting your time? Your aspirations are lowly, your possessions are wretched. Oh, people, the miserable blindness of your soul's eyes, since you are blind to such great light and deaf to such loud voices, failing to see that, while you seek rank and fame, you remain miserable and low, made ignorant and unworthy of such great benefits! There follows the second explanation of "that" given by the soul: "the song of the sweet nightingale."

8. That which is generated in the soul by that "breathing of the air" is the sweet call of her Beloved to her, in which she also sends her delightful jubilation to Him. She here calls both these voices "the song of the nightingale," because, just as the song of Philomel (the nightingale) is heard in spring, after the departure of the chills, rains, and varying winter weather, and the bird pours melody into the ear and refreshment into the spirit, so in this present communication and loving transformation which the bride already enjoys in this life, now protected and free of all earthly disturbances and ups and downs, and stripped and purged of the imperfections, hardships, and mists of her senses and spirit alike, she feels a new springtime in freedom, ease, and cheerfulness of spirit, in

píritu, en la cual siente la dulce voz de el Esposo, que es su *dulce filomena;* con la cual voz renovando y refrigerando la sustancia de su alma, como a alma ya bien dispuesta para caminar a vida eterna, la llama dulce y sabrosamente, sintiendo ella la sabrosa voz que dice: *Levántate, date priesa, amiga mía, paloma mía, hermosa mía, y ven; porque ya ha pasado el invierno, la lluvia se ha ya ido muy lejos; las flores han parecido en nuestra tierra; el tiempo del podar es llegado, y la voz de la tórtola se oye en nuestra tierra* (Cant 2,10–12).

9. En la cual voz de el Esposo que se la habla en lo interior del alma, siente la esposa fin de males y principio de bienes en cuyo refrigerio y amparo y sentimiento sabroso ella también como dulce filomena da su voz con nuevo canto de jubilación a Dios, juntamente con Dios que la mueve a ello; que por eso El da su voz a ella, para que ella en uno la dé junto con El a Dios, porque ésa es la pretensión y deseo de El, que el alma entone su voz espiritual en jubilación a Dios, según también el mismo Esposo se lo pide a ella en los Cantares, diciendo: *Levántate, date priesa, amiga mía, y ven, paloma mía; en los agujeros de la piedra, en la caverna de la cerca, muéstrame tu rostro, suene tu voz en mis oídos* (2,13–14). Los *oídos* de Dios significan aquí los deseos que tiene Dios de que el alma le dé esta voz de jubilación perfecta. La cual voz, para que sea perfecta, pide el Esposo que la dé y suene *en las cavernas de la piedra,* esto es, en la transformación que dijimos de los misterios de Cristo. Que, porque en esta unión el alma jubila y alaba a Dios con el mismo Dios, como decíamos de el amor, es alabanza muy perfecta y agradable a Dios, porque, estando el alma en esta perfección, hace las obras muy perfectas; y así, esta voz de jubilación es dulce para Dios y dulce para el alma. Que por eso dijo el Esposo: *Tu voz es dulce* (Cant 2,14); es a saber, no sólo para ti, sino también para mí, porque, estando conmigo en uno, das tu voz en uno de dulce filomena para mí conmigo.

10. En esta manera es el canto que pasa en el alma en la transformación que tiene en esta vida, el sabor de la cual es sobre todo encarecimiento. Pero, por cuanto no es tan perfecto como el cantar nuevo de la vida gloriosa, saboreada el alma por esto que aquí siente, rastreando por la alteza de este canto la excelencia del que tendrá en la gloria, cuya ventaja es mayor sin comparación, hace memoria de él, y dice que *aquello* que le dará será *el canto de la dulce filomena.* Y dice luego: "el soto y su donaire."

11. Esta es la tercera cosa que dice el alma le ha de dar el Esposo. Por el *soto,* por cuanto cría en sí muchas plantas y animales, entiende aquí a Dios en cuanto cría y da ser a todas las criaturas, las cuales en

which she hears the sweet voice of the Bridegroom, Who is her "sweet nightingale"; renewing and refreshing her soul-substance with that voice, since she is a soul already well prepared for a journey to eternal life, He calls her sweetly and delightfully, she hearing the delightful voice that says: "Arise, make haste, my friend, my dove, my lovely one, and come; for the winter is now over, the rain has moved very far away; the flowers have appeared in our land; pruning time has come; and the voice of the turtledove is heard in our land" ([compare] Song of Solomon 2:10–12).

9. In this voice of the Bridegroom which speaks to her inside her soul, the bride perceives an end to woes and the beginning of good things, and in the refreshment, protection, and delicious feeling of this she too emits her voice like the sweet nightingale with a new song of jubilation to God, together with God, Who incites her to it; for the Bridegroom gives His voice to her so that she in unison will give hers to God together with Him, for this is His aspiration and desire: that the soul intone her spiritual song in jubilation to God, just as the same Bridegroom asks this of her in the Song of Solomon: "Arise, make haste, My friend, and come, My dove; in the clefts of the rocks, in the gap of the hedge, show Me your face, let your voice sound in My ears" ([compare] 2:10–14). What is meant here by God's "ears" are His desires that the soul will send Him that voice of perfect jubilation. For this voice to be perfect, the Bridegroom asks that it may be given and may resound "in the clefts of the rocks"; that is, in the aforesaid transformation of the mysteries of Christ. Because, since in this union the soul jubilantly praises God along with God Himself, as I said about love, it is a very perfect praise and agreeable to God, because when the soul is in this perfection she performs very perfect works; and so, this voice of jubilation is sweet to God and sweet to the soul. That is why the Bridegroom said: "Sweet is thy voice" (Song of Solomon 2:14); that is, not only to you, but also to Me, because, being at one with Me, you pour forth your sweet nightingale's voice for Me in unison with Me.

10. Of such a sort is the song experienced by the soul in the transformation she attains in this life, the savor of which is beyond all praise. But, because it is not as perfect as the new song of life in glory, the soul, given a foretaste by what she feels here and, through the loftiness of this song, perceiving a trace of the excellence of the one she will hear when in glory, which is superior beyond any comparison, takes note of it and states that "that" which she will be given will be "the song of the sweet nightingale." Next she mentions "the grove and its elegance."

11. This is the third thing which the bride says the Bridegroom will give her. By the "grove," because it nurtures many plants and animals within it, she here means God because He nurtures and gives being to all crea-

El tienen su vida y raíz, lo cual es mostrarla a Dios y dársela a conocer en cuanto es Criador. Por el *donaire* de este *soto*, que también pide al Esposo el alma aquí para entonces, pide la gracia y sabiduría y la belleza que de Dios tiene no sólo cada una de las criaturas así terrestres como celestes, sino también la que hacen entre sí en la respondencia sabia, ordenada, graciosa y amigable de unas a otras, así de las inferiores entre sí como de las superiores también entre sí, y entre las superiores y las inferiores, que es cosa que hace al alma gran donaire y deleite conocerla. Síguese lo cuarto, y es: "en la noche serena."

12. Esta noche es la contemplación en que el alma desea ver estas cosas. Llámala *noche,* porque la contemplación es oscura, que por eso la llama por otro nombre *Mística Teología,* que quiere decir sabiduría de Dios secreta o escondida, en la cual, sin ruido de palabras y sin ayuda de algún sentido corporal ni espiritual, como en silencio y quietud, a oscuras de todo lo sensitivo y natural, enseña Dios ocultísima y secretísimamente al alma sin ella saber cómo; lo cual algunos espirituales llaman *entender no entendiendo,* porque esto no se hace en el entendimiento que llaman los filósofos activo, cuya obra es en las formas y fantasías y aprehensiones de las potencias corporales, mas hácese en el entendimiento en cuanto posible y pasivo, el cual, sin recibir las tales formas, etc., sólo pasivamente recibe inteligencia sustancial desnuda de imagen, la cual le es dada sin ninguna obra ni oficio suyo activo.

13. Y por eso llama a esta contemplación *noche,* en la cual en esta vida conoce el alma, por medio de la transformación que ya tiene, altísimamente este divino *soto y su donaire*. Pero, por más alta que sea esta noticia, todavía es noche oscura en comparación de la beatífica que aquí pide, y por eso dice, pidiendo clara contemplación, que este gozar *el soto* y su donaire y las demás cosas que aquí ha dicho, sea *en la noche ya serena,* esto es, en la contemplación ya clara y beatífica, de manera que deje ya de ser noche en la contemplación oscura acá, y se vuelva en contemplación de vista clara y serena de Dios allá; y así, decir *en la noche serena,* es decir en contemplación ya clara y serena de la vista de Dios. De donde David de esta noche de contemplación dice: *La noche será mi iluminación en mis deleites* (Ps 138,11); que es como si dijera: Cuando esté en mis deleites de la vista esencial de Dios, ya la noche de contemplación habrá amanecido en día y luz de

tures, which have their life and root in Him; this is God's showing Himself to her and letting her know He is the Creator.[15] By the "elegance" of this "grove," which the soul here is also asking of her Bridegroom for the future, she is requesting not only the grace, wisdom, and beauty received from God by each of the creatures, whether earthly or heavenly, but also those produced in their interactions by their wise, orderly, gracious, and amiable behavior toward one another, the lower ones among themselves, the higher ones among themselves, and the higher ones with the lower ones; to know this is a great delight and charm to the soul. Her fourth item follows: "in the serene night."

12. This night is the contemplation in which the soul desires to see these things. She calls it night because contemplation is dark, which is why she calls it by the other name of "mystical theology," which means the secret or hidden wisdom of God, in which, without the sound of words or the aid of any bodily or spiritual sense, as if in silence and calm, in the dark as to everything sensory and natural, God instructs the soul very clandestinely and secretly without her knowing how; some spiritual people call this "understanding while not understanding," because this does not occur in the intellect which philosophers call active, and which operates on the forms, imaginings, and perceptions of the bodily powers, but occurs in the possible or passive intellect, which, without receiving these forms, etc., merely passively receives substantial information deprived of images, which is given to it without any work or activity on its part.

13. Therefore she calls this contemplation "night," for in it, in this life, the soul has extremely lofty knowledge of this divine "grove and its elegance" by means of the transformation she has already undergone. But, no matter how lofty this information is, it is still dark night compared to the beatific notification she is here requesting; that is why she asks, requesting clear contemplation, that this enjoyment of the grove and its elegance, and the other things she has mentioned here, be on a night already serene; that is, in contemplation that is now clear and beatific, so that it ceases to be night in the obscure contemplation possible in this life, and becomes clear-sighted and calm contemplation of God as in the next; and so, to say "in the serene night" is to say "in contemplation, now clear and serene, of the sight of God." Hence, David says of this night of contemplation: "The night will be my illumination in my delights" ([compare] Psalm 139:11); which is as if he were saying: "When I have attained my delight in the sight of God in His essence, the night of contemplation will have already

---

15. I here follow the interpretation of an earlier translator, though the Spanish as it stands seems to mean something else (but what?).

mi entendimiento. Síguese lo quinto: "con llama que consume y no da pena."

14. Por la *llama* entiende aquí el amor del Espíritu Santo. El *consumar* significa aquí acabar y perficcionar y el decir el alma que todas las cosas que ha dicho en esta canción se las ha de dar el Amado y las ha ella de poseer con consumado y perfecto amor, absortas todas y ella con ellas en amor perfecto y *que no dé pena;* lo cual dice para dar a entender la perfección entera de este amor, porque, para que lo sea, estas dos propriedades ha de tener, conviene a saber: que consume y transforme el alma en Dios y que no dé pena la inflamación y transformación de esta llama en el alma. Lo cual no puede ser sino en el estado beatífico, donde ya esta llama es amor suave, porque en la transformación de el alma en ella hay conformidad y satisfacción beatífica de ambas partes, y por tanto no da pena de variedad en más o en menos, como hacía antes que el alma llegase a la capacidad de este perfecto amor; porque, habiendo llegado a él, está el alma en tan conforme y suave amor con Dios, que con ser Dios, como dice Moisés, *fuego consumidor* (Deut 4,24), ya no lo sea sino consumador y reficcionador; que no es ya como la transformación que tenía en esta vida el alma, que, aunque era muy perfecta y consumadora en amor, todavía le era algo consumidora y detractiva, a manera del fuego en el ascua, que, aunque está transformada y conforme con ella sin aquel humear que hacía antes que en sí la transformase, todavía, aunque la consumaba en fuego, la consumía y resolvía en ceniza; lo cual acaece en el alma que en esta vida está transformada con perfección de amor, que, aunque hay conformidad, todavía padece alguna manera de pena y detrimento: lo uno, por la transformación beatífica que siempre echa menos en el espíritu; lo otro, por el detrimento que padece el sentido flaco y corruptible con la fortaleza y alteza de tanto amor, porque cualquiera cosa excelente es detrimento y pena a la flaqueza natural; porque, según está escrito, *corpus quod corrumpitur, aggravat animam* (Sap 9,15). Pero en aquella vida beatífica ningún detrimento ni pena sentirá, aunque su entender será profundísimo y su amor muy inmenso, porque para lo uno le dará Dios habilidad y para lo otro fortaleza, consumando Dios su entendimiento con su sabiduría y su voluntad con su amor.

15. Y porque la esposa ha pedido en las precedentes canciones y en la que vamos declarando inmensas comunicaciones y noticias de Dios

yielded to the dawning of the day that will enlighten my understanding."
The fifth item follows: "with flame that consumes but causes no pain."

14. By the "flame" she here means the love of the Holy Spirit. "To con-summate"[16] means here to complete and to perfect; the soul is thereby saying that everything she has mentioned in this stanza will be given to her by her Beloved, and that she will possess them with consummate and perfect love, all of them absorbed in her and she in them in perfect love that "causes no pain." She says this to indicate the entire perfection of this love, because, to be perfect, it must possess these two characteristics: that it should consummate and transform the soul in God, but that the blaze and transformation of this flame in the soul should give no pain. This can-not occur except in the state of bliss, where this flame is now gentle love, because in the soul's transformation in it there is agreement and blissful satisfaction on both sides, and so it does not produce the pain of vicissi-tudes to any degree, as it did before the soul attained the capacity for this perfect love. Once she has reached it, the soul is in such harmonious and gentle love with God that, although God, as Moses says, is "a consuming fire" (Deuteronomy 4:24), He no longer is so, but instead a consummat-ing and restoring one; because this is no longer like the transformation the soul experienced in this life, which, even if it was very perfect and consummating in love, still was somewhat consuming and harmful to her, like fire to a coal: even though the coal has been transformed into con-formity with it, without that smoke it gave off before the fire transformed it into itself, nevertheless, even though it was consummated in fire, it was also consumed and reduced to ashes. This occurs in the soul who in this life is transformed with perfection of love: even though there is harmony, she still suffers some kind of pain and detriment: first, because of the be-atific transformation the lack of which she always feels in her spirit; sec-ond, because of the harm suffered by her weak, corruptible senses from the strength and loftiness of such great love, since any excellent thing is a detriment and pain to the weakness of nature, it being written that the decay of the body burdens the soul (Wisdom of Solomon 9:15). But in that life of bliss she will feel no harm or pain, even if her understanding will be most profound and her love most immense, because for the one thing God will give her ability and, for the other, strength, consummating her intellect with His own wisdom, and her will with His love.

15. And because the bride has requested in the preceding stanzas, and the one being explained here, immense communications and information

---

16. Throughout section 14, there is constant wordplay between *consumir* ("to con-sume") and *consumar* ("to consummate").

con que ha menester fortísimo y altísimo amor para amar según la grandeza y alteza de ellas, pide aquí que todas ellas sean en este amor consumado, perfectivo y fuerte.

Canción 40

Que nadie lo miraba . . .
Aminadab tampoco parecía;
y el cerco sosegaba,
y la caballería
a vista de las aguas descendía.

DECLARACIÓN Y ANOTACIÓN

1. Conociendo, pues, aquí la esposa que ya el apetito de su voluntad está desasido de todas las cosas y arrimado a su Dios con estrechísimo amor, y que la parte sensitiva de el alma con todas sus fuerzas, potencias y apetitos está conformada con el espíritu, acabadas ya y sujetadas sus rebeldías; y que el demonio, por el vario y largo exercicio y lucha espiritual, está ya vencido y apartado muy lejos; y que su alma está unida y transformada con abundancia de riquezas y dones celestiales; y que, según esto, está ya bien dispuesta y aparejada y fuerte, *arrimada en su Esposo,* para subir *por el desierto* de la muerte *abundando en deleites* (Cant 8,5) a los asientos y sillas gloriosas de su Esposo; con deseo que el Esposo concluya ya este negocio, pónele por delante para más moverle a ello todas estas cosas en esta última canción, en la cual dice cinco cosas: la primera, que ya su alma está desasida y ajena de todas las cosas; la segunda, que ya está vencido y ahuyentado el demonio; la tercera, que ya están sujetadas las pasiones y mortificados los apetitos naturales; la cuarta y la quinta, que ya está la parte sensitiva e inferior reformada y purificada, y que está conformada con la parte espiritual, de manera que no sólo no estorbará para recebir aquellos bienes espirituales, mas antes se acomodará a ellos, porque aun de los que agora tiene participa según su capacidad. Dice, pues, ansí: "Que nadie lo miraba."

2. Lo cual es como si dijera: Mi alma está ya desnuda, desasida, sola y ajena de todas las cosas criadas de arriba y de abajo, y tan adentro entrada en el interior recogimiento contigo, que ninguna de ellas alcanza ya de vista el íntimo deleite que en ti poseo, es a saber, a mover mi alma a gusto con su suavidad, ni a disgusto y molestia con su miseria y bajeza, porque, estando mi alma tan lejos de ellas y en tan profundo deleite contigo, ninguna de ellas lo alcanza de vista. Y no sólo eso, pero "Aminadab tampoco parecía."

from God, for which she requires very strong and very sublime love in order to love in proportion to their greatness and sublimity, she here asks that all of them be given in this consummate, perfecting, and strong love.

Stanza 40

> For no one was looking . . .
> nor was Amminadib present;
> and the siege slackened,
> and the cavalry
> was descending in sight of the waters.

EXPLANATION AND COMMENTARY

1. So then, the bride now realizes that the appetite of her will is no longer attached to worldly things, but is supported on her God with most intimate love, and that the sensory part of her soul with all her forces, powers, and appetites is in conformity with her spirit, her rebellions being now finished and subdued; and that the devil, through her long, varied training and spiritual struggle, is now overcome and very distant from her; and that her soul is united and transformed with abundance of riches and heavenly gifts; and that, accordingly, she is now well prepared and ready and strong, "supported by her Bridegroom," to ascend "through the desert" of death "abounding in delights" ([compare] Song of Solomon 8:5 [??]) to her Bridegroom's dwelling and glorious throne. Thus, she desires her Bridegroom to conclude the matter now and sets before him, to incite Him more greatly to do so, all the things mentioned in this final stanza, in which she states five things: first, that her soul is now detached from and alien to all things; second, that the devil is now overcome and frightened away; third, that her passions are subdued and her natural appetites mortified; fourth and fifth, that her sensory lower part is now reformed and purified and is in conformity with her spiritual part, so that not only will it not prevent her from receiving those spiritual benefits, but, on the contrary, will adapt to them, because even of those she now possesses it is partaking as far as it can. So she says: "For no one was looking."

2. Which is as if to say: "My soul is now bare, detached, alone, and foreign to all created things in heaven and on earth, and has entered so deeply into inner seclusion with You that no other woman now attains and sees the intimate delight I possess in You: I can move my soul as I please, gently, with no displeasure or annoyance at her wretchedness and lowness, because, my soul being so far from this and in such profound delight with You, none of them can attain and see this. And not only that, but also: "nor was Amminadib present."

3. El cual *Aminadab* en la Escritura divina (Cant 6,11) significa el demonio (hablando espiritualmente) adversario del alma; el cual la combatía y turbaba siempre con la innumerable munición de su artillería, por que ella no se entrase en esta fortaleza y escondrijo de el interior recogimiento con el Esposo, donde ella, estando ya puesta, está tan favorecida, tan fuerte, tan victoriosa con las virtudes que allí tiene y con el favor del abrazo de Dios, que el demonio no solamente no osa llegar, pero con grande pavor huye muy lejos y no osa parecer; y porque también, por el exercicio de las virtudes y por razón de el estado perfecto que ya tiene, de tal manera le tiene ya ahuyentado y vencido el alma, que no parece más delante de ella; y así: *Aminadab tampoco parecía* con algún derecho para impedirme este bien que pretendo. "Y el cerco sosegaba."

4. Por el cual *cerco* entiende aquí el alma las pasiones y apetitos del alma, los cuales cuando no están vencidos y amortiguados la cercan en derredor, combatiéndola de una parte y de otra, por lo cual los llama *cerco,* el cual dice que también está ya *sosegado,* esto es, las pasiones ordenadas en razón y los apetitos mortificados; que, pues así es, no deje de comunicarle las mercedes que le ha pedido, pues el dicho cerco ya no es parte para impedirlo. Esto dice porque, hasta que el alma tiene ordenadas sus cuatro pasiones a Dios y tiene mortificados y purgados los apetitos, no está capaz de ver a Dios. Y síguese: "y la caballería/a vista de las aguas descendía."

5. Por las *aguas* se entienden aquí los bienes y deleites espirituales que en este estado goza el alma en su interior con Dios. Por la *caballería* entiende aquí los sentidos corporales de la parte sensitiva, así interiores como exteriores, porque ellos traen en sí las fantasmas y figuras de sus objetos; los cuales en este estado dice aquí la esposa que descienden *a vista de las aguas* espirituales, porque de tal manera está ya en este estado de matrimonio espiritual purificada y en alguna manera espiritualizada la parte sensitiva e inferior del alma, que ella con sus potencias sensitivas y fuerzas naturales se recogen a participar y gozar en su manera de las grandezas espirituales que Dios está comunicando al alma en lo interior del espíritu, según lo dio a entender David cuando dijo: *Mi corazón y mi carne se gozaron en Dios vivo* (Ps 83,3).

6. Y es de notar que no dice aquí la esposa que la caballería descendía a gustar las aguas, sino *a vista* de ellas; porque esta parte sensitiva con sus potencias no tienen capacidad para gustar esencial y propiamente de los bienes espirituales no sólo en esta vida, pero ni aun en la otra, sino por cierta redundancia del espíritu reciben sensi-

3. This Amminadib in Holy Scripture (Song of Solomon 6:12) signifies the devil (speaking spiritually), the soul's enemy; he always used to fight her and perturb her with the innumerable pieces of his artillery to keep her from entering that fortress and hiding place of inner seclusion with her Bridegroom; now that she is there, she is so favored, so strong, so victorious with the virtues she has there and with the favor of God's embrace, that not only does the devil not dare to approach, but with great fear he flees very far and does not dare to show himself; and also because, by exercising virtues and because of her present state of perfection, the soul now has him so thoroughly frightened and overcome that he no longer appears to her; therefore: "nor was Amminadib present" with any right to keep me from this good I aspire to. "And the siege slackened."

4. By this "siege" the soul here means her passions and appetites, which, when not overcome and deadened, encircle or besiege her round about, combating her on every side; for this reason she calls them a circle or siege, which she says is also now slackened; that is, her passions are subjected to reason and her appetites are deadened; this being so, let Him not cease to communicate to her the favors she has requested of Him, since the aforesaid siege has no more power to prevent it. She says this because, until her soul has subjected her four passions to God, and has mortified and purged her appetites, she is unable to see Him. There follows: "and the cavalry/was descending in sight of the waters."

5. By "waters" is meant here the benefits and spiritual delights that the soul enjoys in this state within herself with God. By "cavalry" she here means the bodily senses of her sensory part, both inner and outer ones, because they bear in themselves the shapes and figures of their objects; the bride says here that in this state they descend in sight of the spiritual waters, because in this state of spiritual marriage the sensory lower part of her soul is now so purified and, in a way, spiritualized that she and her sensory powers and natural forces concentrate on partaking in and enjoying in their way the spiritual grandeur that God is communicating to the soul within her spirit, as He gave David to understand when he said: "My heart and my flesh enjoyed the living God" ([compare] Psalm 84:2).

6. And it is to be noted that the bride here does not say that the cavalry was descending to taste the waters, but in sight of them; because this sensory part and its powers are unable to taste the spiritual benefits in their essence and true being, not only in this life, but not even in the next, except when through a certain overflow of the spirit they sensorily receive refreshment and delight from them; through this delight these bodily

tivamente recreación y deleite de ellos; por el cual deleite estos sentidos y potencias corporales son atraídos al recogimiento interior, donde
está bebiendo el alma las aguas de los bienes espirituales, lo cual más
es descender a la vista de ellas que a beberlas y gustallas como ellas
son. Y dice aquí el alma que *descendían*, y no dice que *iban* ni otro vo-
cablo, para dar a entender que en esta comunicación de la parte sensitiva a la espiritual, cuando se gusta la dicha bebida de las aguas espirituales, bajan de sus operaciones naturales, cesando de ellas, al
recogimiento espiritual.

7. Todas esta perfecciones y disposiciones antepone la esposa a su
Amado el Hijo de Dios, con deseo de ser por El trasladada del matrimonio espiritual a que Dios la ha querido llegar en esta Iglesia militante, al glorioso matrimonio de la triunfante, al cual sea servido llevar a todos los que invocan su nombre, el dulcísimo Jesús, Esposo de
las fieles almas. Al cual es honra y gloria, juntamente con el Padre y el
Espíritu Santo, *in saecula saeculorum*. Amén.

senses and powers are attracted to inward concentration, in which the soul goes on drinking the waters of the spiritual benefits, which is more like descending to the sight of them than like drinking and tasting them in their essence. And the soul says here that they were "descending," not "going" or any other term, to indicate that in this communication between the sensory and spiritual parts, when the aforesaid draft of spiritual waters is tasted, they descend from their natural functions, abandoning them, into spiritual concentration.

7. The bride displays all these perfections and dispositions to her Beloved, the Son of God, in her desire to be transported from the spiritual marriage to which it has pleased God to bring her in this earthly Church Militant to that glorious marriage in the heavenly Church Triumphant. May it please the most sweet Jesus, Bridegroom of faithful souls, to lead there all who invoke His name. To Whom is honor and glory, together with the Father and the Holy Spirit, world without end. Amen.

Llama de amor viva

Prólogo

1. Alguna repugnancia he tenido, muy noble y devota señora, en declarar estas cuatro canciones que Vuestra Merced me ha pedido; porque, por ser de cosas tan interiores y espirituales, para las cuales comúnmente falta lenguaje (porque lo espiritual excede al sentido), con dificultad se dice algo de la sustancia, porque también se habla mal en las entrañas del espíritu si no es con entrañable espíritu, y por el poco que hay en mí, lo he diferido hasta ahora que el Señor parece que ha abierto un poco la noticia y dado algún calor. Debe ser por el santo deseo que Vuestra Merced tiene, que quizá, como se hicieron para Vuestra Merced, querrá Su Majestad que para Vuestra Merced se declaren. Me he animado, sabiendo cierto que de mi cosecha nada que haga al caso diré en nada, cuánto más en cosas tan subidas y sustanciales. Por eso no será mío sino lo malo y errado que en ello hubiere; y por eso lo sujeto todo al mejor parecer y al juicio de nuestra Madre la Iglesia Católica Romana, con cuya regla nadie yerra. Y con este presupuesto, arrimándome a la Escritura divina, y como se lleve entendido que todo lo que se dijere es tanto menor de lo que allí hay, como lo es lo pintado que lo vivo, me atreveré a decir lo que supiere.

2. Y no hay que maravillar que haga Dios tan altas y extrañas mercedes a las almas que El da en regalar, porque, si consideramos que es Dios y que se las hace como Dios y con infinito amor y bondad, no nos parecerá fuera de razón, pues El dijo que *en el que le amase vendrían el Padre, Hijo y Espíritu Santo, y harían morada en él* (Io 14,23); lo cual había de ser haciéndole a él vivir y morar en el Padre, Hijo y Espíritu Santo en vida de Dios, como da a entender el alma en estas canciones.

3. Que, aunque en las canciones que arriba declaramos hablamos del más perfecto grado de perfección a que en esta vida se puede llegar, que es la transformación en Dios, todavía estas canciones tratan

Living Flame of Love

Prologue

1. I have been somewhat unwilling, most noble and devout lady, to explain these four stanzas at Your Grace's request; because, since they touch on things inward and spiritual, for which usually there are no words (because the spiritual surpasses our senses), it is hard to say anything of substance, because one speaks inadequately about the roots of the spirit unless one is rooted in the spirit, and because of my limited capacity, I have put it off until now, when the Lord seems to have cleared my mind a little and supplied some warmth. It must be for the sake of the devout desire on the part of Your Grace that perhaps, since the poem was written for Your Grace, His Majesty will deign to let me explain it to you. I have taken heart, knowing for a fact that I will say absolutely nothing significant of my own invention, let alone on so lofty and substantive a subject. Therefore only the bad and mistaken things in it will be mine; and for that reason I submit it all to the better opinion and judgment of our mother, the Roman Catholic Church, by whose ruling no one goes astray. And with this assumption, relying on Holy Scripture, and with the understanding that all that will be said here is as inferior to the true state of things as a portrait is to the living subject, I shall make bold to say whatever I know.

2. Nor is it any wonder that God should grant such lofty, unusual favors to the souls whom He chooses to delight, because, if we consider that He is God and is doing this like God, with infinite love and kindness, we shall not think it unreasonable, because He said that to the man who loved Him would come the Father, Son, and Holy Spirit and They would make Their abode in him ([compare] John 14:23); which means making him live and dwell in the Father, Son, and Holy Spirit in a life of God, as the soul indicates in this poem.

3. Although in the poems I explained earlier I spoke of the most perfect degree of perfection attainable in this life—transformation in God—

159

del amor ya más calificado y perficionado en ese mismo estado de transformación, porque, aunque es verdad que lo que éstas y aquéllas dicen todo es un estado de transformación y no se puede pasar de allí en cuanto tal, pero puede con el tiempo y exercicio calificarse (como digo) y sustanciarse mucho más el amor; bien así como, aunque habiendo entrado el fuego en el madero le tenga transformado en sí y está ya unido con él, todavía, afervorándose más el fuego y dando más tiempo en él, se pone mucho más candente e inflamado hasta centellear fuego de sí y llamear.

4. Y en este encendido grado se ha de entender que habla el alma aquí, ya transformada y calificada interiormente en fuego de amor, que no sólo está unida en este fuego, sino que hace ya viva llama en ella. Y ella así lo siente, y así lo dice en estas canciones con íntima y delicada dulzura de amor, ardiendo en su llama, encareciendo en estas canciones algunos efectos que hace en ella; las cuales iré declarando por el orden que las demás: que las pondré primero juntas, y luego, puniendo cada canción, la declararé brevemente, y después, puniendo cada verso, lo declararé de por sí.

Canción 1

¡Oh llama de amor viva,
que tiernamente hieres
de mi alma en el más profundo centro!;
pues ya no eres esquiva,
acaba ya, si quieres;
rompe la tela de este dulce encuentro.

Declaración

1. Sintiéndose ya el alma toda inflamada en la divina unión y ya su paladar todo bañado en gloria y amor, y que hasta lo íntimo de su sustancia está revertiendo no menos que ríos de gloria, abundando en deleites, sintiendo *correr de su vientre los ríos de agua viva,* que dijo el Hijo de Dios que saldrían en semejantes almas (Io 7,38), parece que, pues con tanta fuerza está transformada en Dios y tan altamente dél poseída y con tan ricas riquezas de dones y virtudes arreada, que está tan cerca de la bienaventuranza, que no la divide sino una leve tela; y como ve que aquella llama delicada de amor que en ella arde, cada vez que la está embistiendo, la está como glorificando con suave y fuerte gloria, tanto, que cada vez que la absorbe y embiste le parece que le va a dar la vida eterna, y que va a romper la tela de la vida mor-

this poem discusses a love still more ennobled and perfected in this same state of transformation; because, though it is true that the subject of all these poems is a state of transformation which cannot be exceeded as such, nevertheless, with time and training, as I say, this love can be ennobled and made much more substantive; just as when fire enters a piece of wood: though it has transformed it into itself and is now united to it, nevertheless, the fire growing hotter and the length of time increasing, the wood becomes much more white-hot and blazing until it shoots off sparks and emits a flame.

4. And it is in this blazing degree that the soul should be understood to be speaking here, already transformed and inwardly ennobled into a fire of love; she is not merely united with the fire, but it is now also creating a living flame in her. And she feels this and says so in this poem with intimate and delicate sweetness of love, burning in its flame, emphasizing in this poem some of its effects on her. This poem I shall explain following the same system as for the others: first I shall set it down entirely, then I shall set down each stanza and explain it briefly, and after that I shall set down and explain each line separately.[17]

Stanza 1

**O living flame of love,
you that tenderly wound
the deepest center of my soul!
Since you are no longer harsh,
please complete your task:
rend the veil of this sweet encounter!**

EXPLANATION

1. The soul now feeling that she is entirely afire in the divine union, her palate now entirely bathed in glory and love, and that she is brimming with no less than rivers of glory down to the inmost part of her substance, abounding in delights; and feeling that there flow from her belly those rivers of living water which the Son of God said would gush forth from such souls (John 7:38), it seems to her that, being so powerfully transformed in God, so sublimely possessed by Him, and adorned with such rich wealth of gifts and virtues, she is so close to bliss that only a thin veil separates her from it; and since she sees that that delicate flame of love burning in her is, as it were, glorifying her with gentle but strong glory each time it touches her, so much so, that every time it absorbs her and assails her, it seems about to give her eternal life, and that it is about to

---

17. Here I omit a repetition of poem 3, page 14.

tal, y que falta muy poco, y que por esto poco no acaba de ser glorificada esencialmente, dice con gran deseo a la llama—que es el Espíritu Santo—que rompa ya la vida mortal por aquel dulce encuentro, en que de veras la acabe de comunicar lo que cada vez parece que la va a dar cuando la encuentra, que es glorificarla entera y perfectamente. Y así, dice: "¡Oh llama de amor viva!"

2. Para encarecer el alma el sentimiento y aprecio con que habla en estas cuatro canciones, pone en todas ellas estos términos: ¡oh! y ¡cuán!, que significan encarecimiento afectuoso; los cuales cada vez que se dicen dan a entender del interior más de lo que se dice por la lengua; y sirve el ¡oh! para mucho desear y para mucho rogar persuadiendo, y para entrambos efectos usa el alma dél en esta canción, porque en ella encarece e intima el gran deseo, persuadiendo al amor que la desate.

3. Esta llama de amor es el espíritu de su Esposo, que es el Espíritu Santo, al cual siente ya el alma en sí, no sólo como fuego que la tiene consumada y transformada en suave amor, sino como fuego que, demás de eso, arde en ella y echa llama, como dije; y aquella llama, cada vez que llamea, baña al alma en gloria y la refresca en temple de vida divina. Y ésta es la operación del Espíritu Santo en el alma transformada en amor, que los actos que hace interiores es llamear, que son inflamaciones de amor, en que, unida la voluntad del alma, ama subidísimamente, hecha un amor con aquella llama. Y así, estos actos de amor del alma son preciosísimos, y merece más en uno y vale más que cuanto había hecho en toda su vida sin esta transformación, por más que ello fuese. Y la diferencia que hay entre el hábito y el acto hay entre la transformación en amor y la llama de amor, que es la que hay entre el madero inflamado y la llama dél; que la llama es efecto del fuego que allí está.

4. De donde el alma que está en estado de transformación de amor, podemos decir que su ordinario hábito es como el madero que siempre está embestido en fuego, y los actos de esta alma son la llama que nace del fuego del amor, que tan vehemente sale cuanto es más intenso el fuego de la unión; en la cual llama se unen y suben los actos de la voluntad arrebatada y absorta en la llama del Espíritu Santo, que es como el ángel que se subió a Dios en la llama del sacrificio de Manué (Iud 13,20). Y así, en este estado no puede el alma hacer actos; que el Espíritu Santo los hace todos y la mueve a ellos, y por eso todos los actos de ella son divinos, pues es hecha y movida por Dios; de donde al alma le parece que cada vez que llamea esta llama, hacién

tear the veil of mortal life, and that it will take very little for this to happen, and that only that little keeps her from achieving glorification in her essence: she very ardently asks the flame, which is the Holy Spirit, to rend her mortal life now by that sweet encounter, in which He will truly and finally communicate to her what He seems about to give her at each encounter—that is, her total, perfect glorification. Thus she says: "O living flame of love!"

2. To emphasize the emotion and esteem with which she speaks in these four stanzas, into each one she puts the terms "O!" or "How!" which denote affectionate emphasis; each time they occur they indicate something inward that surpasses what the tongue speaks: the "O!" indicates strong desire and a strong persuasive request, and the soul uses it for both effects in this stanza, because in it she emphasizes and intimates her strong desire, persuading love to unbind her.

3. This flame of love is the spirit of her Bridegroom, which is the Holy Spirit, Whom the soul now feels within her, not only as a fire that has consummated and transformed her in gentle love, but also as a fire that, beyond this, burns in her and emits flame, as I said; and every time this flame flares up, it bathes the soul in glory and refreshes her in the warmth of divine life. And this is the operation of the Holy Spirit in the soul transformed in love: the inward actions He performs are a shooting of flame, blazings of love in which, the soul's will being in union, she loves most sublimely, that flame having changed her into love. And so, these loving actions of the soul are most precious, each of them having more merit and value than everything else she had done all her life before that transformation, however great that may have been. The same difference that exists between a propensity and an action exists between the transformation in love and the flame of love—the same as that between the ignited log and the flaming log; for its flame is the result of the fire that is in it.

4. Hence, we may say that the soul who is in a state of transformation in love has a usual propensity which can be compared to a log always ignited by fire; the actions of this soul are the flame arising from the fire of love, which shoots forth so violently in proportion to the intensity of the fire of union; in this flame there unite and ascend the actions of the will which is enraptured and absorbed in the flame of the Holy Spirit, just like the angel who ascended to God in the flame of Manoah's sacrifice (Judges 13:20). And so, in this state the soul cannot perform actions; the Holy Spirit performs them all and incites her to them, so that all her actions are divine, since she is made and moved by God. Hence, it seems to the soul that, every time this flame flares up, creating delicious love and divine

dola amor con sabor y temple divino, la está dando vida eterna, pues la levanta a operación de Dios en Dios.

5. Y éste es el lenguaje y palabras que trata Dios en las almas purgadas y limpias, todas encendidas como dijo David: *Tu palabra es encendida vehementemente* (Ps 118,140); y el profeta: *¿Por ventura mis palabras no son como fuego?* (Ier 23,29); las cuales palabras, como El mismo dice por san Juan, *son espíritu y vida* (6,64), la cual sienten las almas que tienen oídos para oírla, que (como digo) son las almas limpias y enamoradas; que los que no tienen el paladar sano, sino que gustan otras cosas, no pueden gustar el espíritu y vida de ellas, antes les hacen sinsabor; y por eso, cuanto más altas palabras decía el Hijo de Dios, tanto más algunos se desabrían por su impureza, como fue cuando predicó aquella tan sabrosa, soberana y amorosa doctrina de la sagrada Eucaristía, que muchos de ellos volvieron atrás (Io 6,67).

6. Y no, porque los tales no gusten este lenguaje de Dios (que habla de dentro), han de pensar que no le gustan otros, como aquí se dice; como las gustó san Pedro en el alma cuando dijo a Cristo: *¿Dónde iremos, Señor, que tienes palabras de vida eterna?* (Io 6,69); y la Samaritana olvidó el agua y el cántaro por la dulzura de las palabras de Dios (Io 4,28). Y así, estando esta alma tan cerca de Dios, que está transformada en llama de amor, en que se le comunica el Padre, el Hijo y Espíritu Santo, ¿qué increíble cosa se dice que guste un rastro de vida eterna?; aunque no perfectamente, porque no lo lleva la condición de esta vida. Mas es tan subido el deleite que aquel llamear del Espíritu Santo hace en ella, que la hace saber a qué sabe la vida eterna; que por eso llama a la llama *viva*, no porque no sea siempre viva, sino porque le hace tal efecto, que la hace vivir en Dios espiritualmente y sentir vida de Dios, al modo que dice David: *Mi corazón y mi carne se gozaron en Dios vivo* (Ps 83,3); no porque sea menester decir que sea vivo, pues siempre lo está, sino para dar a entender que el espíritu y sentido vivamente gustaban a Dios, hechos en Dios, lo cual es gustar a Dios vivo, esto es, vida de Dios y vida eterna; ni dijera David allí: *Dios vivo*, sino porque vivamente le gustaba, aunque no perfectamente, sino como un viso de vida eterna. Y así, en esta llama siente el alma tan vivamente a Dios que le gusta con tanto sabor y suavidad, que dice: *¡Oh llama de amor viva,* "que tiernamente hieres!"

7. Esto es, que con tu ardor tiernamente me tocas. Que, por cuanto esta llama es llama de vida divina, hiere al alma con ternura de vida de Dios, y tanto y tan entrañablemente la hiere y enternece, que la de-

warmth for her, it is giving her eternal life, since it uplifts her to the operation of God in God.

5. And this is the speech and wording that God uses to purified, clean souls, totally ignited, as David said: "Your word is violently ablaze" ([compare] Psalm 119:140); while the prophet says: "Is not my word like as a fire?" (Jeremiah 23:29). These words, as He Himself states through Saint John's lips, are the spirit and the life (John 6:63); this life is felt by the souls who have ears to hear it, which (as I say) are the clean, enamored souls; for, those whose palates are not wholesome, but who taste other things, cannot savor the same spirit and life that the others do; on the contrary, they are unpleasant to them. Therefore, the loftier the words spoken by the Son of God, the more some people were displeased because of their own impurity, as occurred when He preached that so delectable, sovereign, and loving doctrine of the Holy Eucharist, and many of His followers turned back (John 6:66).

6. And just because such people dislike this speech of God's (Who speaks from within) they should not think that others do the same, as said here; Saint Peter savored it in his soul when he said to Christ: "Lord, to whom shall we go? thou hast the words of eternal life" (John 6:68); and the woman of Samaria forgot her water and her pitcher because of the sweetness of God's words (John 4:28). And so, this soul being so close to God that she is transformed into a flame of love, in which the Father, Son, and Holy Ghost communicate Themselves to her, why is it unbelievable to say that she is tasting a trace of eternal life?—though not perfectly, because this is not consonant with the condition of this life. Yet the delight which that flaming of the Holy Spirit produces in her is so sublime that it makes her know what eternal life tastes like; therefore she calls the flame "living," not because it is not always living, but because it now has that effect on her, making her live in God spiritually and feel the life in God, in the way David says: "My heart and my flesh enjoyed the living God" ([compare] Psalm 84:2); not that it was necessary to call Him "living," since He always is; it was to indicate that his spirit and senses vividly enjoyed God, having been transformed in God; this it is to enjoy the living God (that is, the life in God and eternal life); nor would David have said "living God" there unless he was vividly enjoying Him, although not perfectly but as a glimmer of eternal life. And so, in this flame the soul feels God so vividly, enjoying Him with so much relish and sweetness, that she says: "O living flame of love, you that tenderly wound!"

7. That is, you that touch me tenderly with your glow. For, since this flame is a flame of divine life, it wounds the soul with the tenderness of life in God, and it wounds her so fiercely and inwardly, making her ten-

rrite en amor, por que se cumpla en ella lo que en la esposa en los
Cantares, que se enterneció tanto, que se derritió, y así dice ella allí:
Luego que el Esposo habló, se derritió mi alma (5,6); porque el habla
de Dios es el efecto que hace en el alma.

8. Mas ¿cómo se puede decir que la hiere, pues en el alma no hay
ya cosa por herir, estando ya el alma toda cauterizada con fuego de
amor? Es cosa maravillosa que, como el amor nunca está ocioso, sino
en continuo movimiento, como la llama está echando siempre llamaradas acá y allá, y el amor, cuyo oficio es herir para enamorar y
deleitar, como en la tal alma está en viva llama, estále arrojando sus
heridas como llamaradas ternísimas de delicado amor, exercitando jo-
cunda y festivalmente las artes y juegos del amor, como en el palacio
de sus bodas, como Asuero con la esposa Ester (2,17ss), mostrando allí
sus gracias, descubriéndola allí sus riquezas y la gloria de su grandeza;
por que se cumpla en esta alma lo que él dijo en los Proverbios, diciendo: *Deleitábame yo por todos los días, jugando delante de él todo
el tiempo, jugando en la redondez de las tierras, y mis deleites estar
con los hijos de los hombres* (8,30–31); es a saber, dándoselos a ellos.
Por lo cual estas heridas que son sus juegos, son llamaradas de tiernos
toques, que al alma tocan por momentos de parte de el fuego de amor,
que no está ocioso. Los cuales, dice, acaecen y hieren "de mi alma en
el más profundo centro."

9. Porque en la sustancia de el alma, donde ni el centro del sentido
ni el demonio puede llegar, pasa esta fiesta de el Espíritu Santo; y por
tanto, tanto más segura, sustancial y deleitable, cuanto más interior
ella es, porque cuanto más interior es, es más pura, y cuanto hay más
de pureza, tanto más abundante y frecuente y generalmente se comunica Dios, y así es tanto más el deleite y el gozar del alma y del espíritu, porque es Dios el obrero de todo, sin que el alma haga de suyo
nada. Que, por cuanto el alma no puede obrar de suyo nada si no es
por el sentido corporal, ayudada de él (del cual en este caso está muy
libre y muy lejos) su negocio es ya sólo recebir de Dios, el cual solo
puede en el fundo de el alma (sin ayuda de los sentidos) hacer obra
y mover al alma en ella, y así, todos los movimientos de tal alma son
divinos, y, aunque son suyos, de ella lo son, porque los hace Dios en
ella con ella, que da su voluntad y consentimiento. Y porque decir:
hiere *en el más profundo centro* de su alma, da a entender que tiene
el alma otros centros no tan profundos, conviene advertir cómo sea
esto.

10. Y, cuanto a lo primero, es de saber que el alma en cuanto espíritu
no tiene alto ni bajo más profundo y menos profundo en su ser, como

der, that it melts her in love, so that there may be fulfilled in her the same as in the bride in the Song of Solomon, who was so softened that she melted, and thus says: "As soon as my Bridegroom spoke, my soul melted" ([compare] Song of Solomon 5:6), because that is the effect which God's words have on the soul.

8. But how can this be said to wound her, since there is nothing in the soul to be wounded any more, she being completely cauterized by the fire of love? It is a marvelous thing that, since love is never idle but in constant motion, like a flame it keeps flaring up here and there. And since Love, whose duty it is to wound in order to enamor and delight, is in bright flame in that soul, he is inflicting his wounds on her like most tender flares of delicate love, merrily and festively practicing his arts and sports, as if in his wedding palace, as Ahasuerus did with his bride Esther (Esther 2:18 ff.), now displaying his charm, now revealing to her his riches and the glory of his greatness; so that there may be fulfilled in this soul what Wisdom said in the Proverbs: "Then I was by him, as one brought up with him: and I was daily his delight, rejoicing always before him; Rejoicing in the habitable part of his earth; and my delights were with the sons of men" (Proverbs 8:30–31); that is, giving those delights to them. Therefore these wounds, which are the sports of love, are flames which touch tenderly, at moments touching the soul on the part of the fire of love, which is not idle. These, she says, occur and wound her in "the deepest center of my soul."

9. Because it is in the substance of the soul, which neither the center of the senses nor the devil can reach, that this festival of the Holy Spirit takes place; and therefore, the more secure, substantial, and delightful it is the more inward it is, because the more inward it is the purer it is, and the more purity there is the more abundantly, frequently, and generally God communicates Himself, and thus the greater are the delight and enjoyment of the soul and the spirit, because God is the artisan of it all, and the soul needs to do nothing on her own. For, since the soul cannot achieve anything on her own except through her bodily senses, with their aid (and in this case she is quite free of and far from them), her task now is only to receive from God, and God alone can operate in the depths of the soul (without the aid of the senses) and move the soul there; and so, all the motions of such a soul are divine, and, though they are His, they are hers, because God causes them in her with her, she giving her will and consent. And because saying that the soul is wounded in her deepest center indicates that the soul has other, less deep centers, it is fitting to note how this can be.

10. In the first place, one must know that, as a spirit, the soul does not have deeper or less deep highs or lows in her being, as three-dimensional

tienen los cuerpos cuantitativos, que, pues en ella no hay partes, no
tiene más diferencia dentro que fuera, que toda ella es de una manera
y no tiene centro de hondo y menos hondo cuantitativo, porque no
puede estar en una parte más ilustrada que en otra, como los cuerpos
físicos, sino toda en una manera en más o en menos, como el aire, que
todo está de una manera ilustrado y no ilustrado en más o en menos.

11. En las cosas, aquello llamamos centro más profundo que es a lo
que más puede llegar su ser y virtud y la fuerza de su operación y
movimiento, y no puede pasar de allí; así como el fuego o la piedra,
que tiene virtud y movimiento natural para llegar al centro de su esfera, y no puede pasar de allí ni dejar de llegar ni estar allí si no es por
algún impedimento contrario y violento. Según esto, diremos que la
piedra cuando en alguna manera está dentro de la tierra, aunque no
sea en lo más profundo de ella, está en su centro en alguna manera,
porque está dentro de la esfera de su centro y actividad y movimiento,
pero no diremos que está en el más profundo de ella, que es el medio
de la tierra, y así siempre le queda virtud y fuerza e inclinación para
bajar y llegar hasta este más último y profundo centro, si se le quita el
impedimento de delante, y, cuando llegare y no tuviere de suyo más
virtud e inclinación para más movimiento, diremos que está en el más
profundo centro suyo.

12. El centro de el alma es Dios, al cual cuando ella hubiere llegado
según toda la capacidad de su ser y según la fuerza de su operación e inclinación, habrá llegado al último y más profundo centro suyo en Dios,
que será cuando con todas sus fuerzas entienda, ame y goce a Dios; y
cuando no ha llegado a tanto como esto, cual acaece en esta vida mortal, en que no puede el alma llegar a Dios según todas sus fuerzas,
aunque esté en este su centro, que es Dios, por gracia y por la comunicación suya que con ella tiene, por cuanto todavía tiene movimiento y
fuerza para más y no está satisfecha, aunque esté en el centro, no empero en el más profundo, pues puede ir al más profundo en Dios.

13. Es, pues, de notar que el amor es la inclinación de el alma y la
fuerza y virtud que tiene para ir a Dios, porque mediante el amor se
une el alma con Dios; y así, cuantos más grados de amor tuviere, tanto
más profundamente entra en Dios y se concentra con El. De donde
podemos decir que cuantos grados de amor de Dios el alma puede
tener, tantos centros puede tener en Dios, uno más adentro que otro,
porque el amor más fuerte es más unitivo, y de esta manera podemos
entender *las muchas mansiones* que dijo el Hijo de Dios *haber en la
casa de su Padre* (Io 14,2). De manera que para que el alma esté en
su centro, que es Dios, según lo que habemos dicho, basta que tenga

bodies do; since she has no parts, there is no difference between her out-side and her inside, for she is all of one kind, without a three-dimensional deep or less deep center, because she cannot be illumined in one part more than in another, like material bodies, but all in one way to a greater or lesser degree, like the air, which is altogether illumined or unillumined to a greater or lesser degree.

11. In material things, we apply the term "deepest center" to the far-thest place attainable by its being and powers and by the strength of its functions and motion, a place that cannot be passed. Take, for example, fire or a stone; the stone has the natural potential and movement to reach the center of its sphere, and cannot pass that center or fail to reach it and remain there, unless there is some strong opposing force. Accordingly, we say that when the stone is inside the earth in some way, even though not in its deepest part, it is in some way at its own center, because it is within the sphere of its center, activity, and movement; but we do not say that it is in the deepest part it can reach, which is the cen-ter of the earth; and so, it is still left with the potential, force, and ten-dency to descend and reach this ultimate, deepest center if the obstacle facing it is removed; whenever it arrives and no longer possesses in itself any further potential or inclination for additional motion, we say it is in its deepest center.

12. The center of the soul is God; when she has reached Him with all the capacity of her being and strength of her operation and inclination, she will have reached her ultimate, deepest center in God; this will be when she understands, loves, and enjoys God with all her might; when she has not yet come so far (as occurs in this mortal life, in which the soul cannot attain God with all her might), she may be at this center of hers, which is God, by His grace and His ongoing communication with her, but, since she still has movement and strength to do more and she is unsatis-fied, though she may be in her center, she is not in the deepest one, since she has yet to reach the deepest one in God.

13. Thus, it is to be noted that love is the soul's inclination and the strength and potential she possesses to reach God, because it is by means of love that the soul is united with God; and so, the higher the degree of love she possesses, the more deeply she enters into God and is centered on Him. Hence, we may say that, the more degrees of love for God the soul can have, the more centers she can have in God, each one deeper than the last, because the stronger love is the more unitive love; in this way we can understand the many mansions that the Son of God said were contained in His Father's house (John 14:2). So that, for the soul to be at her center, which is God, in line with what I have said, it is enough for her

un grado de amor, porque por uno solo se une con El por gracia; si tuviere dos grados, habrá unídose y concentrádose con Dios otro centro más adentro; y si llegare a tres, concentrarse ha como tres; y si llegare hasta el último grado, llegará a herir el amor de Dios hasta el último centro y más profundo de el alma, que será transformarla y esclarecerla según todo el ser y potencia y virtud de ella, según es capaz de recebir, hasta ponerla que parezca Dios. Bien así como cuando el cristal limpio y puro es embestido de la luz, que cuantos más grados de luz va recibiendo, tanto más de luz en él se va reconcentrando, y tanto más se va él esclareciendo, y puede llegar a tanto por la copiosidad de luz que recibe, que venga él a parecer todo luz, y no se divise entre la luz, estando él esclarecido en ella todo lo que puede recebir de ella, que es venir a parecer como ella.

14. Y así, en decir el alma aquí que la llama de amor hiere en su *más profundo centro*, es decir, que cuanto alcanza la sustancia, virtud y fuerza de el alma, la hiere y embiste el Espíritu Santo. Lo cual dice, no porque quiera dar a entender aquí que sea ésta tan sustancial y enteramente como la beatífica vista de Dios en la otra vida, porque, aunque el alma llegue en esta vida mortal a tan alto estado de perfección como aquí va hablando, no llega ni puede llegar a estado perfecto de gloria, aunque por ventura por vía de paso acaezca hacerle Dios alguna merced semejante; pero dícelo para dar a entender la copiosidad y abundancia de deleite y gloria que en esta manera de comunicación en el Espíritu Santo siente. El cual deleite es tanto mayor y más tierno cuanto más fuerte y sustancialmente está transformada y reconcentrada en Dios; que, por ser tanto como lo más a que en esta vida se puede llegar (aunque, como decimos, no tan perfecto como en la otra), lo llama *el más profundo centro*. Aunque, por ventura, el hábito de la caridad puede el alma tener en esta vida tan perfecto como en la otra, mas no la operación ni el fructo; aunque el fructo y la operación de amor crecen tanto de punto en este estado, que es muy semejante al de la otra, tanto que, pareciéndole al alma ser así, osa decir lo que solamente se osa decir de la otra, es a saber: *en el más profundo centro* de mi alma.

15. Y, porque las cosas raras y de que hay poca experiencia, son más maravillosas y menos creíbles, cual es la que vamos diciendo de el alma en este estado, no dudo sino que algunas personas, no lo entendiendo por sciencia ni sabiéndolo por experiencia, o no lo creerán, o lo tendrán por demasía, o pensarán que no es tanto como ello es en sí. Pero a todos éstos yo respondo, que el *Padre de las lumbres* (Iac 1,17), cuya mano no es abreviada (Is 59,1) y con abundancia se infunde sin

to have one degree of love, because even with only one she unites with Him through grace; if she should acquire two degrees, she would unite with and center herself on God one center deeper; and if she were to acquire three, she would reach a third center; and if she attains the ultimate degree, the love of God will come to wound the soul's ultimate and deepest center; this would mean transforming and enlightening her whole being, power, and potential, to the extent of her receptive capacity, until she is so changed that she resembles God. Just as when a clean, pure pane of glass is struck by the light: the more degrees of light it receives the more light is concentrated in it, and the brighter it becomes; this can reach such a degree, through the abundance of light it receives, that it finally looks as if it were all light and it cannot be distinguished from the light, being illumined by it to the extent of its receptive capacity, so that it comes to resemble it.

14. And so, when the soul says here that the flame of love wounds her deepest center, she means that, inasmuch as the Holy Spirit is reaching her substance, potential, and strength, He is wounding and assailing her. She does not say this because she wants to indicate here that this is as substantial and complete a vision as the blissful sight of God in the next world, because even though in this mortal life the soul may reach such a high state of perfection as the one described here, she does not and cannot reach a perfect state of glory, though perhaps God may grant her some similar favor transitorily; rather, she says this to indicate the abundance and fullness of delight and glory which she feels in this kind of communication with the Holy Spirit. This delight is the greater and more tender the more strongly and substantively she is transformed in and concentrated on God. Because it is equivalent to the most that can be attained in this life (though, as I said, not as perfect as in the next life), she calls it the deepest center. Though the soul may perhaps have as perfect a propensity to charitable love in this life as in the next, she does not have the same operation and fruition; although the fruition and operation of love increase so fully in this state, which is very similar to that of the next life, that the soul, believing that it is so, is bold enough to say what can only be asserted of the next life: in the deepest center of my soul.

15. And because unusual things, and those outside normal experience, are more miraculous and incredible, such as what I say here about the soul in this state, I have no doubt but that some people, failing to understand it by their knowledge or to be acquainted with it by experience, either will not believe it or will take it for an exaggeration, or will not believe it is as great as it actually is. But to all these I reply that the "Father of lights" (James 1:17), Whose hand is not shortened (Isaiah 59:1), Who

aceptación de personas (Ephes 6,9) doquiera que haya lugar (como el rayo del sol), mostrándose siempre también él a ellos en los caminos y vías alegremente, no duda ni tiene en poco *tener sus deleites con los hijos de los hombres* de mancomún *en la redondez de las tierras* (Prov 8,31). Y no es de tener por increíble que a un alma ya examinada, probada y purgada en el fuego de tribulaciones y trabajos y variedad de tentaciones, y hallada fiel en el amor, deje de cumplirse en esta fiel alma en esta vida lo que el Hijo de Dios prometió, conviene a saber: que *si alguno le amase, vendría la Santísima Trinidad en él y moraría de asiento en él* (Io 14,23); lo cual es ilustrándole el entendimiento divinamente en la sabiduría de el Hijo, y deleitándole la voluntad en el Espíritu Santo, y absorbiéndola el Padre poderosa y fuertemente en el abrazo abisal de su dulzura.

16. Y si esto usa con algunas almas—como es verdad que lo usa—, de creer es que esta de que vamos hablando no se quedará atrás en estas mercedes de Dios, pues que lo que de ella vamos diciendo, según la operación de el Espíritu Santo que en ella hace, es mucho más que lo que en la comunicación y transformación de amor pasa, porque lo uno es como ascua encendida, y lo otro como, según habemos dicho, como ascua en que tanto se afervora el fuego, que no solamente está encendida, sino echando llama viva. Y así, estas dos maneras de unión: solamente de amor, y unión con inflamación de amor, son en cierta manera comparadas *al fuego de Dios,* que dice Isaías *que esta en Sión, y al horno de Dios que está en Jerusalén* (31,9); que la una significa la Iglesia militante, en que está el fuego de la caridad no en extremo encendido, y la otra significa *visión de paz,* que es la triunfante, donde este fuego está como horno encendido en perfección de amor. Y aunque, como habemos dicho, esta alma no ha llegado a tanta perfección como ésta, todavía, en comparación de la otra unión común, es como horno encendido, con visión tanto más pacífica y gloriosa y tierna, cuanto la llama es más clara y resplandeciente que el fuego en el carbón.

17. Por tanto, sintiendo el alma que esta viva llama del amor vivamente le está comunicando todos los bienes, porque este divino amor todo lo trae consigo; dice: *¡Oh llama de amor viva, que tiernamente hieres!;* que es como si dijera: ¡Oh encendido amor, que con tus amorosos movimientos regaladamente estás glorificándome según la mayor capacidad y fuerza de mi alma!; es a saber, dándome inteligencia divina según toda la habilidad y capacidad de mi entendimiento, y comunicándome el amor según la mayor fuerza de mi voluntad, y deleitándome en la sustancia de el alma con el torrente de tu deleite

copiously infuses Himself with no respect to persons (Ephesians 6:9) wherever there is room (like a sunbeam), and Who in addition always shows Himself to people cheerfully on roads and paths, does not hesitate to, or think it unimportant to, "have His delight with the sons of men," jointly, "in the roundness of the lands" ([complete] Proverbs 8:31). And it should not be considered incredible that, when a soul has already been examined, tested, and purified in the fire of tribulations, toils, and varied temptations, and found to be faithful in love, there should be fulfilled in this life for that faithful soul that which the Son of God promised: that, if anyone loved Him, the Holy Trinity would come into him and take up Their abode in him ([compare] John 14:23); that is, by illumining his intellect divinely in the wisdom of the Son and delighting his will in the Holy Spirit, while the Father absorbs his will mightily and powerfully in the tremendous embrace of His sweetness.

16. And if He does this for some souls—as He really does—it should be believed that the soul we are discussing will not be behindhand in receiving these favors from God, since what I am saying of her, through the working done in her by the Holy Spirit, far surpasses what occurs in the communication and transformation of love, because the latter is like a burning coal, but the former, as I have said, is like a coal in which the heat of the fire is so intense that it not only burns, but emits a living flame. And so these two kinds of union—the union merely of love and the union in a blaze of love—can in a way be compared to the fire of God which Isaiah says is in Zion and to the furnace of God which is in Jerusalem (Isaiah 31:9); the former connotes the Church Militant, in which the fire of charity is not yet lighted to an extreme, while the latter connotes the "vision of peace," the Church Triumphant, in which this fire is like a furnace blazing in the perfection of love. And though, as I have said, this soul has not attained such great perfection as that one, nevertheless, compared to that other ordinary union, she is like a blazing furnace, with a vision the more pacific, glorious, and tender the more the flame is brighter and more resplendent than the fire hidden in the coal.

17. Therefore, the soul, feeling that this living flame of love is vividly communicating all good things to her, because all this is a concomitant of that divine love, says: "O living flame of love, you that tenderly wound!"—as if to say: "O blazing love, which with your loving motions are delightfully glorifying me to my greatest capacity and power!"—that is, by giving me divine knowledge to the greatest capacity and ability of my intellect, and communicating love to me to the greatest power of my will, and delighting me in my substance with the torrent of your delight at your divine contact and substantive juncture in proportion to the greatest purity

en tu divino contacto y junta sustancial según la mayor pureza de mi sustancia y la capacidad y anchura de mi memoria. Y esto acaece así, y más de lo que se puede y alcanza a decir, al tiempo que se llevanta en el alma esta llama de amor; que por cuanto el alma, según su sustancia y potencias: memoria, entendimiento y voluntad, está bien purgada, la sustancia divina, que, como dice el Sabio (Sap 7,24), *toca en todas partes por su limpieza,* profunda y sutil y subidamente con su divina llama la absorbe en sí, y en aquel absorbimiento de el alma en la sabiduría, el Espíritu Santo exercita los vibramientos gloriosos de su llama. Por ser tan suave, dice el alma luego: "pues ya no eres esquiva."

18. Es a saber, pues ya no afliges, ni aprietas, ni fatigas como antes hacías. Porque conviene saber que esta llama de Dios cuando el alma estaba en estado de purgación espiritual, que es cuando va entrando en contemplación, no le era tan amigable y suave como ahora lo es en este estado de unión. Y en declarar cómo esto sea nos habemos de detener algún tiempo.

19. En lo cual es de saber que, antes que este divino fuego de amor se introduzga y se una en la sustancia de el alma por acabada y perfecta purgación y pureza, esta llama, que es el Espíritu Santo, está hiriendo en el alma, gastándole y consumiéndole las imperfecciones de sus malos hábitos; y ésta es la operación de el Espíritu Santo, en la cual la dispone para la divina unión y transformación de amor en Dios. Porque es de saber que el mismo fuego de amor que después se une con el alma glorificándola, es el que antes la embiste purgándola; bien así como el mismo fuego que entra en el madero es el que primero le está embistiendo e hiriendo con su llama, enjugándole y desnudándole de sus feos accidentes, hasta disponerle con su calor, tanto, que pueda entrar en él y transformarle en sí. Y esto llaman los espirituales *vía purgativa;* en el cual exercicio el alma padece mucho detrimento y siente graves penas en el espíritu (que de ordinario redundan en el sentido), siéndole esta llama muy esquiva. Porque en esta disposición de purgación no le es esta llama clara, sino oscura, que, si alguna luz le da, es para ver sólo y sentir sus miserias y defectos; ni le es suave, sino penosa, porque, aunque algunas veces le pega calor de amor, es con tormento y aprieto; y no le es deleitable, sino seca, porque, aunque alguna vez por su benignidad le da algún gusto para esforzarla y animarla, antes y después acaece lo lasta y paga con otro tanto trabajo; ni le es reficionadora y pacífica, sino consumidora y argüidora, haciéndola desfallecer y penar en el conocimiento propio; y así, no le es gloriosa, porque antes la pone miserable y amarga en luz espiritual que la da de propio conocimiento, *enviando Dios fuego,* como dice

of my substance and the capacity and breadth of my memory. And this occurs, in a way beyond what can be said and described, when this flame of love arises in the soul; for when the soul, in her substance and in her powers of memory, intellect, and will, is thoroughly purified, the substance of God, which, as the sage says, touches all places because of its cleanness (Wisdom of Solomon 7:24), profoundly, subtly, and sublimely absorbs her into itself with its divine flame, and in that absorption of the soul into wisdom, the Holy Spirit manifests the glorious flickerings of His flame. Because this is so gentle, the soul next says: "since you are no longer harsh."

18. That is, since you no longer afflict, oppress, or fatigue me as you did before. Because one must know that when the soul was in the state of spiritual purification, which is when it was entering into contemplation, this flame of God was not as friendly and gentle to her as it now is in this state of union. To explain how this is, I must tarry for a while.

19. Regarding this, one must know that, before this divine fire of love is introduced and merged into the soul's substance through her excellent and perfect purgation and purity, this flame, which is the Holy Spirit, has been wounding the soul, wearing away and consuming the imperfections of her evil propensities; this is the working of the Holy Spirit, in which He prepares her for the divine union and loving transformation in God. Because one must know that the fire of love which later unites with the soul, glorifying her, is the same fire that was formerly assailing her and purifying her; just as the fire that enters the log is the same fire that previously was assailing it and wounding it with its flame, drying it out and burning away its ugly irregularities, until it made it so ready with its heat that it could enter it and transform it into itself. This is what spiritual people call the purgative way; in the course of it the soul suffers much harm and feels severe pains in her spirit (which usually flow over into her senses), this flame being very harsh to her. Because in this purificatory preparation it is not a bright flame to her, but a dark one, which, if it gives her any light, it is only enough to see and feel her wretchedness and her defects; nor is it gentle to her, but painful, because, even though it occasionally lends her the warmth of love, it is with torment and oppression; and it is not delightful to her, but arid, because, though in its kindness it occasionally gives her some pleasure to encourage and enliven her, before and after this happens it exacts retribution with an equal amount of travail; nor is it restorative and peaceful to her, but consuming and contradictory, making her swoon and suffer from self-knowledge; thus, it is not glorious for her, because, on the contrary, it makes her miserable and bitter by the spiritual light of self-knowledge it gives her, just as "God sends

Jeremías, *en sus huesos, y enseñándola* (Thren 1,13), y, como también dice David, *examinándola en fuego* (Ps 16,3).

20. Y así, en esta sazón padece el alma acerca del entendimiento grandes tinieblas, acerca de la voluntad grandes sequedades y aprietos, y en la memoria grave noticia de sus miserias, por cuanto el ojo espiritual está muy claro en el conocimiento propio; y en la sustancia de el alma padece desamparo y suma pobreza, seca y fría, y a veces caliente, no hallando en nada alivio, ni un pensamiento que la consuele, ni aun poder levantar el corazón a Dios, habiéndosele puesto esta llama tan esquiva como dice Job que en este exercicio hizo Dios con él, diciendo: *Mudado te me has en cruel* (30,21); porque, cuando estas cosas juntas padece el alma, verdaderamente le parece que Dios se ha hecho cruel contra ella y desabrido.

21. No se puede encarecer lo que el alma padece en este tiempo, es a saber, muy poco menos que un purgatorio. Y no sabría yo ahora dar a entender esta esquivez cuánta sea ni hasta dónde llega lo que en ella se pasa y siente, sino con lo que a este propósito dice Jeremías con estas palabras: *Yo, varón, que veo mi pobreza en la vara de su indignación; hame amenazado y trájome a las tinieblas y no a la luz: tanto ha vuelto y convertido su mano contra mí. Hizo envejecer mi piel y mi carne y desmenuzó mis huesos; cercóme en derredor, y rodeóme de hiel y trabajo; en tenebrosidades me colocó como muertos sempiternos; edificó en derredor de mí por que no salga; agravóme las prisiones; y, demás de esto, cuando hubiere dado voces y rogado, ha excluido mi oración; cerróme mis caminos con piedras cuadradas, y trastornó mis pisadas y mis sendas* (Thren 3,1–9). Todo esto dice Jeremías, y va allí diciendo mucho más. Que, por cuanto en esta manera está Dios medecinando y curando al alma en sus muchas enfermedades para darle salud, por fuerza ha de penar según su dolencia en la tal purga y cura; porque aquí le pone Tobías el corazón sobre las brasas, para que en él se extrique y desenvuelva todo género de demonio (Tob 6,8); y así, aquí van saliendo a la luz todas sus enfermedades, poniéndoselas en cura y delante de sus ojos a sentir.

22. Y las flaquezas y miserias que antes el alma tenía asentadas y encubiertas en sí, las cuales antes no veía ni sentía, ya con la luz y calor del fuego divino las ve y las siente; así como la humedad que había en el madero no se conocía hasta que dio en él el fuego y le hizo sudar, humear y respender; y así hace el alma imperfecta cerca de esta llama. Porque, ¡oh cosa admirable!, levántanse en el alma a esta sazón contrarios contra contrarios: los de el alma contra los de Dios, que embisten el alma, y, como dicen los filósofos, unos relucen cerca de los

fire into her bones, to instruct her," as Jeremiah says ([compare] Lamentations 1:13), and as David also says, "testing her in fire" ([compare] Psalm 17:3).

20. And so, at this time the soul suffers great darkness in her intellect, great aridity and oppression in her will, and weighty notice of her wretchedness in her memory, because her spiritual eye is very clear in self-knowledge; and in her substance she suffers abandonment and dire poverty; she is arid and cold, at times hot, finding no relief in anything, nor any thought to comfort her, nor even being able to raise up her heart to God, this flame having become as harsh as the one Job says God directed against him in his trials: "Thou art become cruel to me" (Job 30:21); because, when the soul suffers all these things together, it truly seems to her that God has become cruel and surly to her.

21. One cannot exaggerate what the soul suffers at that time—not much less than a purgatory. And I would be unable now to indicate the magnitude of this harshness or the extent of what befalls the soul, or what she feels, except with these words spoken by Jeremiah on this subject: "I am the man that hath seen affliction by the rod of his wrath. He hath led me, and brought me into darkness, but not into light. Surely against me is he turned; he turneth his hand against me all the day. My flesh and my skin hath he made old: he hath broken my bones. He hath builded against me, and compassed me with gall and travail. He hath set me in dark places, as they that be dead of old. He hath hedged me about, that I cannot get out; he hath made my chain heavy. Also when I cry and shout, he shutteth out my prayer. He hath inclosed my ways with hewn stone, he hath made my paths crooked" (Lamentations 3:1–9). Jeremiah says all this, and goes on to say much more. For, since God is in this way doctoring and curing the soul in her many infirmities to give her health, she must necessarily suffer in proportion to her ailment in that purge and cure; because in this situation Tobias places the fish's heart on the coals, so that all sorts of demons may writhe out of it and leave it free (Tobit 6:8); and so, in this case all the soul's infirmities come to light, being cured for her and visible to her eyes.

22. And the weakness and wretchedness formerly lodged and hidden within the soul, which she previously did not see or feel, she now sees and feels in the light and heat of the divine fire; just as the dampness contained in the log was not recognized until the fire touched it, making it sweat, smoke, and glow; such is the reaction of the imperfect soul to this flame. Because (O wondrous thing!) at this time there arise in the soul one set of opponents against another: the soul's fighters against God's, which assail the soul; and, as the philosophers say, one set makes the

otros y hacen la guerra en el sujeto de el alma, procurando los unos expeler a los otros por reinar ellos en ella, conviene saber: las virtudes y propiedades de Dios en extremo perfectas contra los hábitos y propiedades del sujeto del alma en extremo imperfectos, padeciendo ella dos contrarios en sí; porque, como esta llama es de extremada luz, embistiendo ella en el alma, su luz luce en las tinieblas de el alma, que también son extremadas, y el alma entonces siente sus tinieblas naturales y viciosas, que se ponen contra la sobrenatural luz y no siente la luz sobrenatural, porque no la tiene en sí como sus tinieblas, que las tiene en sí, *y las tinieblas no comprehenden a la luz* (Io 1,5). Y así, estas tinieblas suyas sentirá en tanto que la luz las embistiere, porque no pueden las almas ver sus tinieblas si no embistiere en ellas la divina luz, hasta que, expeliéndolas la luz, quede ilustrada el alma y vea la luz en sí transformada, habiendo sido limpiado y fortalecido el ojo espiritual con la luz divina. Porque inmensa luz en vista impura y flaca totalmente le era tinieblas, sujetando en eminente sensible la potencia; y así, érale esta llama esquiva en la vista del entendimiento.

23. Y porque esta llama de suyo es amorosa en extremo y tierna y amorosamente embiste en la voluntad, y la voluntad de suyo es seca y dura en extremo, y lo duro se siente cerca de lo tierno, y la sequedad cerca del amor, embistiendo esta llama amorosa y tiernamente en la voluntad, siente la voluntad su natural dureza y sequedad para con Dios; y no siente el amor y ternura de la llama estando ella prevenida con dureza y sequedad, en que no caben estos otros contrarios de ternura y amor, hasta que, siendo expelidas por ellos, reine en la voluntad amor y ternura de Dios. Y de esta manera era esta llama esquiva a la voluntad, haciéndola sentir y padecer su dureza y sequedad. Y, ni más ni menos, porque esta llama es amplísima e inmensa y la voluntad es estrecha y angosta, siente su estrechura y angostura la voluntad en tanto que la llama la embiste, hasta que, dando en ella, la dilate y ensanche, y haga capaz de sí misma. Y porque también esta llama es sabrosa y dulce, y la voluntad tenía el paladar del espíritu destemplado con humores de desordenadas afecciones, érale desabrida y amarga y no podía gustar del dulce manjar del amor de Dios. Y desta manera también siente la voluntad su aprieto y sinsabor cerca de esta amplísima y sabrosísima llama, y no siente el sabor de ella, porque no la siente en sí, sino lo que tiene en sí, que es su miseria. Y, finalmente, porque esta llama es de inmensas riquezas y bondad y deleites, y el alma de suyo es pobrísima y no tiene bien ninguno ni de qué se satisfacer, conoce y siente claramente sus miserias y pobreza y malicia cerca de estas riquezas y bondad y deleites, y no conoce las riquezas,

other manifest, and they wage war in the soul's identity, one set trying to drive out the other to prevail in her; that is, the extremely perfect virtues and qualities of God versus the extremely imperfect propensities and qualities of the soul's identity—so that she suffers from their combat within her. Because, when this flame, which consists of extreme light, assails the soul, its light shines in the soul's darkness, which is also extreme, and then the soul feels her natural sinful darkness, which opposes the supernatural light, and she does not sense the supernatural light, because she does not have it within her as she has the darkness within her, and "darkness does not understand the light" ([compare] John 1:5). And so, she will feel this darkness of hers as long as the light assails it, because souls cannot see their own darkness unless the divine light strikes them, until it is driven out by the light, and the soul is left illumined and can see the light transformed into her, her spiritual eye having been cleansed and strengthened by the divine light. Because the immense light on her unclear, weak sight was totally darkness to her, subduing her sensory power extensively; thus, this flame was harsh to her in the sight of her intellect.

23. And because this flame is per se extremely loving and tender, and strikes the will tenderly, while the will is per se extremely arid and hard, and hardness is felt when placed alongside softness, and aridity when placed alongside love, whenever this flame strikes the will lovingly and tenderly, the will feels its own natural hardness and aridity toward God; and it does not feel the flame's love and tenderness, being clad in hardness and aridity, which cannot absorb those opposites, tenderness and love, until the former are driven out by the latter and God's love and tenderness reign in the will. And in this way this flame was harsh to the will, making it feel, and suffer from, its hardness and aridity. And in the same way, because this flame is very ample and immense, while the will is narrow and tight, the will feels its narrowness and tightness when the flame strikes it, until, entering the will, it expands and widens it, making it able to contain the flame. And though this flame is also delectable and sweet, because the palate of the will's spirit was distempered with the humors of disordered affections, the flame was unpleasant and bitter to it, and the will was unable to savor the sweet food of God's love. And in this way the will also feels its oppression and incapacity for enjoyment when placed alongside this most ample and delectable flame, and fails to savor it, because it does not feel it within itself, but feels only what it does contain: its own wretchedness. And, lastly, because this flame is immensely rich in goodness and delights, while the soul per se is very poor and owns no goods or anything to content her, she clearly recognizes and feels her misery, poverty, and wickedness when placed alongside this wealth of good-

bondad y deleites de la llama, porque la malicia no comprehende a la bondad, ni la pobreza a las riquezas, etc., hasta tanto que esta llama acabe de purificar el alma y con su transformación la enriquezca, glorifique y deleite. De esta manera le era antes esquiva esta llama al alma sobre lo que se puede decir, peleando en ella unos contrarios contra otros: Dios, que es todas las perfecciones, contra los hábitos imperfectos de ella, para que, transformándola en sí, la suavice y pacifique y esclarezca, como el fuego hace al madero cuando ha entrado en él.

24. Esta purgación en pocas almas acaece tan fuerte; sólo en aquellas que el Señor quiere levantar a más alto grado de unión, porque a cada una dispone con purga más o menos fuerte, según el grado a que la quiere levantar, y según también la impureza e imperfección de ella. Y así, esta pena se parece a la del Purgatorio, porque así como se purgan allí los espíritus para poder ver a Dios por clara visión en la otra vida, ansí, en su manera, se purgan aquí las almas para poder transformarse en El por amor en ésta.

25. La intensión de esta purgación y cómo es en más y cómo en menos, y cuándo es según el entendimiento y cuándo según la voluntad, y cómo según la memoria y cuándo y cómo también según la sustancia del alma, y también cuándo todo y según todo, y la purgación de la parte sensitiva, y cómo se conocerá cuándo la es la una y la otra, y a qué tiempo y punto o sazón de camino espiritual comienza, porque lo tratamos en la *Noche oscura de la Subida de el Monte Carmelo* y no hace ahora a nuestro propósito, no lo digo. Baste saber ahora que el mismo Dios que quiere entrar en el alma por unión y transformación de amor, es el que antes está embistiendo en ella y purgándola con la luz y calor de su divina llama, así como el mismo fuego que entra en el madero es el que le dispone antes, como habemos dicho; y así, la mesma que ahora le es suave estando dentro embestida en ella, le era antes esquiva estando fuera embistiendo en ella.

26. Y esto es lo que quiere dar a entender cuando dice el alma el presente verso: *Pues ya no eres esquiva,* que en suma es como si dijera: Pues ya no solamente no me eres oscura como antes, pero eres la divina luz de mi entendimiento, que te puedo ya mirar; y no solamente no haces desfallecer mi flaqueza, mas antes eres la fortaleza de mi voluntad con que te puedo amar y gozar, estando toda convertida en amor divino; y ya no eres pesadumbre y aprieto para la sustancia de mi alma, mas antes eres la gloria y deleites y anchura de ella, pues que de mí se puede decir lo que se canta en los divinos Cantares, di-

ness and delights, but does not recognize the riches, goodness, and delights of the flame because wickedness cannot understand goodness, nor poverty wealth, etc., until this flame achieves the purification of the soul, and enriches, glorifies, and delights her in her transformation. And so, previously, this flame was harsher to her than any words can tell, while two sets of opposites were fighting inside her: God, Who is every perfection, versus her own imperfect propensities, so that, transforming her in Himself, he might soften, pacify, and enlighten her, as the fire does to the log once it has entered it.

24. Only in a few souls is this purification so strong, only in those whom it pleases the Lord to raise to a higher degree of union, because He prepares each one with a more or less powerful purging, in proportion to the degree to which He wishes to raise her, and also in proportion to her impurity and imperfection. And so, this suffering resembles that of Purgatory, because, just as spirits are purified there so that they can see God with clear sight in the next life, thus, in their way, souls are purified here so they can be transformed in Him through love in this life.

25. The intensity of this purgation; the different degrees of it; when it affects the intellect, when it affects the will, and when it affects the memory, and also when and how it affects the substance of the soul, and also when it affects her entirely; and the purification of her sensory part, and how to recognize when it affects both her sensory and her spiritual parts, and at what time, point, or moment of the spiritual journey it begins—all these matters I shall not discuss here, because I have already handled them in the *Dark Night* division of my *Ascent of Mount Carmel* and they are not to our purpose now. Let it suffice to know now that it was God (Who now wishes to enter the soul by loving union and transformation) Who was formerly assailing her and purifying her with the light and heat of His divine flame, just as the fire that enters the log is the same fire that prepares it previously, as I have said; and so, the flame that is now gentle to the soul, having already assailed her and now being within her, is the same flame that was formerly harsh to her while it was outside assailing her.

26. And this is what the soul wishes to indicate when she speaks the present line: "since you are no longer harsh," which is a brief equivalent to saying: "Then, you are now not only not dark to me as you were before, but also you are the divine light of my intellect, so that I can now behold you; and not only do you not make my weakness grow faint, but, on the contrary, you are the strength of my will so that I can love and enjoy you, being now completely changed into divine love; and you are no longer a heaviness and oppression to my substance, but, on the contrary, you are its glory, delight, and amplitude, since that can be said of me which is sung in the divine Song

ciendo: *¿Quién es esta que sube de el desierto abundante de deleites, estribando sobre su Amado, acá y allá vertiendo amor?* (8,5). Pues esto es ansí, "acaba ya, si quieres."

27. Es a saber: acaba ya de consumar conmigo perfectamente el matrimonio espiritual con tu beatífica vista—porque ésta es la que pide el alma—; que, aunque es verdad que en este estado tan alto está el alma tanto más conforme y satisfecha cuanto más transformada en amor, y para sí ninguna cosa sabe ni acierta a pedir, sino todo para su Amado (pues *la caridad,* como dice san Pablo [1 Cor 13,5], *no pretende para sí sus cosas,* sino para el amado), porque vive en esperanza todavía, en que no se puede dejar de sentir vacío, tiene tanto de gemido (aunque suave y regalado) cuanto le falta para la acabada posesión de la adopción de los hijos de Dios (Rom 8,23), donde, consumándose su gloria, se quietará su apetito; el cual, aunque acá más juntura tenga con Dios, nunca se hartará ni quietará hasta que parezca su gloria (Ps 16,15), mayormente tiniendo ya el sabor y golosina de ella, como aquí se tiene; que es tal, que, si Dios no tuviese aquí favorecida también la carne, amparando al natural con su diestra—como hizo con Moisés en la piedra, para que sin morirse pudiese ver su gloria (Ex 33,22)—, a cada llamarada de éstas se corrompería el natural y moriría, no tiniendo la parte inferior vaso para sufrir tanto y tan subido fuego de gloria.

28. Y por eso este apetito y la petición de él no es aquí con pena, que no está aquí el alma capaz de tenerla; sino con deseo suave y deleitable pidiéndolo en conformidad de su espíritu y sentido: que por eso dice en el verso: *acaba ya si quieres,* porque está la voluntad y apetito tan hecho uno con Dios, que tiene por su gloria complirse todo lo que Dios quiere. Pero son tales las asomadas de gloria y amor que en estos toques se trasluce quedar a la puerta por entrar en el alma, no cabiendo por la angostura de la casa terrestre, que antes sería poco amor no pedir entrada en aquella perfección y cumplimiento de amor. Porque, demás de esto, ve allí el alma que en aquella fuerza de deleitable comunicación de el Esposo la está el Espíritu Santo provocando y convidando con aquella inmensa gloria que le está propuniendo ante sus ojos, con maravillosos modos y suaves afectos, diciéndole a su espíritu lo que en los Cantares a la esposa; lo cual refiere ella, diciendo: *Mirad lo que me está diciendo mi Esposo: Levántate y date priesa, amiga mía, paloma mía, hermosa mía, y ven; pues ya ha pasado el invierno, y la lluvia se fue y alejó, y las flores han parecido en nuestra tierra, y ha llegado el tiempo del podar. La voz de la tortolilla se ha oído en nuestra tierra; la higuera ha producido sus fructos,*

of Solomon: 'Who is this who ascends from the wilderness, abounding in delights, leaning on her Beloved, pouring forth love all around?' ([compare] Song of Solomon 8:5). Since this is so: 'please complete your task.'"

27. That is: complete your task of consummating perfectly the spiritual marriage between me and the beatific sight of you—because it is this that the soul is requesting. For, though it is true that in this very lofty state the soul is the more in conformity and satisfied the more she is transformed in love, and cannot come to ask anything for herself, but everything for her Beloved (since charity, as Saint Paul says [I Corinthians 13:5], "seeketh not her own," but the good of the loved one), nevertheless, since she is still living in hope, and still cannot avoid feeling empty, she has as much moaning (though gentle and comforting) as she needs for the complete possession of the "adoption" of the children of God (Romans 8:23), in which, her glory being consummated, her appetite will be appeased; no matter how closely she is joined to God in this life, it will never be sated or appeased until His glory appears (Psalm 17:15), especially since she already has a taste and yearning for it, as stated here; this yearning is so great that, if God were not here favoring the flesh, as well, and protecting the soul's body with His right hand—as he did with Moses in the rock, so he could see His glory without dying (Exodus 33:22)—at each flaring up of these yearnings her body would be corrupted and die, her lower part not having the capacity to undergo such great and sublime fire of glory.

28. Therefore the request to still this appetite is not made here with pain, because here the soul is unable to feel any, but with a gentle, delightful desire, a request in conformity with the soul's spirit and senses; this is why she says in this line: "please complete your task." Because her will and appetite are now so at one with God that she considers it her glory to fulfill all of God's wishes. But so powerful are the sudden flashes of glory and love which in these moments of contact evidently remain outside the soul's door, and cannot enter because the narrowness of her earthly house cannot contain them, that it would, on the contrary, betoken a lack of love not to ask entry into that perfection and fulfillment of love. Because, besides this, the soul sees here that in this force of delightful communication with her Bridegroom, the Holy Spirit is inciting and inviting her with that immense glory which He is setting before her eyes, in wondrous ways and sweet affections, saying to her spirit what He says in the Song of Solomon to His bride, who cites it in these words: "My beloved spake, and said unto me, Rise up, my love, my fair one, and come away. For, lo, the winter is past, the rain is over and gone; The flowers appear on the earth; the time of the singing of birds is come, and the voice of the turtle is heard in our land; The fig tree putteth forth her green figs, and the vines with the ten-

las floridas viñas han dado su olor. Levántate, amiga mía, graciosa mía, y ven, paloma mía, en los horados de la piedra, en la caverna de la cerca; muéstrame tu rostro, suene tu voz en mis oídos, porque tu vos es dulce y tu rostro hermoso (2,10–14). Todas estas cosas siente el alma y las entiende distintísimamente en subido sentido de gloria, que la está mostrando el Espíritu Santo en aquel suave y tierno llamear, con gana de entralle en aquella gloria; y por eso ella aquí, provocada, responde diciendo: *Acaba ya si quieres;* en lo cual le pide al Esposo aquellas dos peticiones que él nos enseñó en el Evangelio, conviene saber: *Adveniat regnum tuum; fiat voluntas tua* (Mt 6,10); y así, es como si dijera: *Acaba,* es a saber, de darme este reino; *si quieres,* esto es, según es tu voluntad.

29. Y para que así sea, "rompe la tela de este dulce encuentro"; la cual tela es la que impide este tan grande negocio, porque es fácil cosa llegar a Dios quitados los impedimentos y rompidas las telas que dividen la junta entre el alma y Dios. Las telas que pueden impedir a esta junta, y que se han de romper para que se haga y posea perfectamente el alma a Dios, podemos decir que son tres, conviene a saber: temporal, en que se comprehenden todas las criaturas; natural, en que se comprehenden las operaciones e inclinaciones puramente naturales; la tercera, sensitiva, en que sólo se comprehende la unión del alma con el cuerpo, que es vida sensitiva y animal, de que dice san Pablo: *Sabemos que, si esta nuestra casa terrestre se desata, tenemos habitación de Dios en los cielos* (2 Cor 5,1). Las dos primeras telas, de necesidad se han de haber rompido para llegar a esta posesión de unión de Dios, en que todas las cosas del mundo están negadas y renunciadas, y todos los apetitos y afectos naturales mortificados, y las operaciones de el alma de naturales ya hechas divinas; todo lo cual se rompió e hizo en el alma por los encuentros esquivos de esta llama cuando ella era esquiva, porque en la purgación espiritual que arriba hemos dicho acaba el alma de romper en estas dos telas, y de ahí viene a unirse con Dios como aquí está, y no queda por romper más que la tercera de la vida sensitiva. Que por eso dice aquí *tela,* y no *telas;* porque no hay más que ésta que romper, la cual, por ser ya tan sutil y delgada y espiritualizada con esta unión de Dios, no la encuentra la llama rigurosamente como a las otras dos hacía, sino sabrosa y dulcemente. Que por eso aquí le llama *dulce encuentro,* el cual es tanto más dulce y sabroso, cuanto más le parece que le va a romper la tela de la vida.

30. Donde es de saber que el amor natural de las almas que llegan

der grape give a good smell. Arise, my love, my fair one, and come away. O my dove, that art in the clefts of the rock, in the secret places of the stairs, let me see thy countenance, let me hear thy voice; for sweet is thy voice, and thy countenance is comely" (Song of Solomon 2:10–14). The soul feels and understands all these things very clearly in her sublime glorified senses, things the Holy Spirit is showing her in that gentle and tender flaming, desiring to let her enter that glory; therefore here she is incited and replies: "please complete your task." Therewith she makes of the Bridegroom those two requests which He taught us in the Gospels: "Thy kingdom come. Thy will be done" (Matthew 6:10); and so, it is as if she were saying: "complete your task" (that is, of giving me this kingdom), "please" (that is, according to Your will).

29. And in order that this may be so, "rend the veil of this sweet encounter!" It is this veil which hinders this great task, because it is easy to reach God once the obstacles are removed and the veils torn which stand between the juncture of the soul and God. We may say that there are three veils that can hinder this juncture, and have to be torn if the soul is to adapt to God and possess Him perfectly: a worldly veil, comprising all the created things; a natural veil, comprising the purely natural functions and inclinations; and, third, the sensory veil, consisting solely in the union between soul and body, which is the sensory, animal life of which Saint Paul says: "We know that, if this earthly house of ours dissolves, we have the abode of God in heaven" ([compare] II Corinthians 5:1). The first two veils must necessarily have been torn to attain this possession of union with God, in which all worldly things are denied and renounced, every natural appetite and affection mortified, and the soul's functions already changed from natural to divine; all of this tearing was done in the soul by the harsh attacks of that flame while it was still harsh, because in the spiritual purification I have described above the soul finally tears those two veils, thus coming to unite with God in this life; only the third veil of bodily life remains to be torn. That is why she here says "veil" and not "veils"; because there is only this one left to tear. But, because it is now so subtle, thin, and spiritualized by this union with God, the flame does not attack it severely as it did the first two, but delightfully and sweetly. That is why she here calls this a "sweet encounter," being the sweeter and the more delightful to her the more she believes that it is going to rend the veil of her life.

30. Hence, one must know that when souls attain this state,[18] although

---

18. I here omit the reference in the Spanish text to the "natural love" of these souls, which is apparently either intrusive in the text, or a false start to the sentence.

a este estado, aunque la condición de su muerte en cuanto el natural es semejante a las demás, pero en la causa y en el modo de la muerte hay mucha diferencia, porque, si las otras mueren muerte causada por enfermedad o por longura de días, éstas, aunque en enfermedad mueran o en cumplimiento de edad, no las arranca el alma sino algún ímpetu y encuentro de amor mucho más subido que los pasados y más poderoso y valeroso, pues pudo romper la tela y llevarse la joya de el alma. Y así, la muerte de semejantes almas es muy suave y muy dulce, más que les fue la vida espiritual toda su vida; pues que mueren con más subidos ímpetus y encuentros sabrosos de amor, siendo ellas como el cisne, que canta más suavemente cuando se muere. Que por eso dijo David que *era preciosa la muerte de los santos en el acatamiento de Dios* (Ps 115,15), porque aquí vienen en uno a juntarse todas las riquezas de el alma, y van allí a entrar los ríos de el amor del alma en la mar, los cuales están allí ya tan anchos y represados, que parecen ya mares; juntándose lo primero y lo postrero de sus tesoros para acompañar al justo que va y parte para su reino, oyéndose ya las alabanzas desde los fines de la tierra, que, como dice Isaías, *son gloria del justo* (24,16).

31. Sintiéndose, pues, el alma a la sazón de estos gloriosos encuentros tan al canto de salir a poseer acabada y perfectamente su reino, en las abundancias que se ve está enriquecida—porque aquí se conoce pura y rica y llena de virtudes y dispuesta para ello, porque en este estado deja Dios al alma ver su hermosura y fíale los dones y virtudes que le ha dado, porque todo se le vuelve en amor y alabanzas, sin toque de presunción ni vanidad, no habiendo ya levadura de imperfección que corrompa la masa—, y como ve que no le falta más que romper esta flaca tela de vida natural en que se siente enredada, presa e impedida su libertad, *con deseo de verse desatada y verse con Cristo* (Phil 1,23), haciéndole lástima que una vida tan baja y flaca la impida otra tan alta y fuerte, pide que se rompa, diciendo: *Rompe la tela de este dulce encuentro.*

32. Y llámale *tela* por tres cosas: la primera, por la trabazón que hay entre el espíritu y la carne; la segunda, porque divide entre Dios y el alma; la tercera, porque así como la tela no es tan opaca y condensa que no se pueda traslucir lo claro por ella, así en este estado parece esta trabazón tan delgada tela, por estar ya muy espiritualizada e ilustrada y adelgazada, que no se deja de traslucir la Divinidad en ella. Y como siente el alma la fortaleza de la otra vida, echa de ver la flaqueza de estotra, y parécele mucho delgada tela, y aun tela de araña, como le llama David, diciendo: *Nuestros años como la araña*

the condition of their death, in accordance with nature, is similar to that of all other souls, nevertheless in the cause and manner of their death there is a great difference: if the others die a death caused by illness or length of days, these souls, even when dying of illness or completing their life span, are not wrenched from the body except by some impetus and encounter of love much more sublime than the past ones, and more powerful and bold, since it was able to rend the veil and carry off that jewel of a soul. And so, the death of such souls is very gentle and sweet, more than their spiritual life was, as long as they lived; because they die from a more sublime impetus and delightful, loving encounters, being like the swan, which sings more sweetly when it dies. That is why David said: "Precious in the sight of the Lord is the death of his saints" (Psalm 116:15), because here all the riches of the soul come to be joined together, and there the rivers of the soul's love go to enter the sea, those rivers being now so broad (from being dammed up) that they resemble seas; the first and the last of the righteous man's treasures join together to accompany him as he leaves and departs for his kingdom, his praises now being heard from one end of the earth to another; as Isaiah says, they are "glory to the righteous" (Isaiah 24:16).

31. So then, since the soul at the moment of these glorious encounters feels that she is on the verge of sallying out to possess her kingdom completely and perfectly, in the abundance with which she finds herself enriched (because here she realizes she is pure, wealthy, filled with virtues, and prepared for all this, since in this state God lets the soul see her beauty and entrusts her with the gifts and virtues He has given her, everything turning into love and praise, with no trace of presumption or vanity, with no more leaven of imperfection to spoil the dough), and since she sees that all that remains for her to do is to rend this weak veil of natural life in which she feels ensnared and caught, with her freedom obstructed, "having a desire to depart and to be with Christ" (Philippians 1:23), finding it a pity that a life so low and weak is keeping her from another so high and strong: she asks that it be ripped: "Rend the veil of this sweet encounter!"

32. She calls it "veil" for three reasons: first, because the spirit and the flesh are interwoven; second, because it separates God from the soul; and third, because just as a veil is not so opaque and thick that brightness cannot filter through it, so in this state this interweaving seems to be such a thin veil (because it is now very spiritualized, illumined, and thinned) that Deity does not cease to filter through it. And as the soul feels the power of the next life, she realizes the weakness of this one, and the veil seems very thin to her, practically a spiderweb, as David calls it: "Our years will be considered like the spider" ([compare] Psalm 90:9); and it is even

meditarán (Ps 89,9); y aun es mucho menos delante de el alma que así
está engrandecida, porque, como está puesta en el sentir de Dios,
siente las cosas como Dios, delante del cual, como también dice
David, *mil años son como el día de ayer que pasó* (Ps 89,4), y según
Isaías, *todas las gentes son como si no fuesen* (40,17). Y ese mesmo
tomo tienen delante de el alma, que todas las cosas le son nada, y ella
es para sus ojos nada. Sólo su Dios para ella es el todo.

33. Pero hay aquí que notar: ¿Por qué razón pide aquí más que
rompa la tela, que la *corte* o que la *acabe,* pues todo parece una cosa?
Podemos decir que por cuatro cosas: la primera, por hablar con más
propiedad, porque más propio es del encuentro romper que cortar y
que acabar. La segunda, porque el amor es amigo de fuerza de amor
y de toque fuerte e impetuoso, lo cual se ejecuta más en el romper
que en el cortar y acabar. La tercera, porque el amor apetece que el
acto sea brevísimo, por que se cumple más presto, y tiene tanta más
fuerza y valor cuanto es más breve y más espiritual, porque la virtud
unida más fuerte es que esparcida; e introdúcese amor al modo que la
forma en la materia, que se introduce en un instante, y hasta entonces
no había acto sino disposiciones para él; y así, los actos espirituales
como en un instante se hacen en el alma, porque son infusos de Dios,
pero los demás que el alma de suyo hace más se pueden llamar disposiciones de deseos y afectos sucesivos, que nunca llegan a ser actos
perfectos de amor o contemplación, sino algunas veces cuando (como
digo) Dios los forma y perficciona con gran brevedad en el espíritu;
por lo cual dijo el Sabio que *el fin de la oración es mejor que el principio* (Eccl. 7,9), y lo que comúnmente se dice: que la oración breve
penetra los cielos (Ecli 35,21). De donde el alma que ya está dispuesta, muchos más y más intensos actos puede hacer en breve
tiempo que la no dispuesta en mucho, y aun, por la gran disposición
que tiene, se suele quedar harto en acto de amor o contemplación; y
a la que no está dispuesta todo se le va en disponer el espíritu, y aun
después se suele quedar el fuego por entrar en el madero, ahora por
la mucha humedad dél, ahora por el poco calor que dispone, ahora
por lo uno y lo otro; mas en el alma dispuesta, por momentos entra el
acto de amor, porque la centella a cada toque prende en la enjuta
yesca; y ansí, el alma enamorada más quiere la brevedad de el *romper*
que el espacio de el *cortar* y *acabar.* La cuarta es por que se acabe más
presto la tela de la vida, porque el cortar y acabar hácese con más
acuerdo, porque se espera que la cosa esté sazonada o acabada o algún
otro término, y el *romper* no espera al parecer madurez y ni nada de
eso.

much less in the eyes of the soul who has become so enlarged, since, being placed in the sensation of God, she feels things as God does, in Whose sight, as David also says, "a thousand years . . . are but as yesterday when it is past" (Psalm 90:4), and, according to Isaiah: "all nations before him are as nothing" (Isaiah 40:17). And they have the same importance in the eyes of the soul, for all things are nothing to her, and she is nothing in her own eyes. Only her God is her all.

33. But here it is to be noted: Why does she here ask that the veil be "rent," rather than "cut" or "consumed," which all seem to be the same thing? We may say that there are four reasons: first, in order to use a more appropriate term, because it is more characteristic of this encounter, or collision, to tear rather than cut or consume. Second, because love is a friend to loving force and a strong, impetuous contact, which results in tearing rather than cutting or consuming. Third, because love desires the action to be very brief so it is over sooner; it will have all the more power and boldness the briefer and more spiritual it is, because united forces are stronger than scattered ones, and love introduces itself just as form introduces itself into matter—in an instant. Until then there was no action, but merely preparedness for it. And so, spiritual actions take place in the soul as if instantaneously, because they are infused by God, whereas the other actions undertaken by the soul on her own may rather be called preparations through desires and a sequence of affections, which never come to be perfect actions of love or contemplation, unless (as I say) God occasionally shapes and perfects them very quickly in the spirit; that is why the sage said: "Better is the end of a thing than the beginning thereof" (Ecclesiastes 7:8), and that which is often quoted: that a short prayer enters heaven (Ecclesiasticus 35:21). Hence, the soul that is already prepared can perform many more, and more intense, actions in a brief time than an unprepared one in a long time, and, what is more, because of her great preparedness she generally lingers in an action of love or contemplation for quite a while; whereas all the time of the unprepared soul is taken up with preparing her spirit, and even later the fire generally takes a long time to enter the log, at times because the log is very damp, at times because the fire fails to apply enough heat, at times for both reasons. But into the prepared soul the action of love enters in a moment, because at each contact the spark ignites the dry tinder. And so, the soul that is in love prefers the brevity of "tearing" to the longer process of "cutting" or "consuming." The fourth reason is the desire to have the veil of life destroyed more quickly, because cutting and consuming presuppose more planning, since one must wait for its object to be "ripened" or fully formed, or for some other deadline, whereas tearing apparently does not await maturity or anything similar.

34. Y esto quiere el alma enamorada, que no sufre dilaciones de que se espere a que naturalmente se acabe la vida ni a que en tal o tal tiempo se corte; porque la fuerza del amor y disposición que en sí ve la hacen querer y pedir se rompa luego la vida con algún encuentro o ímpetu sobrenatural de amor. Sabe muy bien aquí el alma que es condición de Dios llevar antes de tiempo consigo las almas que mucho ama, perficionando en ellas en breve tiempo por medio de aquel amor lo que en todo suceso por su ordinario paso pudieran ir ganando. Porque esto es lo que dijo el Sabio: *El que agrada a Dios es hecho amado; y, viviendo entre pecadores, fue trasladado; arrebatado fue por que la malicia no mudara su entendimiento, o la afición no engañara su alma. Consumido en breve, cumplió muchos tiempos. Porque era su alma agradable a Dios, por tanto, se apresuró a sacarle de medio,* etc. (Sap 4,10–14). Hasta aquí son palabras de el Sabio, en las cuales se verá con cuánta propiedad y razón usa el alma de aquel término, *romper,* pues en ellas usa el Espíritu Santo de estos dos términos: *arrebatar* y *apresurar,* que son ajenos de toda dilación. En el *apresurarse* se da a entender la priesa con que Dios hizo perficionar en breve el amor del justo, y en el *arrebatar* se da a entender llevarle antes de su tiempo natural. Por eso es gran negocio para el alma exercitar en esta vida los actos de amor, por que, consumándose en breve, no se detenga mucho acá o allá sin ver a Dios.

35. Pero veamos ahora por qué también a este embestimiento interior del Espíritu le llama *encuentro* más que otro nombre alguno. Y es la razón porque, sintiendo el alma en Dios infinita gana (como habemos dicho) de que se acabe la vida, y que, como no ha llegado el tiempo de su perfección, no se hace, echa de ver que para consumarla y elevarla de la carne, hace él en ella estos embestimientos divinos y gloriosos a manera de encuentros, que, como son a fin de purificarla y sacarla de la carne, verdaderamente son encuentros con que siempre penetra, endiosando la sustancia de el alma, haciéndola divina, en lo cual absorbe al alma sobre todo ser a ser de Dios. Y la causa es porque la encontró Dios y la traspasó Dios en el Espíritu Santo vivamente, cuyas comunicaciones son impetuosas cuando son afervoradas, como lo es este encuentro. Al cual, porque el alma vivamente gusta de Dios, llama *dulce,* no porque otros muchos toques y encuentros que en este estado reciben dejen de ser dulces, sino por eminencia que tiene sobre todos los demás, porque lo hace Dios (como habemos dicho) a fin de desatarla y glorificarla presto, de donde a ella le nacen alas para decir: *Rompe la tela,* etc.

36. Resumiendo, pues, ahora toda la canción, es como si dijera: ¡Oh

34. And this is what the soul in love wants: not to suffer delays while awaiting the natural end of life, nor to have it cut short at some future moment; because the force of love and readiness she finds in herself make her wish and request that her life be torn immediately by some supernatural encounter or impetus of love. The soul here is well aware that it is God's way to take to Himself prematurely the souls that He loves greatly, perfecting in them briefly, by means of that love, whatever they might gain at all events in their ordinary life span. Because this is what the sage said: "The man pleasing to God has become beloved; and, living amid sinners, he has been transported to heaven, snatched away before evil could alter his understanding, or affections deceive his soul. Quickly consumed, he completed a long period of time. Because his soul was pleasing to God, He hastened to take him away," etc. ([compare] Wisdom of Solomon 4:10–14). Up to this point these are the words of the sage, in which it will be seen how appropriately and with what good reason the soul uses the term "rend," because in this quotation the Holy Spirit uses the two terms "snatched away" and "hastened," which are the opposite of delaying. "Hastened" indicates God's hurry to perfect the righteous man's love swiftly, and "snatched away" indicates that he was taken before his natural time. Therefore it is of great purport to the soul to practice the actions of love in this life, so that, when she is quickly consummated, she will not be greatly delayed, on earth or in heaven, before seeing God.

35. But now let us see why she also calls this inward assault by the Spirit an "encounter" rather than anything else. This is because the soul in God feeling an infinite desire (as I have said) for her life to end, but the time of her perfection not having arrived, this does not occur, she realizes that, for her to be consummated and uplifted from the flesh, He makes these divine and glorious assaults on her in the manner of encounters (or collisions, or clashes), which, since their aim is to purify her and take her out of the flesh, are truly encounters by which He always penetrates, deifying the soul's substance, making her divine, and therewith absorbing the soul beyond all being into the being of God. And this is because God encountered her and pierced her vividly in the Holy Spirit, Whose communications are impetuous when they are fervent, as in the case of this encounter. Since the soul is taking vivid pleasure in God, she calls this encounter "sweet," not because many other contacts and encounters received in this state are not also sweet, but because this one so far surpasses all the rest, since it is God doing it (as I have said) in order to release her and glorify her quickly, so that she is stimulated to say: "Rend the veil," etc.

36. So then, now summarizing the entire stanza, it is equivalent to say-

llama del Espíritu Santo, que tan íntima y tiernamente traspasas la sustancia de mi alma y la cauterizas con tu glorioso ardor!, pues ya estás tan amigable que te muestras con gana de dárteme en vida eterna, si antes mis peticiones no llegaban a tus oídos, cuando con ansias y fatigas de amor, en que penaba mi sentido y espíritu por la mucha flaqueza e impureza mía y poca fortaleza de amor que tenía, te rogaba me desatases y llevases contigo, porque con deseo te deseaba mi alma, porque el amor impaciente no me dejaba conformar tanto con esta condición de vida que tú querías que aún viviese; y si los pasados ímpetus de amor no eran bastantes, porque no eran de tanta calidad para alcanzarlo, ahora que estoy tan fortalecida en amor, que no sólo no desfallece mi sentido y espíritu en ti, mas antes, fortalecidos de ti, *mi corazón y mi carne se gozan en Dios vivo* (Ps 83,2), con grande conformidad de las partes, donde lo que tú quieres pida pido, y lo que tú no quieres no quiero, ni aun puedo ni me pasa por pensamiento querer; y, pues son ya delante de tus ojos más válidas y estimadas mis peticiones, pues salen de ti y tú me mueves a ellas, y con sabor y gozo en el Espíritu Santo te lo pido, *saliendo ya mi juicio de tu rostro* (Ps 16,2), que es cuando los ruegos precias y oyes, rompe la tela delgada de esta vida y no la dejes llegar a que la edad y años naturalmente la corten, para que te pueda amar desde luego con la plenitud y hartura que desea mi alma, sin término ni fin.

ing: "O flame of the Holy Spirit, which so intimately and tenderly pierces the substance of my soul, cauterizing it with your glorious ardor, since you are now so friendly that you manifest the desire of giving yourself to me in eternal life, if in the past my requests did not reach your ears, when with amorous longings and labors, in which my senses and spirit suffered because of my great weakness and impurity and my lack of steadfastness in love, I would pray to you to release me and take me with you, because my soul desired you greatly, since impatient love would not let me conform closely enough to that way of life you wanted me to follow for all the time I still had left to live, and if the former assaults of love were insufficient, because they lacked the quality to merit this; now that I am so strengthened in love that not only do my senses and spirit not faint in you, but, on the contrary, strengthened by you, 'my heart and my flesh enjoy the living God' ([compare] Psalm 84:2) with great agreement between my parts, so that I request what you want me to request, and I do not want what you do not want me to want (nor am I able to want it, nor does it even enter my mind to want it); and since my requests are now more valid and esteemed in your eyes because they come from you and you incite me to them, and with pleasure and joy in the Holy Spirit I ask it of you, now that 'my judgment issues from your face' ([compare] Psalm 17:2), which is when you esteem prayers and listen to them: rend the thin veil of this life and do not let it tarry until old age and many years cut it short naturally, so that I may love you immediately with the fullness and amplitude that my soul desires, without term or ending!"

A CATALOG OF SELECTED
DOVER BOOKS
IN ALL FIELDS OF INTEREST

A CATALOG OF SELECTED DOVER
BOOKS IN ALL FIELDS OF INTEREST

CONCERNING THE SPIRITUAL IN ART, Wassily Kandinsky. Pioneering work by father of abstract art. Thoughts on color theory, nature of art. Analysis of earlier masters. 12 illustrations. 80pp. of text. 5⅜ x 8½. 0-486-23411-8

CELTIC ART: The Methods of Construction, George Bain. Simple geometric techniques for making Celtic interlacements, spirals, Kells-type initials, animals, humans, etc. Over 500 illustrations. 160pp. 9 x 12. (Available in U.S. only.) 0-486-22923-8

AN ATLAS OF ANATOMY FOR ARTISTS, Fritz Schider. Most thorough reference work on art anatomy in the world. Hundreds of illustrations, including selections from works by Vesalius, Leonardo, Goya, Ingres, Michelangelo, others. 593 illustrations. 192pp. 7⅛ x 10¼. 0-486-20241-0

CELTIC HAND STROKE-BY-STROKE (Irish Half-Uncial from "The Book of Kells"): An Arthur Baker Calligraphy Manual, Arthur Baker. Complete guide to creating each letter of the alphabet in distinctive Celtic manner. Covers hand position, strokes, pens, inks, paper, more. Illustrated. 48pp. 8¼ x 11. 0-486-24336-2

EASY ORIGAMI, John Montroll. Charming collection of 32 projects (hat, cup, pelican, piano, swan, many more) specially designed for the novice origami hobbyist. Clearly illustrated easy-to-follow instructions insure that even beginning papercrafters will achieve successful results. 48pp. 8¼ x 11. 0-486-27298-2

BLOOMINGDALE'S ILLUSTRATED 1886 CATALOG: Fashions, Dry Goods and Housewares, Bloomingdale Brothers. Famed merchants' extremely rare catalog depicting about 1,700 products: clothing, housewares, firearms, dry goods, jewelry, more. Invaluable for dating, identifying vintage items. Also, copyright-free graphics for artists, designers. Co-published with Henry Ford Museum & Greenfield Village. 160pp. 8¼ x 11. 0-486-25780-0

THE ART OF WORLDLY WISDOM, Baltasar Gracian. "Think with the few and speak with the many," "Friends are a second existence," and "Be able to forget" are among this 1637 volume's 300 pithy maxims. A perfect source of mental and spiritual refreshment, it can be opened at random and appreciated either in brief or at length. 128pp. 5⅜ x 8½. 0-486-44034-6

JOHNSON'S DICTIONARY: A Modern Selection, Samuel Johnson (E. L. McAdam and George Milne, eds.). This modern version reduces the original 1755 edition's 2,300 pages of definitions and literary examples to a more manageable length, retaining the verbal pleasure and historical curiosity of the original. 480pp. 5³⁄₁₆ x 8¼. 0-486-44089-3

ADVENTURES OF HUCKLEBERRY FINN, Mark Twain, Illustrated by E. W. Kemble. A work of eternal richness and complexity, a source of ongoing critical debate, and a literary landmark, Twain's 1885 masterpiece about a barefoot boy's journey of self-discovery has enthralled readers around the world. This handsome clothbound reproduction of the first edition features all 174 of the original black-and-white illustrations. 368pp. 5⅜ x 8½. 0-486-44322-1

CATALOG OF DOVER BOOKS

STICKLEY CRAFTSMAN FURNITURE CATALOGS, Gustav Stickley and L. & J. G. Stickley. Beautiful, functional furniture in two authentic catalogs from 1910. 594 illustrations, including 277 photos, show settles, rockers, armchairs, reclining chairs, bookcases, desks, tables. 183pp. 6½ x 9¼.   0-486-23838-5

AMERICAN LOCOMOTIVES IN HISTORIC PHOTOGRAPHS: 1858 to 1949, Ron Ziel (ed.). A rare collection of 126 meticulously detailed official photographs, called "builder portraits," of American locomotives that majestically chronicle the rise of steam locomotive power in America. Introduction. Detailed captions. xi+ 129pp. 9 x 12.   0-486-27393-8

AMERICA'S LIGHTHOUSES: An Illustrated History, Francis Ross Holland, Jr. Delightfully written, profusely illustrated fact-filled survey of over 200 American lighthouses since 1716. History, anecdotes, technological advances, more. 240pp. 8 x 10¾.
                                                      0-486-25576-X

TOWARDS A NEW ARCHITECTURE, Le Corbusier. Pioneering manifesto by founder of "International School." Technical and aesthetic theories, views of industry, economics, relation of form to function, "mass-production split" and much more. Profusely illustrated. 320pp. 6⅛ x 9¼. (Available in U.S. only.)   0-486-25023-7

HOW THE OTHER HALF LIVES, Jacob Riis. Famous journalistic record, exposing poverty and degradation of New York slums around 1900, by major social reformer. 100 striking and influential photographs. 233pp. 10 x 7⅞.   0-486-22012-5

FRUIT KEY AND TWIG KEY TO TREES AND SHRUBS, William M. Harlow. One of the handiest and most widely used identification aids. Fruit key covers 120 deciduous and evergreen species; twig key 160 deciduous species. Easily used. Over 300 photographs. 126pp. 5⅜ x 8½.   0-486-20511-8

COMMON BIRD SONGS, Dr. Donald J. Borror. Songs of 60 most common U.S. birds: robins, sparrows, cardinals, bluejays, finches, more—arranged in order of increasing complexity. Up to 9 variations of songs of each species.
                                   Cassette and manual 0-486-99911-4

ORCHIDS AS HOUSE PLANTS, Rebecca Tyson Northen. Grow cattleyas and many other kinds of orchids—in a window, in a case, or under artificial light. 63 illustrations. 148pp. 5⅜ x 8½.   0-486-23261-1

MONSTER MAZES, Dave Phillips. Masterful mazes at four levels of difficulty. Avoid deadly perils and evil creatures to find magical treasures. Solutions for all 32 exciting illustrated puzzles. 48pp. 8¼ x 11.   0-486-26005-4

MOZART'S DON GIOVANNI (DOVER OPERA LIBRETTO SERIES), Wolfgang Amadeus Mozart. Introduced and translated by Ellen H. Bleiler. Standard Italian libretto, with complete English translation. Convenient and thoroughly portable—an ideal companion for reading along with a recording or the performance itself. Introduction. List of characters. Plot summary. 121pp. 5¼ x 8½. 0-486-24944-1

FRANK LLOYD WRIGHT'S DANA HOUSE, Donald Hoffmann. Pictorial essay of residential masterpiece with over 160 interior and exterior photos, plans, elevations, sketches and studies. 128pp. 9¼ x 10¾.   0-486-29120-0

CATALOG OF DOVER BOOKS

THE CLARINET AND CLARINET PLAYING, David Pino. Lively, comprehensive work features suggestions about technique, musicianship, and musical interpretation, as well as guidelines for teaching, making your own reeds, and preparing for public performance. Includes an intriguing look at clarinet history. "A godsend," *The Clarinet,* Journal of the International Clarinet Society. Appendixes. 7 illus. 320pp. 5⅜ x 8½. 0-486-40270-3

HOLLYWOOD GLAMOR PORTRAITS, John Kobal (ed.). 145 photos from 1926-49. Harlow, Gable, Bogart, Bacall; 94 stars in all. Full background on photographers, technical aspects. 160pp. 8⅜ x 11¼. 0-486-23352-9

THE RAVEN AND OTHER FAVORITE POEMS, Edgar Allan Poe. Over 40 of the author's most memorable poems: "The Bells," "Ulalume," "Israfel," "To Helen," "The Conqueror Worm," "Eldorado," "Annabel Lee," many more. Alphabetic lists of titles and first lines. 64pp. 5³⁄₁₆ x 8¼. 0-486-26685-0

PERSONAL MEMOIRS OF U. S. GRANT, Ulysses Simpson Grant. Intelligent, deeply moving firsthand account of Civil War campaigns, considered by many the finest military memoirs ever written. Includes letters, historic photographs, maps and more. 528pp. 6⅛ x 9¼. 0-486-28587-1

ANCIENT EGYPTIAN MATERIALS AND INDUSTRIES, A. Lucas and J. Harris. Fascinating, comprehensive, thoroughly documented text describes this ancient civilization's vast resources and the processes that incorporated them in daily life, including the use of animal products, building materials, cosmetics, perfumes and incense, fibers, glazed ware, glass and its manufacture, materials used in the mummification process, and much more. 544pp. 6¹⁄₈ x 9¹⁄₄. (Available in U.S. only.) 0-486-40446-3

RUSSIAN STORIES/RUSSKIE RASSKAZY: A Dual-Language Book, edited by Gleb Struve. Twelve tales by such masters as Chekhov, Tolstoy, Dostoevsky, Pushkin, others. Excellent word-for-word English translations on facing pages, plus teaching and study aids, Russian/English vocabulary, biographical/critical introductions, more. 416pp. 5⅜ x 8½. 0-486-26244-8

PHILADELPHIA THEN AND NOW: 60 Sites Photographed in the Past and Present, Kenneth Finkel and Susan Oyama. Rare photographs of City Hall, Logan Square, Independence Hall, Betsy Ross House, other landmarks juxtaposed with contemporary views. Captures changing face of historic city. Introduction. Captions. 128pp. 8¼ x 11. 0-486-25790-8

NORTH AMERICAN INDIAN LIFE: Customs and Traditions of 23 Tribes, Elsie Clews Parsons (ed.). 27 fictionalized essays by noted anthropologists examine religion, customs, government, additional facets of life among the Winnebago, Crow, Zuni, Eskimo, other tribes. 480pp. 6⅛ x 9¼. 0-486-27377-6

TECHNICAL MANUAL AND DICTIONARY OF CLASSICAL BALLET, Gail Grant. Defines, explains, comments on steps, movements, poses and concepts. 15-page pictorial section. Basic book for student, viewer. 127pp. 5⅜ x 8½. 0-486-21843-0

THE MALE AND FEMALE FIGURE IN MOTION: 60 Classic Photographic Sequences, Eadweard Muybridge. 60 true-action photographs of men and women walking, running, climbing, bending, turning, etc., reproduced from rare 19th-century masterpiece. vi + 121pp. 9 x 12. 0-486-24745-7

CATALOG OF DOVER BOOKS

ANIMALS: 1,419 Copyright-Free Illustrations of Mammals, Birds, Fish, Insects, etc.,
Jim Harter (ed.). Clear wood engravings present, in extremely lifelike poses, over
1,000 species of animals. One of the most extensive pictorial sourcebooks of its kind.
Captions. Index. 284pp. 9 x 12.   0-486-23766-4

1001 QUESTIONS ANSWERED ABOUT THE SEASHORE, N. J. Berrill and
Jacquelyn Berrill. Queries answered about dolphins, sea snails, sponges, starfish,
fishes, shore birds, many others. Covers appearance, breeding, growth, feeding,
much more. 305pp. 5¼ x 8¼.   0-486-23366-9

ATTRACTING BIRDS TO YOUR YARD, William J. Weber. Easy-to-follow guide
offers advice on how to attract the greatest diversity of birds: birdhouses, feeders,
water and waterers, much more. 96pp. 5³⁄₁₆ x 8¼.   0-486-28927-3

MEDICINAL AND OTHER USES OF NORTH AMERICAN PLANTS: A
Historical Survey with Special Reference to the Eastern Indian Tribes, Charlotte
Erichsen-Brown. Chronological historical citations document 500 years of usage of
plants, trees, shrubs native to eastern Canada, northeastern U.S. Also complete identifying information. 343 illustrations. 544pp. 6½ x 9¼.   0-486-25951-X

STORYBOOK MAZES, Dave Phillips. 23 stories and mazes on two-page spreads:
Wizard of Oz, Treasure Island, Robin Hood, etc. Solutions. 64pp. 8¼ x 11.
                                                            0-486-23628-5

AMERICAN NEGRO SONGS: 230 Folk Songs and Spirituals, Religious and
Secular, John W. Work. This authoritative study traces the African influences of songs
sung and played by black Americans at work, in church, and as entertainment. The
author discusses the lyric significance of such songs as "Swing Low, Sweet Chariot,"
"John Henry," and others and offers the words and music for 230 songs.
Bibliography. Index of Song Titles. 272pp. 6½ x 9¼.   0-486-40271-1

MOVIE-STAR PORTRAITS OF THE FORTIES, John Kobal (ed.). 163 glamor,
studio photos of 106 stars of the 1940s: Rita Hayworth, Ava Gardner, Marlon
Brando, Clark Gable, many more. 176pp. 8⅜ x 11¼.   0-486-23546-7

YEKL and THE IMPORTED BRIDEGROOM AND OTHER STORIES OF
YIDDISH NEW YORK, Abraham Cahan. Film Hester Street based on *Yekl* (1896).
Novel, other stories among first about Jewish immigrants on N.Y.'s East Side. 240pp.
5⅜ x 8½.   0-486-22427-9

SELECTED POEMS, Walt Whitman. Generous sampling from *Leaves of Grass.*
Twenty-four poems include "I Hear America Singing," "Song of the Open Road," "I
Sing the Body Electric," "When Lilacs Last in the Dooryard Bloom'd," "O Captain!
My Captain!"–all reprinted from an authoritative edition. Lists of titles and first lines.
128pp. 5³⁄₁₆ x 8¼.   0-486-26878-0

SONGS OF EXPERIENCE: Facsimile Reproduction with 26 Plates in Full Color,
William Blake. 26 full-color plates from a rare 1826 edition. Includes "The Tyger,"
"London," "Holy Thursday," and other poems. Printed text of poems. 48pp. 5¼ x 7.
                                                            0-486-24636-1

THE BEST TALES OF HOFFMANN, E. T. A. Hoffmann. 10 of Hoffmann's most
important stories: "Nutcracker and the King of Mice," "The Golden Flowerpot," etc.
458pp. 5⅜ x 8½.   0-486-21793-0

THE BOOK OF TEA, Kakuzo Okakura. Minor classic of the Orient: entertaining,
charming explanation, interpretation of traditional Japanese culture in terms of tea
ceremony. 94pp. 5⅜ x 8½.   0-486-20070-1

FRENCH STORIES/CONTES FRANÇAIS: A Dual-Language Book, Wallace Fowlie. Ten stories by French masters, Voltaire to Camus: "Micromegas" by Voltaire; "The Atheist's Mass" by Balzac; "Minuet" by de Maupassant; "The Guest" by Camus, six more. Excellent English translations on facing pages. Also French-English vocabulary list, exercises, more. 352pp. 5⅜ x 8½. 0-486-26443-2

CHICAGO AT THE TURN OF THE CENTURY IN PHOTOGRAPHS: 122 Historic Views from the Collections of the Chicago Historical Society, Larry A. Viskochil. Rare large-format prints offer detailed views of City Hall, State Street, the Loop, Hull House, Union Station, many other landmarks, circa 1904-1913. Introduction. Captions. Maps. 144pp. 9⅜ x 12¼. 0-486-24656-6

OLD BROOKLYN IN EARLY PHOTOGRAPHS, 1865-1929, William Lee Younger. Luna Park, Gravesend race track, construction of Grand Army Plaza, moving of Hotel Brighton, etc. 157 previously unpublished photographs. 165pp. 8⅞ x 11¾. 0-486-23587-4

THE MYTHS OF THE NORTH AMERICAN INDIANS, Lewis Spence. Rich anthology of the myths and legends of the Algonquins, Iroquois, Pawnees and Sioux, prefaced by an extensive historical and ethnological commentary. 36 illustrations. 480pp. 5⅜ x 8½. 0-486-25967-6

AN ENCYCLOPEDIA OF BATTLES: Accounts of Over 1,560 Battles from 1479 B.C. to the Present, David Eggenberger. Essential details of every major battle in recorded history from the first battle of Megiddo in 1479 B.C. to Grenada in 1984. List of Battle Maps. New Appendix covering the years 1967-1984. Index. 99 illustrations. 544pp. 6½ x 9¼. 0-486-24913-1

SAILING ALONE AROUND THE WORLD, Captain Joshua Slocum. First man to sail around the world, alone, in small boat. One of great feats of seamanship told in delightful manner. 67 illustrations. 294pp. 5⅜ x 8½. 0-486-20326-3

ANARCHISM AND OTHER ESSAYS, Emma Goldman. Powerful, penetrating, prophetic essays on direct action, role of minorities, prison reform, puritan hypocrisy, violence, etc. 271pp. 5⅜ x 8½. 0-486-22484-8

MYTHS OF THE HINDUS AND BUDDHISTS, Ananda K. Coomaraswamy and Sister Nivedita. Great stories of the epics; deeds of Krishna, Shiva, taken from puranas, Vedas, folk tales; etc. 32 illustrations. 400pp. 5⅜ x 8½. 0-486-21759-0

MY BONDAGE AND MY FREEDOM, Frederick Douglass. Born a slave, Douglass became outspoken force in antislavery movement. The best of Douglass' autobiographies. Graphic description of slave life. 464pp. 5⅜ x 8½. 0-486-22457-0

FOLLOWING THE EQUATOR: A Journey Around the World, Mark Twain. Fascinating humorous account of 1897 voyage to Hawaii, Australia, India, New Zealand, etc. Ironic, bemused reports on peoples, customs, climate, flora and fauna, politics, much more. 197 illustrations. 720pp. 5⅜ x 8½. 0-486-26113-1

THE PEOPLE CALLED SHAKERS, Edward D. Andrews. Definitive study of Shakers: origins, beliefs, practices, dances, social organization, furniture and crafts, etc. 33 illustrations. 351pp. 5⅜ x 8½. 0-486-21081-2

THE MYTHS OF GREECE AND ROME, H. A. Guerber. A classic of mythology, generously illustrated, long prized for its simple, graphic, accurate retelling of the principal myths of Greece and Rome, and for its commentary on their origins and significance. With 64 illustrations by Michelangelo, Raphael, Titian, Rubens, Canova, Bernini and others. 480pp. 5⅜ x 8½. 0-486-27584-1

LIGHT AND SHADE: A Classic Approach to Three-Dimensional Drawing, Mrs. Mary P. Merrifield. Handy reference clearly demonstrates principles of light and shade by revealing effects of common daylight, sunshine, and candle or artificial light on geometrical solids. 13 plates. 64pp. 5⅜ x 8½. 0-486-44143-1

ASTROLOGY AND ASTRONOMY: A Pictorial Archive of Signs and Symbols, Ernst and Johanna Lehner. Treasure trove of stories, lore, and myth, accompanied by more than 300 rare illustrations of planets, the Milky Way, signs of the zodiac, comets, meteors, and other astronomical phenomena. 192pp. 8⅜ x 11. 0-486-43981-X

JEWELRY MAKING: Techniques for Metal, Tim McCreight. Easy-to-follow instructions and carefully executed illustrations describe tools and techniques, use of gems and enamels, wire inlay, casting, and other topics. 72 line illustrations and diagrams. 176pp. 8¼ x 10⅞. 0-486-44043-5

MAKING BIRDHOUSES: Easy and Advanced Projects, Gladstone Califf. Easy-to-follow instructions include diagrams for everything from a one-room house for bluebirds to a forty-two-room structure for purple martins. 56 plates; 4 figures. 80pp. 8¾ x 6⅜. 0-486-44183-0

LITTLE BOOK OF LOG CABINS: How to Build and Furnish Them, William S. Wicks. Handy how-to manual, with instructions and illustrations for building cabins in the Adirondack style, fireplaces, stairways, furniture, beamed ceilings, and more. 102 line drawings. 96pp. 8¾ x 6⅜. 0-486-44259-4

THE SEASONS OF AMERICA PAST, Eric Sloane. From "sugaring time" and strawberry picking to Indian summer and fall harvest, a whole year's activities described in charming prose and enhanced with 79 of the author's own illustrations. 160pp. 8¼ x 11. 0-486-44220-9

THE METROPOLIS OF TOMORROW, Hugh Ferriss. Generous, prophetic vision of the metropolis of the future, as perceived in 1929. Powerful illustrations of towering structures, wide avenues, and rooftop parks–all features in many of today's modern cities. 59 illustrations. 144pp. 8¼ x 11. 0-486-43727-2

THE PATH TO ROME, Hilaire Belloc. This 1902 memoir abounds in lively vignettes from a vanished time, recounting a pilgrimage on foot across the Alps and Apennines in order to "see all Europe which the Christian Faith has saved." 77 of the author's original line drawings complement his sparkling prose. 272pp. 5⅜ x 8½. 0-486-44001-X

THE HISTORY OF RASSELAS: Prince of Abissinia, Samuel Johnson. Distinguished English writer attacks eighteenth-century optimism and man's unrealistic estimates of what life has to offer. 112pp. 5⅜ x 8½. 0-486-44094-X

A VOYAGE TO ARCTURUS, David Lindsay. A brilliant flight of pure fancy, where wild creatures crowd the fantastic landscape and demented torturers dominate victims with their bizarre mental powers. 272pp. 5⅜ x 8½. 0-486-44198-9

Paperbound unless otherwise indicated. Available at your book dealer, online at **www.doverpublications.com**, or by writing to Dept. GI, Dover Publications, Inc., 31 East 2nd Street, Mineola, NY 11501. For current price information or for free catalogs (please indicate field of interest), write to Dover Publications or log on to **www.doverpublications.com** and see every Dover book in print. Dover publishes more than 500 books each year on science, elementary and advanced mathematics, biology, music, art, literary history, social sciences, and other areas.